THE *of* G.I. JOURNAL SERGEANT GILES

by JANICE HOLT GILES

The Enduring Hills
Miss Willie
Tara's Healing
40 Acres and No Mule
The Kentuckians
Hill Man
The Plum Thicket
Hannah Fowler
The Believers
The Land Beyond the Mountains
Johnny Osage
Savanna
Voyage to Santa Fe
A Little Better than Plumb (with Henry Giles)
Run Me a River
The G. I. Journal of Sergeant Giles (editor)
The Great Adventure
Shady Grove
Six-Horse Hitch
The Damned Engineers
Around Our House (with Henry Giles)
The Kinta Years
Wellspring
Act of Contrition

THE G.I. JOURNAL
of
SERGEANT GILES

THE 291ST ENGINEER COMBAT BATTALION IN
WORLD WAR II, 1943-1945

EDITED BY

JANICE HOLT GILES

Commonwealth Book Company
ST. MARTIN, OHIO
2019

FRONT COVER PHOTOGRAPH: Company C, 291st Engineers, near Malmedy, 1944

REAR COVER PHOTOGRAPH: Paul LaCoste & Henry Giles

To
Company A
especially the three
who didn't come back

Pvt. Merion A. Priester
Pvt. Arnold K. Hall
Pfc. Wiley A. Holbrook

JANICE HOLT GILES (1905–1979) was born in Arkansas and raised there and in Oklahoma. In 1941 she accepted a position at Presbyterian Theological Seminary in Frankfort, Kentucky. On a bus trip to Arkansas in 1943 she happened to sit next to a soldier returning to Camp Swift, Texas, from a furlough at his home in Adair County, Kentucky. After 48 hours on the bus together, Henry Giles and Janice Holt would not see each other again until 1945. But when Henry shipped out to Boston and then to England to participate in the Normandy invasion, he and Janice began a correspondence that would last through the war, and resulted in their marriage in 1945. In 1949 Janice published her first novel, *The Enduring Hills*. Over the next three decades she produced over twenty novels, mostly set in Kentucky and the frontier west, and was one of the most beloved authors of the mid-twentieth century.

Henry's wartime letters to Janice numbered over six hundred and, along with a detailed journal he kept, formed the basis of a project dear to Janice, her edited publication of *The G. I. Journal of Sergeant Giles*. Henry was a sergeant in the 291st Engineer Combat Battalion, a small unit that played a pivotal role in stemming the German counter-offensive in the Battle of the Bulge in 1944. Following extensive research and countless interviews, and expanding on her work with *G. I. Journal*, Janice published in 1970 the critically well-received history of the 291st Engineers in World War II, *The Damned Engineers*. Together, these two books offer no mere accounting of events, causes, and results, but rather they convey the real experiences of ordinary men who, when placed in extraordinary circumstances, displayed the courage and fortitude to get the job done. And, as Janice wrote, the 291st Engineers not only got the job done, but they "gave a damned good account of themselves."

Acknowledgments

To EVERY man of Company A, 291st Engineer Combat Battalion, with whom we made contact, our grateful thanks. Many took the time and trouble to write their personal memories of action they were in during the Battle of the Bulge. Others felt they could not rely well enough on their memories, after twenty years, to write an account; but every man we reached was in one way or another helpful to us, by giving us leads to other men, by recalling dates and places of action, by lending us photographs, and the like. The section on the Battle of the Bulge is much richer because of their cheerful, willing cooperation.

The Lake Cumberland Regional Library was once again tirelessly helpful in locating for me every book I needed for background and interpretative reading. They also located much difficult, hard-to-find data and material concerning general military affairs. I am very much in their debt.

To General Telephone of Kentucky, a great big thank you! We reached most of the men of the 291st by telephone. The patience, the unfailing courtesy, the interest and the untiring efforts of the night long distance operators went far "beyond the call of duty." I cannot express my gratitude enough.

I owe thanks to two authors for permission either to quote directly from them or to interpret from them. First, the paragraph quoted on p. 197 from *Dark December,* Ziff-Davis Publishing Company, is quoted with Mr. Merriam's permission.

Second, Lt. Col. Ken Hechler, now Congressman Hechler, allowed me to lean very heavily on his book *The Bridge at Remagen,* Ballantine Books, Inc., for my editorial interpretation.

JANICE HOLT GILES

Contents

Maps and Illustrations

ILLUSTRATIONS
following page 194
Note: The photographs were
furnished largely by John Coupe,
a few by Jeff Elliott and Bob
Billington.

THE G.I. JOURNAL
of
SERGEANT GILES

From England to Cherbourg Peninsula

[THIS *Journal* is compiled from a notebook which Henry Giles kept during World War II and excerpts from his letters to me during the two years he was overseas. I have thought it best, as editor, not to indicate where the notebook leaves off and the letter excerpts are introduced. The whole makes up the *G.I. Journal of Sergeant Giles*. The letters, except for military information, were almost a complete journal in themselves, and the notebook supplied the factual and military details.

At the time this *Journal* begins, Henry Giles was Weapons Sergeant of 2nd platoon, Company A, 291st Engineer Combat Battalion. This continued to be his job throughout the war.

The 291st had been in England since October, 1943. They had been on construction work for the most part during the eight months in England. A notebook was kept during that time but it deals largely with routine which would be of little interest.

Around the 1st of March, 1944, however, the 291st was shifted from construction to an intensive program of combat training at Highnam Court, Gloucester. All of the men believed this meant preparation for the invasion.

The *Journal* begins in May as the unknown, but inevitable, invasion date drew nearer and nearer. After its initial opening, the first entry contains a compilation of several earlier notebook entries which we believed necessary as a background for a better understanding of Sergeant Giles and his position and situation.]

Highnam Court
Gloucester
Sunday, May 7, 1944

THE invasion jitters have really hit us, & it's no wonder. You can't pick up a paper of any kind that isn't full of it & it's all anybody talks about. *Stars & Stripes* has been plugging it for weeks, the British papers are quite newsy about it & the papers from the States are predicting when & where. It's enough to give anybody the shakes.

Tonight Hinkel [1] & I have been talking about how jittery the whole outfit[2] is. We went in town today, ate dinner at the Red Cross canteen, prowled around a little looking for a movie we hadn't seen, had no luck, so we came on back to camp early. Nobody else much back from pass yet so we had the tent to ourselves. Both of us had mail, then we both wrote our letters & still had some time for talk.

It can't be long before this big show begins for the days are getting longer & warmer & the summer season is just around the corner. Stands to reason we'll hit the continent in plenty of time for a long summer. If you use your head you know we'll have to make most of our gains before winter & I don't happen to be one of those who thinks the Wehrmacht is going to fold just because we land & hit them. I asked Paul how he felt about it. He grinned & said, "Hell, you know how I feel. I hope we're not tabbed to hit the beaches — but I know we have to go. That's what we're over here for. But I think the outfit's ready. I think the boys can take it."

I think they can, too. But like Paul, I hope we aren't tabbed for the assault, either.

There's been much speculation about the invasion since we were pulled off construction & sent here for combat training, for

---

1 S/Sgt. Paul J. Hinkel, platoon sergeant, 2nd platoon, Company A.
2 By "the outfit" Henry Giles always means Company A.

that's what it's been — pure combat training & mighty damned intensive at that. Road building, night problems, Bailey bridges, classes in map reading, mine detection & dismantling, mine laying & grenade work, & all Weapons Sgts. have conducted classes in machine gunnery. The only thing we haven't had yet is beach training. There may be time for that yet, but I'm beginning to doubt it.

When Loftis & Wall [3] came home, the four of us talked a little longer about it, then Hinkel went on back to his own tent. This is the first time since we've been overseas & almost the first time since he came into the army in 1942 that Hinkel & I haven't been roommates. But it seemed best for the Weapons Sgts. to be together here, so Wall & Loftis & I have shared a tent. Hinkel comes around every night, however, to shoot the breeze or write his letter.

Arlie & Jack have hit the sack now, but four cups of coffee have got me wide-eyed & I'm not sleepy yet. Thinking ahead, I suppose, is also making me think back a lot. There are times when you need to know where you stand & why.

Where I stand is in the middle of a war. How I got there is by enlisting in the old army back in 1939. But when I enlisted, I must admit, I didn't even think about a war. I enlisted for a good many reasons. For one, the depression hadn't ended down our way & I was sick & tired of the scrabbling & the shame of the commodity lines & no jobs but the WPA. You couldn't find a day's work in a month of Sundays.

But it was more than that. It was the way we'd always lived, hand to mouth, scrabbling along. Nobody knows what the army meant to me — security & pride & something fine & good. The first step to becoming a soldier is putting on the uniform. In my case putting on that uniform not only meant that for the first

[3] Sgt. Jack Loftis, 3rd platoon; Sgt. Arlie Wall, 1st platoon. Both were Weapons Sergeants, as was Henry Giles.

time in my life I had clothes I wasn't ashamed of, but for the first time in my life I was *somebody*. That uniform stood for something to me — and it still does, something pretty grand and fine, for *I* chose it, *it* didn't choose me.

By the time of Pearl Harbor, I was an NCO. Shortly afterward the first draftees began coming in. They came in bitching about this & that, regulations, the food, a cot instead of an innerspring mattress, barracks instead of private rooms. Sometimes I felt like wringing their necks. If they had gone as lean as I had, army food would have tasted good to them. If they had gone cold as often as I had, warm barracks would have felt wonderful. If they had slept on a cornshuck mattress in an attic where snow drifted in on your bed, army cots would have felt fine. I don't think I was a particularly hard platoon sergeant, but they weren't there for fun & somebody had to begin making soldiers out of them.

In the old army there were many things about soldiering I liked. The army system made sense to me. It was tidy & orderly & you knew where you were. It wasn't all messed up or fouled up like the civilian world. And I guess I was born a sucker for the flag. I never saw it ripple down at Retreat without a sense of pride. And there's no better feeling in the world than taking your platoon through a good close order drill, watching them step out sharp & with snap, execute the commands perfectly. It came as natural to me as breathing.

A green S/Sgt was taking his boys through close order one day & he was not only pretty green, he was scared stiff because the Col.[4] was present. I knew how he felt. He wanted to bring it off fine. But he was so scared he loused it up. He finally had the boys so bewildered they were going in all directions at once. The Col. gave him his chance to pull them together, but he just

[4] Lt. Col. David E. Pergrin, Battalion Commander, 291st Engineers.

got worse & worse. All at once the Col. had enough of it. "Sgt. Giles, get in there & straighten that mess out." It felt good to know I could do it.

Maybe I did wrong by turning down my chances to go to OCS, but I don't think so & believe I would do it the same way again. I took my IQ test at Fort Ord. Qualified as officer material. Was called in & asked if I wanted to go to Belvoir. No, sir. If there is anything lower on the totem pole than an OCS 2nd looey, I don't know of it. He not only gets the dirty end of the stick from the officers, he doesn't have the respect of the men. I already had what I wanted — line Sgt.

Went on my first cadre when Camp Crowder was set up.[5] A month later was called in again & asked if I wanted to go to Belvoir. Turned it down again. Then I made S/Sgt.

The next cadre was McCoy in Wisconsin.[6] Same deal. Did I want to go to Belvoir. Same answer.

Next cadre was Swift.[7] Same old rigamarole. Four times I turned down Belvoir. But by Swift I had talked to too many who had gone & then bitterly regretted it. One said to me, "Don't ever go. Don't let 'em talk you into it. I had it made as a top NCO, but I had to let the idea of a bar on my shoulder go to my head & I wish I was rid of the damned thing."

But that's the past. And it's past, too, that when I made the cadre to Swift & the 291st was activated, I decided it was time for me to take a good long look at the TO & find myself the job I could do best & would like best to do, for this outfit was going. With my crocky knees, it wasn't platoon Sgt.[8] It had to be weap-

---

[5] Camp Crowder, Neosho, Missouri, early 1942.

[6] Camp McCoy, Sparta, Wisconsin, fall of 1942.

[7] Camp Swift, Austin, Texas, January of 1943.

[8] Henry Giles had some remote, undiagnosed illness when he was eleven years old which left him with rheumatic knees. How he ever passed the physical to enlist in the army has always been a mystery to me.

ons. So I busted myself from S/Sgt back to Pvt. Nine days later was called in & asked if I would take Cpl. On one condition — next step was Weapons Sgt. Four weeks later, I had it.

We had nine months at Swift, then moved out to Port of Embarkation. These things have a way of happening when you least want them to. I met Janice[9] on my furlough in June & the last thing I wanted right then was to leave the States. Maybe you're not ever ready to go to war but I don't think I would have minded so much earlier. The way it was, I felt sick at my stomach when we walked up the gangplank & sicker yet when I watched the U.S. fade out of sight. Seemed to me I was saying goodbye forever to all that meant the most to me & might never see again. There is something awfully final about going aboard a troop ship & sailing away from your own country. Like a one-way ticket to hell. But you live through it even though you feel like you're not going to.

We left Boston Harbor on Oct. 8th on the *Santa Elena.* At first, sweating out the chow lines took almost all the time we had. But a day or two out & seasickness took care of the long chow lines. I had some uneasy moments but didn't miss a meal. Made up my mind if I was going to be seasick I was going to do it on a full stomach. It must have worked, or something did, for although there were some meals that didn't much appeal to me, I didn't miss a one & I didn't lose one, either.

We had an uneventful crossing except for one hell of a big storm that lasted four days & a few submarine scares. Of course, everytime we were alerted we had to fall out topside with full field pack, rifle & all. Since we were about as far down in the hold as you could get, it meant climbing all those damned stairs

---

[9] Janice or J: Myself, at this time Janice H. Moore, secretarial assistant to Dean Lewis J. Sherrill, Louisville Presbyterian Seminary. With my young daughter, Libby Moore, I lived at 1437 Hepburn Avenue, Louisville, Kentucky. Henry and I were not engaged yet when he first went overseas in October of 1943, but by May of 1944, we had decided to be married when he returned.

every time. Speedy[10] got so sick of lugging his pack & rifle & stuff up & down & back & forth that the last time we were alerted he just quietly dumped it all overboard — pack, rifle, everything! Just fed it to the Atlantic! It threw us into convulsions, but it's what we all felt like doing. If that ship had been hit we'd have drowned like rats we were packed in so close. Slept in shifts, three to one bunk. But, by God, the military meant us to go down, if we had to, under full arms & equipment.

With nothing better to do & nothing much to read, I played a lot of very low stake poker. Won in all, $80.00.

We landed at Liverpool on the 19th of October, made two or three stands until we got shook down & assigned to the jobs. Built a camp at Emborough Pond,[11] another at Plymouth, then came here the 1st of March. So here I am and this looks like the real thing to all of us.

Thursday, May 11, 1944

Hinkel & I went in to town for a few beers, but came home early to see if we had any mail. Found the tent full, and the bunch in here tonight are unusually noisy. So much arguing & yelling going on I can't hear myself think. Took me two hours to get my letter to J. written & I don't know whether I'll make it very far in this notebook.

Seems like our tent is like a pub for a bunch to gang up in. But all the boys know they can come here & sit around & talk, get a poker game going, or if they've come in off pass & are restless they can work it off a little before going to bed. There's usually one grouch in every tent who wants it quiet so he can sleep. I can sleep with all hell busted loose if I want to, & Jack & Arlie are O.K. too.

10 Pfc. Louis Dymond, 2nd platoon.
11 Emborough Pond was near the city of Bath, also the smaller town of Shepton Mallett.

In here tonight are Billington, Pigg, Black Mac, LaCoste & one or two others.[12] All talking about the invasion & arguing about it, when it's going to take place, where it's going to take place, how rough it's going to be, and of course, are *we* going to hit the beaches. Everybody has an opinion & they're all different.

Billington — not too big a guy, twenty-two, I think — dark hair, put together sort of loose & talks & acts a little slow & easy. From New York state. Good guy in every way & better educated than most. Always talking about Sherlock Holmes & saying, "Elementary, my dear Watson, elementary." Reads a lot, but A. Conan Doyle seems to be a great favorite of his.

Pigg — short, sort of squarebuilt, wears a small dark moustache. Good with the pat word or phrase, sometimes unprintable — but a very good man with his boys.

Black Mac. Now there's a man after my own heart. From Louisiana. Slow talking, easy going, doesn't have too much to say & can he ever play a guitar! Knows that New Orleans jazz from way back, but he knows my hillbilly songs, too. Big man & very dark-skinned. He's a guy to go down the river with, any old day.

LaCoste. One of the best. Also from Louisiana. Says he's a "swamp angel." We call him "Cajun." Jabbers French like a native. Built slim & trim, highstrung, very excitable. A good-looking kid, with a neat little black moustache.

Hinkel — my best friend in the whole outfit. He can act the fool with the best of them but he's got a real head on his shoulders.

One of the other boys is the fellow who got the summary courtmartial last fall at Emborough Pond. Fingered a jeep to go into Bath, got drunk & wrecked it. A line man is a fool to finger a jeep himself. The motor pool boys can get by with it.

12 Sgt. R. C. Billington; Sgt. Edwin Pigg; Cpl. Isaac O. McDonald; Pfc. Paul LaCoste, all 2nd platoon.

They can always say they're on a job for some officer. But a line man seldom has any business with one. Anyway, he got a summary & thirty days in the brig.

He is a good friend of mine, a very good friend, & damned if they didn't pick me to guard him to the stockade! Had to load up my gun with live ammunition & guard one of my own buddies to the damned guardhouse. It made me sick at my stomach. He took it all right. Tried to make a joke of it. Asked me what I would do if he was crazy enough to try to make a break for it. Would I really shoot him? I said, "Sure. Right through the guts." But it made me nearly puke just to have to make that long walk with him. I made up my mind right then if I was ever ordered to do such a thing again, I wouldn't. They could courtmartial me for disobeying an order.

He's made it fine, though — got his stripes back & doing well.

But the truth is, if there's another platoon in this man's army you can get more out of for a longer time than 2nd platoon, I've not seen it. Very few eightballs. They're not kids, but they are all some younger than I am. Sometimes, watching them & listening to them they make me feel like Grandpa Jones back home. Outside of Love & McCarl,[13] both old army like myself, I'm just about the oldest man in the outfit. I saw most of these boys come in as rookies & slowly turn into soldiers & played, by God, a little part in helping turn them into soldiers.

I was still platoon sergeant then. And we had it rough at Swift for a while. That first CO we had thought he was another General Patton & he ran a concentration camp instead of a training camp. As rookies the boys couldn't ever clean their rifles well enough. Every inspection the outfit got gigged because somebody's rifle wouldn't pass. I got tired of it myself, but felt sorrier for them.

---

[13] S/Sgt. T. P. Love, Supply Sergeant, Company A; S/Sgt. Carl McCarl, Mess Sergeant, Company A.

There's only one way to get a rifle clean & that's with steel wool, but it's strictly against regulations. Let an officer find that first tiny little shred of the stuff in a rifle barrel & as platoon sergeant you've had it. Summary courtmartial. But I stuck my neck out — called the squad leaders together & told them to pass it on to the boys but to, by God, be *certain* there never was any telltale shred of wool left in the barrel. We never had a dirty rifle again & there never was that first little piece of wool to give us away. We had a happy platoon, as far as inspections were concerned.

I saw most of these boys make their first stripes. I'd been on so many cadres & helped train so many rookies by then I could pick them inside two weeks — the ones who would steady up & shake down & make it. The ones who would do all right & the ones who would be eightballs to the day they died. They've worked out just about the way I figured them.

As a platoon, these boys are as tough as they come now. They can take care of themselves. As one pub keeper told me the other day, "They're the toughest lot of little lads I ever saw." You can't help being proud of them.

S & S had an article today about how everyone was waiting for the man in Radio City to press the button & make the big announcement. It's what has everybody teed off tonight. "You really think we'll be tabbed?"

"God, yes! Bound to be. What the hell you think we've had all this training for? They got us pinpointed!"

"Sure. We'll be the suckers who hit the beaches."

"They say Engineers will take 90% casualties."

"Goddamn! Do you *have* to talk about it? Ain't it bad enough without bringing it up all the time?"

"Well, look, now — this is the way I see it. Must be a hundred or two engineer outfits on this damn island. Say our chances of being picked are 150 to 1. That's pretty damn good odds, I'd say."

LaCoste, shuffling the cards, says, "If they was 1,000 to 1, I'd still have the shakes."

Me, I don't know. No way of knowing. We don't want to be picked & make no bones about it. I haven't heard a man shooting off his mouth trying to be a hero. We just want to get this damn mess over with & get home. Only B Company has had duck training[14] & I'm going to try not to get too worked up until the whole Battalion has had it. That will be the real tip-off, far as I'm concerned.

Sunday, May 14, 1944

Slept until 10:00 but got up in time for breakfast. Next meal isn't until four. Think I won't go into town tonight.

There was a Company dance last night & I went. I don't dance much. Too old for this jitterbugging & my kind of dancing is out of style nowadays. But I like to watch the fellows & I like to listen to the band. Loftis plays bass fiddle & they've really got a hot little outfit.

Billington & I were sitting together last night & he got to kidding me about another Company dance, back at Marston Manor, I think, anyway shortly after we got to England. He & I & a girl were sitting on a bench along the wall. I had a pack of Luckies, which were scarcer than hen's teeth at that time. I offered one to Billington, then to the girl. She took one, looked at the pack to see what make they were, then oooohed, "Ooooh, I just *adore* those Lucky Stripes!" And with my Luckies, I was on my way!

Mail call. Two letters from J. She is beginning to be pretty worried & not able to hide it as well as at first. Ordinarily she

14 Training in assault landings.

doesn't cry the blues much but sweating out this invasion is getting her down. And I've not been much help to her. Doing too much of my own kind of sweating. I've been restless the last couple of weeks & have been writing her twice a day too often. She's too smart not to know what that means. I did the same thing just before we shipped out & she figured it then. I don't usually have the time to write twice a day. Have written her twice already today & have an almost uncontrollable desire to write again. Even sent her a poem I cut out of S & S, about waiting & the miles & the time. A dead giveaway, but I let it go through. Why the hell I can't handle this I don't know, but I can't.

Sort of wish now I had gone ahead & given her a ring, but she didn't want one. She said the little silver Engineer insignia & chain I gave her Christmas were her engagement ring. She thought we ought to save the money & I know she's right. With both of us saving all we can we won't have too much to make a start with. We each have other responsibilities. She has Libby & an apartment to keep. I have to help my folks.

I've got myself cut down so short with a $60 allotment for savings & the $25 a month to the folks I haven't been able to go anywhere or do anything here in England. Only draw $20 a month. Sometimes I have been ashamed with the fellows. Couldn't do the things they do, or go where they've gone. Know they've thought many times I was a dull clod who didn't care about going to London & the other places. I do, but a three-day pass anywhere would have taken my whole pay & I'd have been broke the rest of the month. I don't mind borrowing a shilling now & then, but when you get into borrowing big you're behind forever. I haven't cut down the savings allotment because our future (if we have any) is more important to me than anything else.

Bunch of fellows in here as usual. They are composing and

improvising new verses of an old song. In their versions she did everything for an Engineer. I don't know when I've laughed so much. I must say they leave little to the imagination. Some of the least objectionable verses are:

> Around her thigh she wore a purple ribbon,
> She wore it in the winter and the merry month of May;
> And when I asked her why the hell she wore it,
> She wore it for an Engineer who's far, far away.

> Cho: Far away, far away
>   She wore it for an Engineer who's far, far away.

> In her cellar she keeps a baby buggy,
> She keeps it in the winter and the merry month of May;
> And when I asked her why the hell she kept it,
> She kept it for an Engineer who's far, far away.

> Cho:

> Behind the door her father keeps a shotgun,
> He keeps it in the winter and the merry month of May;
> And when I asked him why the hell he kept it,
> He kept it for that Engineer so far, far away.

That last far away is sung very mournfully & long drawn out. Black Mac's face trying to express woe is enough to put you in stitches.

Thursday, May 18, 1944

Well, today it came. We are alerted for movement & any fool knows what the movement is — Goodbye England, Hello France!

There are some worried faces & some sad ones. Several of the fellows have met nice English girls here they are serious about. John Coupe[15] has met one he's very fond of. For him & some others, leaving here will hurt.

The whole outfit now has a very bad case of invasion shakes. Very little talk about anything but assault landings, what it will be like, what the casualties will be, etc. Any way you look at it, it's not going to be any piece of cake. After the alert this morning I caught myself several times looking around & wondering for the hundredth time how the hell I got *here* & what the hell I'm doing here — me, Henry Giles, an old farmer boy from Caldwell Ridge, Knifley, Kentucky! For the first time in years a uniform doesn't seem to fit me. A little too tight.

I'm not made of hero material & I don't mind admitting I dread like everything getting into this thing. I think a man would be a liar to say he didn't. I haven't heard a one say but that he was scared as hell. In fact, several have said they don't expect to come out of it alive.

To show how jittery I am, I took a shower tonight. When I went to dress, for some reason I checked my dogtags & St. Christopher. The medal was wet & had clung to the back of one of the dogtags. For one frantic moment I thought I'd lost it & I never felt so naked and scared. A Catholic friend of J's had her pastor bless it & today I began to know how much it means to me. J. said St. Christopher was the patron saint of travelers. *This* traveler is going to need all the luck he can get.

For some reason it's very quiet in our tent tonight. Nobody hanging around. Don't know where Wall & Loftis are but there's only Hinkel and me. We're writing at the same table & each have a candle for light. Cool enough for a fire & the stove makes the tent cozy & warm. I like an evening like this once in

[15] T/4 (Sgt) John Coupe, H/S platoon (Headquarters & Service), Company A.

a while. I like all the fellows, but sometimes you just want to be quiet.

I think maybe, tonight, everybody wants to be quiet — everybody, like me, a little scared. It's a moment of truth. Hinkel & I were talking about how good our chances are of making it all the way through. I think, & so does he, they're pretty good if we don't have to make the assault. We're Engineers, not Infantry or Armor. We're Combat Engineers, sure — & we're going to be under fire. But I feel pretty hopeful that most of us will make it & don't much think I'm just talking to make a noise. It's a very strange feeling, though, to know you're heading for war — really on your way — a very queer, helpless, frightening feeling. But the rent's due & we have to move on.

Mail call. Four letters tonight, an old one, April 20, & three recent ones. She says that beginning with my letter of May 4, each letter has been opened by the base censor & resealed. That has never happened before, so she has had her "alert" too.

But I had to laugh. Hinkel's wife & Janice are both always asking what they can send us — what we need, etc. There's nothing we really need but some extra smokes & something sweet. We get a little hungry for good cookies & candy & cake, etc. But one night they both happened to ask, for about the 100th time, what they could send. For some reason we thought it would be cute to say, "Send us a dish of icecream." Only I went further & said, "Make it chocolate with pecan sauce." The *sauce* was in the letter of April 20th!

She has a neat way of telling me off. Not naggy or nasty — but rather blunt & straight & then it's over. When she gets through, though, you damn well know you've been told off. My lady has a temper — but I wouldn't give a dime for anybody who doesn't have at least a little. I've apologized. It was a damn fool thing to do.

Sunday, May 28, 1944

Nothing yet. Still sitting here. No work, just a hell of a lot of recreation — baseball, volleyball, basketball, etc. The days are really long now. Doesn't get dark until ten o'clock.

Everybody tries for a pass every night these days. As usual, most of us NCOs do without & let the boys have them. We only get so many for the outfit & we know the ropes too well to have to have a pass to go out. All we do is tell the guard we're going & when we'll be back. Only risk is the very slight one of running into some eager beaver MP who wants to check your pass, or getting fouled up some way & being late for bedcheck.

But Hinkel & I went in together last night & for once I thought our luck had run out. Both of us were well in our cups & for some reason Hinkel went crazy wild. We came out of the pub to head back to camp & he got to singing & yelling & kicking things over & stopping civilians & shouting at them & I couldn't do a damn thing with him.

I saw a squad of MPs down the street & knew we were in trouble if Hinkel didn't quiet down. They're usually pretty good joes & don't really want to haul you in but if you're drunk & disorderly they have to. But I've used a bold front with them before & had it work, so even though we didn't have passes & if they checked we'd be in trouble, I decided it was better to risk it than to go on trying to quiet Hinkel down. I already wasn't getting anywhere with that.

I took him by the arm & marched him down to them, told them we'd both had too much to drink, were about to be late, & we'd appreciate it if they'd run us out to camp. They did *and* didn't ask to see our passes. But durned if I'm not going to take a muzzle along for Hinkel next time.

First time I ever tried that approach was at Crowder. There was a redlight district in Joplin that was off limits. Well, I never in my life made use of a redlight district & wasn't there for the purpose then. But "off limits" is a natural invitation to see what it's all about. I spotted two MPs about the same time they spotted me. I was in trouble & knew it & having nothing to lose walked over to them, told them I was lost & would appreciate it if they would get me back into the main part of town. They checked my pass (I had one that night) & drove me back to the main street. I've used it half a dozen times since & found that if you're polite, if you're handling your liquor well, they'll cooperate. Glad it worked again last night.

Three letters tonight & one from Irene.[16] J. still showing tension. Irene worried because Charlie is in sick bay. Wonder if there is a living soul in the whole world who isn't worried tonight.

Sunday, June 4, 1944

Nothing yet. And nerves are sure wearing thin. I lost my bet on the invasion date & can't say I'm sorry.

Two letters today, May 30 & 31st. Mine to her still being checked by the base censor, but since May 18 (the day we were alerted) my letters have stopped coming.

She knows what it means. She knows two other women with men in England. They have put their heads together & have come up with — invasion, very near. Looks to me as if the top brass might as well have taken full page ads in all the big newspapers & announced the news. Women aren't fools. Stop their mail & they begin to add two & two & come up with four. I think such close security is its own biggest gossip.

We have heard all of southern England has been sealed off, also. No civilian travel allowed into or out of it. That's another dead giveaway. But to top it all, news of an invasion was flashed everywhere today, then denied. Must have been a hell

16 Irene Scott, Henry's oldest sister. Her husband, Charles Scott, was in the Navy.

of a security leak somewhere. Then they worry about what we'll say in our letters.[17]

Had a guitar in my hands tonight for the first time since leaving the States. Found I hadn't forgotten how to play one. We've been sitting around, a bunch of us, singing everything we could think of for a couple of hours. The boys seem to like my hillbilly songs. It's funny. I can never think of a song until I get an instrument in my hands. Then I never have to think. I can go from one to another for hours. Guess just having my hands on the strings brings them out. My kind of music isn't to everybody's liking but there are quite a few of the fellows that seem to enjoy it.

When the music ended & everybody left Hinkel & I settled down to write our letters. He was in the mood tonight. Propped his wife's picture up on the table in front of him & began talking to it. What he said was guaranteed either to keep me from thinking or make me think *too* damn much. What a guy he is.

Flash: We had chicken for chow tonight & I had a wing besides my usual neck. GI chickens are very peculiar birds. They only have wings & necks. Would like to see one alive.

D-day!

Tuesday, June 6, 1944

This is it! No false alarm today. This is D-day. The invasion is on. I would guess the first thing most of us thought was, thank God we missed it! I did & am not ashamed to admit it. I had a wonderful feeling of relief. Some other poor Engineer sonsabitches are catching it & having it rugged, but a miracle

---

[17] This was one of the most curious security breaks of the war. An AP teletype operator, who knew nothing at all about the invasion, was practicing on an idle machine to improve her speed. She typed a flash message saying Allied forces had landed in France. By error the perforated tape was sent out. It was caught immediately, but too late. The news had gone round the world.

happened & it wasn't us. Whatever we get when we go, it can't be as rough as today.

We've been listening to BBC on the radio most of the morning. It says Allied forces are landing on the northern coast of France. No place identified beyond that. We've been trying to guess where & most of the boys think Calais. It's the shortest distance.

Gen. Eisenhower released a message saying we would accept nothing less than full victory.

We have seen some of the big transport planes coming back. There must have been some parachute drops. These were C47s & the guide ropes were still dangling.[18]

We have heard Churchill's speech to the House of Commons. The old boy was really excited. His voice was sort of squeaky & trembly. He said over 4,000 ships are taking part in the landings & over 11,000 planes. He said, as best I can remember, "So far the commanders who are engaged report that everything is proceeding according to plan. And *what* a plan." We could hear the cheering as he spoke & when he had finished.

After the first excitement & realizing we'd been passed over for the time being, we've been fairly quiet. Just sitting around listening to the radio, thinking about those poor guys, & at the same time as relieved as hell it's not us. It could have been. Just a piece of luck, I suppose.

It's the middle of the afternoon here, now, so guess it's early morning at home & they are beginning to get the news. I'm wondering what Janice is doing, how she's taking it — & the folks. It will make Mama sick, for she looks on the dark side of things anyway. Have written them both & hope they begin to let our letters go through *fast* now.

Later: Listened to the radio again tonight & it looks as if they

18 Airborne troops of the 82nd and 101st Divisions had been dropped on the Cherbourg peninsula during the night of June 5th.

have got on. They've been telling about several beaches, all taken now. Some trouble at one, but nobody has got thrown back. What a hell of a big, big show it was!

Seemed a little queer to go to a movie here in camp tonight, just as if nothing had happened. Jack & Arlie & I talked about whether we ought to go. It seemed somehow disrespectful. Loftis finally said, "Hell, let's make the most of what we've got while we've got it. We can't do any good by not going & we'll be over there next."

It was an Abbott & Costello comedy & I don't suppose any of us ever laughed harder. Came out feeling pretty good, but it soon wore off. Tent is full tonight, everybody guessing when we'll go, too excited about the events of the day to settle down. It's hit me differently. I feel awfully tired, as if I'd worked hard all day. It's the let-down, I suppose.

Friday, June 9, 1944

Played volleyball all afternoon. Nice day for it, warm & sunny.

S & S today identified the beaches & said things were really rugged on the one called Omaha Beach. There was a hell of a lot more German strength there than they'd expected & the terrain was bad for breaking out. Some high land overlooked the beach & the Krauts were there in fortifications. Poured heavy fire down on the boys.

There was a map, too, in S & S & it showed the landings between Le Havre & Cherbourg. Omaha Beach, where the going was the toughest, is in the middle. The British landed on the left near Caen. American forces landed at Omaha & Utah beaches. The landing places are called Utah, Omaha, Gold, Juno & Sword. Wonder who thinks of names for these things? Somebody from Utah & somebody from Omaha must have wanted those names to go down in history. Depends how it comes out how pleasant they will be to remember.

S & S denies heavy casualties, but BBC says the Germans are claiming very heavy damage & many prisoners taken. You can never believe what the Krauts say, but I don't know that you can believe our propaganda, either.

Two letters today, May 22 & 29th. A little old. I hope to God she begins to get some mail soon. If the situation were reversed I'd be out of my mind.

Enclosed in one letter was the clipping from the Fort Smith newspaper announcing our engagement. We decided some time ago to be married when I get home, but there didn't seem much point in announcing it. Then I got to wanting it made official & formal, so she had her mother announce it. The Holts are so well known in Fort Smith that the paper really played it up big with a good picture of Janice, etc. I showed it to Hinkel & then put it in my wallet. For some reason it gives me an awfully good feeling. I knew she would wait for me without it, once she said she would. But I'm so damned proud of her I just wanted everybody who knew her to know she was mine.

Been reading Ernie Pyle's book, *Here Is Your War*. To me, he is the best of the war correspondents. I had read many of these columns back in the States, but have enjoyed reading them again. Then I worked on the crossword in the *Courier* a while. Sleepy, now, & tired from the volleyball.[19]

Sunday, June 11, 1944

Pretty today & most of us went to church — me for the first time since we got to England. Either I should be ashamed for

---

[19] I sent Henry a copy of the Louisville *Courier-Journal* once a week, mostly so he would have at least one crossword puzzle each week, but also to keep him abreast of Kentucky news.

not going earlier or for going today. I guess most of us had some notion we might feel better if we went. It didn't make me feel much better, though.

You can't help thinking what it's going to be like & will I be able to stand up to it & what kind of guts have I really got. I *hope* I've got enough but won't know till I get there.

I dread going without mail, too. Even here in England when we've moved there's been a lag & it stands to reason it will be longer in France. It all looks like sweat to me.

Played a doubleheader of softball this afternoon & my right arm is sore now. Two games is a little too much for the "old man."

Wrote J. this morning & again tonight.

Had chicken for chow with everything good to go with it. Billington said, "They're fattening us up for the kill." Bloody thought!

Mail call. Three letters & a package. I'll be so damned glad when she begins getting mail again. I don't know how she's stood it, but she's doing awfully well. The package was another of those good fruitcakes like she sent Christmas. June 23rd is my birthday. Long ago she asked what I'd like for it. I asked for another fruitcake. So here it is — a little early but welcome. Hinkel went to the kitchen for coffee & he & Black Mac & La-Coste & I have been having a real treat.

One letter from home tonight, too. Mama is so disheartened about me she can hardly write. She hasn't had any mail, either, naturally. Said she hadn't heard from J. the week before & was wondering why. I think I know. Janice writes her each week, tells her how many letters she's had & what the general news is. She didn't want Mama to know she hadn't heard. It's all a bloody mess & nothing but heartache for anybody. Wish to God somebody had clobbered Hitler before he started it.

Monday, June 12, 1944

I met Janice one year ago today. As crazy as it sounds, even with a war on, it's been the happiest year of my life. I wouldn't have missed it for the world even though I've had to pay a hell of a price in longing & wishing.

Black Mac came in a while ago with a letter from his girl. He said, "Isn't June 12th the anniversary of the day you met Janice?" I told him it was. He read me part of his letter & his girl was reminding him it was their anniversary.

It figures. Mac & I both went on furlough last June. We both got back to camp the same night, one day early. He met his girl on that furlough & I met J. though I don't suppose we told each other at the time. But both of us were laughing tonight over going into Austin on our extra time & drinking everything from muddy water to Old Crow trying to get a buzz & neither of us could. Worst pass we ever went on together.

Played more volleyball today. Weather very beautiful. We have cussed the English weather all winter but the old island seems to be turning on all its charms for us as we get ready to leave. I don't suppose any of us will ever forget England. We've had to work hard, but we've also had some wonderful times. I'm going to miss the pubs. I wish we had them back home. They're more like a social club than a bar or tavern.

But we didn't come over here to take out naturalization papers & it's time to be moving on.

Thursday, June 15, 1944

All passes cancelled today & it's definite we'll move within a few days, three or four at the most. Much wailing & gnashing of teeth. Many are the broken hearts, real or fancied, most I'd guess soon to be mended by the mademoiselles of France. Men have died & worms have eaten them, but not for love. Who said that?

There was a chapel service earlier tonight & most of the fellows went, including me. I have a strange, queer feeling of being awfully alone, or lonely, if there's any difference & of not wanting to be alone. Went to chapel mostly, I think, just to be with the others, for with my mixed up feelings about religion it couldn't be expected to do me any good. I *wish* I could believe as I was taught to believe. It would be very comforting right now. But I don't & can't. All I know is that I never in my whole life ever had a prayer answered & I have prayed for some good, not selfish things. I believe in God, of course, but not the personal God I was taught to believe in. It's very vague with me as yet. Some kind of force, but not especially any loving force, behind life. I don't see much evidence of any divine love or care right now, for instance. I think I trust J's St. Christopher more than anything, but that I suppose is because she believes. She is a Presbyterian, but I happen to know she wishes she had been born a "cradle" Catholic. She says it's too late, now. Her mind questions too much of their theology. But if she had been born into the Catholic church, it would never have questioned.

Been laughing at the sudden rush of letter writing tonight. Men who haven't written a letter for a month are suddenly as busy as beavers, coming in to borrow paper, ink, stamps, anything to get a letter off. Last minute conscience? Could be, but I'd guess it's last minute realization that the fun is over, that home is after all pretty good & a hell of a long way off.

Have just burned the last of J.'s letters. Have no way to keep them. And I've just written her. Hard to do & keep nothing from showing through.

Great shakedown of much collected clutter. Being a firm believer in traveling light, I've not had much to discard. A few odds & ends that could be put in the fire is all. To me very little is worth the trouble to haul around. Besides, I've been too broke to acquire anything.

Felt very sorry for a kid that was in here a while ago. He's met a very nice girl here in Gloucester & at least *thinks* he is deeply & seriously in love. Had a date tonight, couldn't keep it, couldn't even call her. About ready to cry over it. Told him to write to her & he'd probably hear from her before we get across.

Been thinking of an old song I used to hear Muh sing sometimes.[20] Don't remember much of it but it was something about,

> Gloucester maids are sweet and fair,
> Gloucester maids are waiting there . . .

Of course that was the Gloucester in the States, but maybe some of the English Gloucester maids will wait for those who want them to.

Southampton
Tuesday, June 20, 1944

We are in the marshaling area in Southampton. A big tent city divided up into sub-areas out in the edge of the town. We had a hell of a convoy here with much traffic on the roads & many delays & long waits. Finally got here & it was raining & blowing & we couldn't find our sub-area. Wandered all over the damn place then we ran across it in some woods.

If we were prisoners of war we couldn't be more closely guarded. There's not only a barbed wire fence all around the camp but there are guards posted everywhere to keep civilians from coming anywhere near. By george, when you come through that gate & get behind this wire it really hits you that

[20] Muh was the family name for Henry's grandmother Giles.

the only way out is through France & Germany. It's strictly a one-way road.

This storm is delaying our departure, they say. Don't know when we'll get away. There is a big tent where movies are shown round the clock to help pass the time. We can also write, but mail won't go out until we have sailed.

We have been more or less briefed, given three seasickness pills, issued French money, a French language phrase book & an army publication pamphlet telling us how to behave in France. This last is a real lulu. For instance, "Some French are good & some are bad." Billington said, "What do they do? Put arm bands on 'em so we can tell 'em apart?"

And this, "You probably won't be meeting any of the better class Frenchmen." One guy said, "Who wants to? All I want is to meet some of the lower class French women!"

And this, "Don't think every pretty girl you see is interested in you. Maybe she isn't?"

And a guy with a slow drawl & a definite way with women says, "How ya gonna know unless you try?"

Wonder why they put out poop like that?

The French phrase book has given us some fun, too. One fellow was thumbing through it muttering to himself, "Ou est la . . . ou est la . . . ou est la . . ." then he looks up at LaCoste, who is Louisiana French, & says, "What the hell is the French word for whorehouse?"

LaCoste, pretending insult, draws himself up & says, "The French do not have whorehouses."

The guy slams his phrase book shut & says, "Then I'm not going to France. This trip ain't necessary for me."

I don't believe many of us are going to get very far with French, but as long as we have LaCoste we ought to do all right. He has taught me to say "oeufs" and "vin" and "comment allez vous," and he has run through every form of "amour" for all the guys!

The boys are carrying it off with a light touch. Discipline & training really show in them & the 291st has always had plenty of both. Some think too much. They should have been in the *old* army.

Mail call. Two letters, June 6 & 7th. Had to go off by myself to finish reading them. Was afraid I would cry. I hope to God she never has to go through anything again like she did on the 6th.

From Carentan to St. Lô

Aboard LST #311
Wednesday, June 21, 1944

IF THIS storm lets up enough we'll shove off today or tonight. The Battalion has been split up for the crossing. Don't know where the rest of the outfits are. Only Company A is on this ship.

I don't feel as nervous as I thought I would. Not nearly as nervous as when we left the States. I'm not as cool as a cucumber — I notice I'm chain smoking — but I'm not as shaky as I thought I might be.

Everybody went to church this morning before we loaded on. So did I. But I couldn't pray except for courage, for I don't believe one man is saved in answer to prayer & another man who may have prayed just as hard & deserved to live perhaps better, gets killed. I don't believe God operates that way. I don't know exactly what I believe, but I have never seen any evidence that God interferes at all. If you're in the right place at the right time & a bullet or shell comes your way, you're going to get it. All I can see is take care of yourself as best you can.

I do believe in some kind of hereafter, although I don't know what. That's also very vague with me. I just think it will be all right, whatever it is, for since I don't believe in heaven, neither do I believe in hell.

Area 4, France

Sunday, June 25, 1944

We landed yesterday afternoon, the 24th, at Omaha Beach & are now in an assembly area back of the beach waiting for the rest of the Battalion.

Spent my birthday crossing the channel. Only thought of it once — sometime during the morning. Thought perhaps it was the strangest birthday I'd ever spent or was likely ever to spend. Only hope I'm still around for the next one.

We came over combat loaded & rode ashore in our trucks which had been waterproofed in England. It was a moment of truth when that ramp went down & the trucks began to move out. I had a wild feeling all at once of wanting off — it was like a nightmare that I was actually riding into a shooting war. Like some crazy dream. I sure didn't feel like singing "Onward, Christian Soldiers" I can tell you — or like marching as to war. It was the first test of guts for me. I sat there & swallowed the chunk in my throat & tried to show nothing. It's a one-way ticket, & even if it doesn't get punched somewhere along the line, it's going all the way — no stopovers or delays enroute.

It's been 19 days since D-day but that beach is still one hell of a mess to see. Burned out vehicles, tanks, trucks, jeeps, half-tracks, rolls of wire, curious looking obstacles, posts stuck in the sand, abandoned equipment, every kind of junk you can think of strowed around. A lot of stuff was floating in the water. They say the big storm washed away tons of supplies that had been unloaded on the beach. All the troops, or nearly all, & most of the supplies have to be unloaded there & ships were unloading as we came in.

We are bivouacked behind the top of that hill where the Krauts were entrenched & poured so much fire onto the beach. The road comes up the side of the hill. There was a lot of traffic on it as we came up & impossible to keep intervals. Infantry just unloaded were moving along the road, too. They had to keep left & right & razzed everybody who was riding. Well, they're as new & green as we are right now.

We rolled up into this field, with what's left of an apple orchard over to one side. We stopped & First Sarge climbed out of the Company truck & came back down the line, saying, "All right, boys, this is it. Unload. Unload." He went off where the officers were.

We piled out, some of the boys still shaky on their legs from the rough crossing. Dumped our stuff & just stood there looking around, talking a little, waiting to see what came next. It was drizzling rain & pretty cool. And not much to see — just this field with a lot of shell holes in it, some burned out tanks & half-tracks & stuff. There were some old clots of manure. This must have been a pasture before the invasion.

All at once Hinkel leaned down & picked up a handful of dirt & sifted it through his fingers. Looked over at me & laughed. "French soil," he said. "Just wanted to make sure."

I laughed, too, & said, "No different from my old place in Kentucky. Dirt's dirt no matter where you find it."

Sgt. Smith[1] yelled for Hinkel & the other platoon leaders & they went over. Stood around talking a minute & I heard Hinkel say, "Nuts."

Then he came back & told us there'd be no kitchen set up. "K-rations," he said, "whenever you get hungry, but first dig, and dig good and deep."

Billington said, "Why? Haven't they got the Krauts pushed back far enough yet?"

---

[1] 1/Sgt. William H. Smith, Company A.

Hinkel said, "Don't ask me. All I know is it's an order. Dig!"

Pigg said, "Can't we eat first? I'm getting pretty damned hungry. That Navy food has done wore off."

Hinkel said, "According to what our good friend First Sarge said you'd better dig first & eat later."

Everybody bitched a little but began digging.

Hinkel & I looked over the ground & picked us out a good place, a little high & we thought it might be fairly dry. We talked about digging separate trenches. I asked if we had to. He said, "No. He didn't say anything about that."

So we decided to dig us a two-man trench so we could use our shelter halves for cover in case it rained harder during the night. We could also put down two blankets & have two for cover by sharing them.

It took us about an hour & then we began to hit seepage & had to quit not more than a foot down. Hinkel went off to see if he could scrounge a tarp & came back with a torn shelter half. Best he could do, he said. We put that down & laid our blankets in & just pulled our shelter halves over to keep the hole dry until we could put them up later.

It was after ten o'clock by then, but the army is on double summer time so dark doesn't come until nearly eleven. We decided to eat. We were supposed to have been issued C-rations, but most of us got K, one each for breakfast, dinner & supper. Black Mac came over & said he had three breakfasts. I traded him a dinner for one of his breakfasts. Then Geary[2] & Cornes[3] & Pigg came over & we hunkered down & ate. Habit, I suppose, made me open a supper. K-rations would keep you alive, I guess, but they sure wouldn't keep you happy. I think they use embalming fluid to preserve the stuff.

We were just finishing up & Hinkel was saying keep the joint

2 Sgt. Joseph H. Geary, 1st squad leader, 2nd platoon.
3 Sgt. Tommy Cornes, 2nd squad leader, 2nd platoon.

clean, we didn't want First Sarge on our tails, when we heard some planes. Didn't think anything about it, didn't even look up. But about that time all hell busted loose. Every kind of gun the army uses opened up on those planes. Ack-ack, machine guns, antitank, even 105s from the way it sounded. The noise was terrific. It rocked you back on your heels. The ground shook, your stomach caved in, your ears hurt.

Then hot iron began falling all over the place. I remember thinking, what the hell! Then it dawned on me they were enemy planes, our guns were firing & it was shrapnel from our own guns that was falling all around us. About that time I picked up my feet & traveled. Hinkel got to our trench first & we got scrambled like eggs. I landed on top of him & heard him give a "Whoomph," & next thing I knew I was trying to unwrap one of his legs from around my neck. I lost my helmet for a minute — think I ran out from under it when I jumped — but I found it & clamped it on.

We got ourselves unlocked finally & stayed scrooched, waiting for the bombs. After a while we realized none were falling — not in our area anyway — & the firing was beginning to die down. We crawled out. I told Hinkel we had to dig that hole a hell of a lot deeper. I felt like my tail had stuck up an exposed mile & I didn't like the idea of having it shaved off. He grinned & said, "Why didn't you put your helmet on your tail instead of your head?" If I'd thought of it, I would have. We dug a little more but there really wasn't any use. We were down to water already.

Everybody was digging & wondering what the hell had happened. The Krauts hadn't dropped any bombs but the shrapnel from our own guns had fallen all over the place.

We got settled down finally. The guns let off two or three more times during the night & believe me it felt mighty good to be down in a hole in the ground. It needs a stouter roof than a puptent, though. I'm going to get real fancy & lay some brush or logs over, pile the dirt on top. That ought to do it.

Today we've heard it was "Bedcheck Charley" & his pals. They tell us he comes over every night around dark & lays a few eggs, mostly they say trying to knock out the shipping. But he might mistake his target some night & I mean to be ready for him.

Things in general still snafu today — equipment lost, duffle bags missing, nobody knowing where anything is. It always happens in moving. You'd think in a Company, less than 200 men, somebody could keep track of the stuff. But no — there's always a foul-up. A kitchen of sorts has been set up, though, so we'll have hot chow tonight.

Still drizzling rain today & mighty chilly for this time of year. Wrote J. & home tonight. First chance I've had. Not a hell of a lot I can tell them but they have to know I'm "Somewhere in France." The kind of censorship imposed on us seems pretty stupid to me when the papers at home are printing maps of the fighting areas & S & S identifies areas & units just a few days after some piece of action. No use arguing with the army, though.

Near Vierville
Wednesday, June 28, 1944

Moved here yesterday, near what's left of a little village. Battalion was here & sent for us. They came over on an LST as we did. B & C Companies haven't showed yet. They are on regular troop ships.

Nobody has to be told to dig any more! Soon as we unloaded the first tool grabbed was a shovel. Hinkel & I dug us a very fancy trench this time. It's drier here & we got it good & deep. Then we found some planks & boards in some rubbish & laid

them over, piled the dirt back on good & thick. Over that we
put our puptent. We felt very secure in it last night & I slept
right through Bedcheck Charley & all the guns for once.

Saw my first Germans today. We don't have any work details
yet, no assignments & I've already checked out the guns,[4] so Mac
& LaCoste & I went prowling around late in the afternoon.
There's a PW cage not far from here & on the road we saw a
patrol bringing in about twenty prisoners. If they are "supermen" we've fallen for a lot of propaganda. They looked lousy
& undersized & scurvy & dirty, with greasy hair & flat mouths &
short necks. I looked good as they passed, trying to find at least
one who looked like a real Nazi, such as I had read about.
There weren't any. Their uniforms are rough & shoddy & they
were shuffling along, looking miserable. Black Mac laughed
suddenly & said, "Well, there they are, Adolf's supermen."

Suddenly one of the prisoners saw us & grinned, pointed at
his chest & yelled, "Russki! Russki!" A guard poked him with
his bayonet & he scrambled on by. We didn't know what he
meant but today we've heard that the Krauts have been using
Russian & Polish prisoners of war in their lines in this area.

We went on into the town. The weather has cleared up a
little & it has turned warmer & we had nothing better to do.
Felt a little foolish lugging our Mıs along but orders are, under arms at all times. Been a long time since I've had to sling a
Garand over my shoulder. But we'll get used to it.

This was the first time we had ever seen a real bombed-out
town. Not a building left whole. Just walls, sometimes only
one wall, a big chimney or smokestack standing all by itself, the
streets full of rubble. There is not one house in the village left

---

4 2nd platoon had a .30-caliber machine gun for each squad and one .50-caliber
which the Weapons Sergeant operated. As Weapons Sergeant, it was Henry Giles'
responsibility to see that all the machine guns were kept clean and in firing
order. His own .50-caliber was usually mounted on the platoon Hq. truck.

intact. It gave me a curious, displaced feeling to look at the damage that can be done.

We found one house with just the roof caved in. It was a two-story house, built of stone. We went inside on the lower floor. There was a small hall & a room opening off each side. Sort of tiptoeing we went through. One must have been a living room. There was a sofa, wet & ruined, some tables & chairs, a fireplace with a clock on the mantel. It had stopped at ten minutes to four. We wondered if that was about the time the Navy opened up its big guns on D-day. Across the hall was a dining room. We didn't go any farther. It smelled so sour & it somehow turned your stomach. I kept thinking, somebody lived here. This was somebody's home — and now look at it. I said, "Let's get out of here."

Black Mac said, "Hell, yes. It gives me the creeps."

But the people have begun to come back. You wouldn't think they would. What's there to come back to? But when we went out of the house we saw several coming down the street. They would stop & look at a pile of rubbish, shake their heads & walk on. LaCoste spoke to them. They jabbered back & forth a while. He said they hadn't gone far away. Just back in the country a little way. Now they were coming home. Home?

Some, they told him, never left the town. Just holed up in cellars. They'll keep on living in their cellars till they can find a little of their stuff & begin trying to fix up their homes again.

I can already tell my French phrase book isn't going to do me much good. Even if I could make the people understand me, I couldn't understand them. They talk too fast.

We came on back to the area, then. Most of us pretty hungry these days. The cooks haven't been able to come up with anything but stew & hash. We have stew one meal, hash the next.

No mail yet. Probably won't be for some time.

Carentan

Friday, June 30, 1944

We got our work assignments yesterday & moved here into a right pretty orchard near this town. Seems that most of the traffic, & what a hell of a lot there is of it, comes through this town — from the beaches where everything is unloaded, going north toward Cherbourg, & west to the other front. The Battalion's assignment is to keep the sector of the Isigny–Cherbourg road open from Carentan to Ste. Mère Eglise. Our outfit is assigned to maintain the bridge here. It's called Tucker Bridge, after some officer who was killed on it. A lot of other people are liable to get killed on it, too, including us. We found that out for ourselves today.

We were working near the bridge when we heard some shells whistling around & saw some bursts up the road a piece. We kept on working, thinking (at least I did) that it was our own artillery. They're up on a ridge of land not very far away. Finally a shell screamed in & landed about a 100 yards away, right on the road.

I think it was Holbrook straightened up & said, "What the hell's going on here?" [5]

The next hit was damned close & we all got the idea about the same time, but Hinkel yelled, "Hit the dirt! Hit the dirt! The damned Krauts are shooting at us!"

We hit the ditches & it didn't take us long & they began laying it up & down the road. Let me tell you, artillery fire is hell let loose. There comes this long, wild screeching noise that gets louder & louder until you think your ears will burst. You're lying there trying to make yourself as little as possible, trying to get down in the dirt, trying to dig in with your belly & thighs. And you know the damned thing is going to hit somewhere & you wait & feel like it's got eyes & can see *you!* You wait & then

[5] Pfc. Wiley A. Holbrook, 2nd platoon.

there is this huge, enormous crash & explosion & it feels as if the whole earth just rose up & fell back under you.

Then it gets quiet & the shrapnel begins to hit against the buildings & the road & you know it's red hot & if a piece of it hits you in the right place you're a gone gosling. Then here it comes again — the long screech, the noise, & maybe it's closer this time, & dirt & pebbles spray all over your back. I scrooched my eyes so tight they hurt — as if that would do any good. Clenched my jaws so tight they wouldn't come open. I don't know what I thought — don't think I thought anything, really. Just lay there & hung on & hung on. Finally they got tired & quit. Waited a little longer to make sure.

Then we got up & checked around. Nobody hurt. But we sure were shook. Speedy Dymond is a Virginia boy & slow as molasses. Nobody ever saw him get in a hurry about anything. He doesn't even talk in a hurry. When we got up & were brushing ourselves off, Speedy took his helmet off, wiped his face, looked around & took a good breath. Then he said, "Why doesn't somebody tell us these things? Why, a man could get himself killed on this durned bridge!" Coming from Speedy it sounded so funny & he looked so offended, it got a laugh. And that was good.

Now we've learned the Krauts shell the bridge & the road all the time trying to knock out the bridge & the supply line. Nice little assignment we've drawn. Well, we just have to get used to being shook. They say this bridge is very important.[6]

---

[6] General Bradley considered the Carentan bridge vital and there was considerable worry about it for some time. If the Germans decided to break through and retake it, the Allied supply line would have been sliced in two, as well as the armies. The Cherbourg harbor was so badly wrecked by the Germans that it was many weeks before it could be made useful for unloading troops and supplies. All supplies and troops were therefore unloaded at Omaha Beach and moved up and across the peninsula over the Carentan road and bridge. See *World War II, a Photographic Record of the War in Europe from D-Day to V-E Day*, edited by Ralph G. Martin and Richard Harrity.

Last night, which was the first night we were here, Hinkel &
I dug our trenches over near the hedgerow. We knew there was
some outfit on the other side but since they were "friendly" we
didn't pay any attention. Damned if when old Bedcheck Charley came over, right on time, an anti-tank gun didn't cut loose
right over our heads. Every time it fired we could see the
flame & every time it fired it almost bounced us out of our hole.
That thing has really got concussion. It rolled us around like a
pair of dice. We stayed with it all night but got up this morning feeling pretty beat. And we moved today. Billington was
just down the row from us & he said he got up this morning feeling like somebody had been using him for a rubber ball.

Haven't had a chance to write J. for a couple of days but did
tonight. Jeff [7] brought some cider around a while ago. Somebody found a big vat of it. It's helping a lot. He's a wild, crazy
kid, good for a laugh a minute — crazy about motors, cars, anything that will run. He's dying to get his hands on one of these
Kraut tanks that will still run. He's driving for the Lieut. [8]
right now & has a chance to get around & do a little "liberating."
Damned generous with it, too.

Saturday, July 1, 1944

We're still getting it pretty hot on the road & bridge. Even
the MPs who direct the traffic hate this bloody stretch of the
road. They stay behind sandbag bunkers as much as they can &
only come out if things get in such a snarl they have to. And
the traffic does get balled up. There's so much of it, so many
trucks & so much supply going up, they can't keep intervals.
Some tinhat officer is always coming around bellering about
keeping intervals, keeping intervals. The speed limit across the

[7] T/4 Jeff Elliott, 2nd platoon roster, but motor pool.
[8] 1/Lt. Alvin E. Edelstein, platoon commander, 2nd platoon.

bridge is supposed to be 20 mph, but nobody wants to crawl across that bridge. They gun it & get across as quick as they can, then get slowed up in a jam on the other side. Saw a truck stalled right on the bridge today & was that driver ever sweating! Leaning out the window yelling for something to get moving, get going, get the hell out of the way. An MP finally had to go out & get the foul-up straightened out.

We were glad of those sandbag bunkers ourselves today. Bunch of us were working on the bridge approach this afternoon when we heard that high, whining scream coming in. A bunker was handy so five or six of us made a flying tackle for it. We flattened & lay there. The Krauts threw one 88 after another in, all over the damned place. We thought we'd had it this time. One came in noisier than the others, headed straight for us. It got louder & louder until it was right on top of us & a thousand boxcars with locomotives attached couldn't have been noisier — at least to me. Then we heard a thud & I came as close to dying from fear as I ever will, waiting for it to blow us all to pieces. Nothing. No explosion. Just quiet. And that was the last of the barrage. We waited to make sure, then crawled up, still shaking.

Nobody said anything for a minute, then Schommer said, right peevishly, "Sometimes I feel like Willie. I'd like to get my hands on the guy who invented that damned 88." [9]

It brought a laugh. We all would like to get our hands on him. You get the feeling the damned things can all but go around corners. Billington brushed himself off & said, "By God, if my nose had been a shovel I'd have been speaking Chinese in another five minutes."

When we went around from behind the bunker we saw the

[9] Cpl. A. C. Schommer, 2nd platoon. The reference he made to "Willie" was from a Bill Mauldin cartoon in *Stars & Stripes*. Willie was standing grimly by as a German prisoner was being interrogated. The interrogation officer was saying to him, "I'll let you know, Willie, if we find the one who invented the 88."

dud stuck right in the middle of the sandbags. The one that would have got us — and it was a dud. Very awesome, believe me. A moment of truth. LaCoste laughed all at once & said, "Anybody want it for a souvenir?" It made me shudder. It came too damn close to being a final souvenir to suit me.

Schommer has it really rough. He's one of our radiomen & he has to stick right at that bridge every day. The rest of us draw other details sometimes, but Schommer has to take it every day. He doesn't like it a damn bit & I don't blame him. But it's his job & he does it.[10]

What a day. Only good thing about it is the mail finally came. There were ten letters from J. — June 10 through June 17, with two for the 11th & 16th. She was getting the letters held up after May 18, but was still sweating out D-day. By the 16th she was feeling some better. She & the folks had an arrangement if they got a telegram with bad news one of them, Irene probably, would go into town & call her. She believed by the 16th or 17th they would have heard if anything happened to me on D-day.

Tonight the whole outfit got their hair clipped clear to the skull. It's a sort of initiation rite, I guess you could call it. It marks an old "Peninsular" — one who's been baptized by fire.

From what I've seen of France so far I don't think I would much like it even in peacetime. England was a little like home but France is really a foreign country. The fields around here are little, some of them not much bigger than a good-sized barn lot back home & they're fenced with these hedgerows. Looks as if the people had thrown up a kind of dirt wall & planted these

[10] Al Schommer says about Tucker Bridge: "I spent most of that period in an abandoned German foxhole on the river bank which we set up as a radio station. Three radio operators manned this station on eight hour shifts for several weeks. Our job was to call Bn. Hqs. each time the bridge was hit by artillery so a work crew could be dispatched for repairs. Several MPs were killed at this bridge."

hedges & now they've grown up tall & thick & bristly. Make very good hiding places for Kraut snipers, too.

Everything here is so old, too. The buildings, what's left of them, look like they'd been here since time began. Saw a S & S today & it said Normandy was the "milk bucket" of France. From what I've seen so far the milk bucket has been kicked over. All I've seen have been dead cows. If I ever find a live one I aim to tie her to a tree & milk her just to see what fresh milk tastes like. Have had none since we left the States.

Cloudy & drizzly again today. I drew Sgt. of the Guard tonight. Lt. Hayes is officer of the guard.[11] Have to get the password & get it set up now.

Monday, July 3, 1944

My big news tonight is that I saw Gens. Eisenhower & Bradley today. They passed over our bridge in a jeep. I was so busy trying to execute my best salute when I saw the four stars I barely recognized them. I didn't know any of the top brass were over here but some of the fellows say they have heard that Gen. Bradley has been here since the day after D-day.

I know one thing for sure about France. They have the biggest & the most mosquitoes I ever saw in my life. I guess it's all these canals & the low, swampy country, but I honestly saw a column down on the road today that looked black & just like a swarm of bees. And I could swear they are as big as blackbirds. Bite? My God, when they zero in on you, you feel it.

We had a little fun today firing at some Kraut planes that came over. We don't see many in the daytime for our boys keep them pretty well scared off, but a few wandered over today. Everybody was shooting like crazy — Arlie's boys, Jack's and

11 1/Lt. Frank R. Hayes, Mess & Supply officer, Company A. Also Company censor.

ours. Don't figure the .30s would have much effect but my .50 is a pretty lethal weapon, with that long black barrel & a bullet half an inch in diameter. You could bring a plane down with it if you got it in a vulnerable spot. But these boys stayed up too high.

Hinkel will have to let me have a gun-cleaning detail tomorrow.

Saw a dogfight between a Spitfire & a Kraut 109 today, too. They were all over the sky, turning & wheeling & chasing. Don't know how it came out. They went out of sight, but my money would be on the Spit. He was faster & looked to be out-maneuvering the Kraut.

All the fellows are trying to find parachute nylon for scarves. They're in style these days. There's plenty of the stuff, from the drop the day before D-day. Don't think I'll follow the fashion. I'm not exactly the flyboy type.

We have such a long twilight here it's pretty good. Black Mac & LaCoste are sitting on a tarp in front of my tent right now. Mac, easy as always, LaCoste jabbering away. Both are cleaning their rifles. You spend most of your free time cleaning your gun or trying to keep it from getting wet, or drying it out if it does get wet, scrubbing the rust off, cleaning the bore.

LaCoste talks so much & so fast that his tongue gets away from him & when he can't think of the right word he just makes one up. He just now said, "Sgt. Giles, why don't you get me off that bumbdaddling road?"

I said, "What the hell's bumbdaddling?"

"It's got bombs & it addles you."

Makes sense. I said, "All right. Want to clean guns tomorrow?"

LaCoste says, "Sure. Sure. I'll clean guns."

Well, it may be tedious, but it's not a bad detail to draw.

Mail call. Three for me & one from home. J's letters are

old, before the last ones — but every one so good & welcome. She thinks she chatters too much. If she thinks that, I have failed to make her understand how much it means to me to know what dress she wore to the office, that she had trouble putting her hair up, what she had for lunch, what she worked on at the office that day. She keeps herself so real to me. And she tells me all the foolishness between herself & Libby. I never knew a mother & daughter like them before. They have so much fun together. They seem to like each other better than anyone else, better than their other friends. But J. was so young when Libby was born I suppose it's natural they would have a lot of the same interests.

Thursday, July 6, 1944

Drew charge of a work detail in Carentan yesterday. Orders came down to begin to clean the town up, get the streets cleaned of rubble & patched so traffic can get through. Hinkel asked me to take it. I've got Rog, McCutcheon, Pink, Street, Implazo, Gregory, Morello & Marucci — all 3rd squad boys.[12]

The Krauts are still shelling the town. A dozen times today we had to quit work & take shelter. Sometimes they're too blamed close for comfort, other times not so near. Gregory grins when they're hot & when the dust has settled & we're all still in one piece, he says, "Damn poor shots, those Krauts. They didn't get us *that* time."

Implazo says, "I hope to God they don't ever improve."

So do I!

B and C Companies are building a bypass to help take care of the bottleneck, too. Heard today one of the C Company boys

---

12 The Battalion history does not have a complete roster of all men with their first names and ranks. Except for John Pink and Walter Street, Henry does not now remember the other first names. All of the men were Privates or Pfcs, however.

got hurt pretty badly by a mine. He was clearing the road shoulder.[13]

Carentan is a mess but it's not in as bad shape as Vierville was. Most of the buildings have been hit but they've not been flattened. There's a roof left or three walls or something to hold them up. And durned if the people aren't milling around all over the place, cleaning it out, trying to open up for business again. You wouldn't think anybody who didn't *have* to stay around here would, but they do. It's a funny war, with civilians all mixed up in it.

I found a meat market open for business today and bought a couple of steaks for Hinkel and me. We're still getting too much hash & stew to suit me & I fancied a steak tonight. I think they're butchering these dead cows but as long as they don't stink, I don't mind. It's still beef. Also found a bakery & got some bread.

Hinkel had a hard day down on the road today. Speedy and some of the boys also had a narrow escape.[14] Nearly got it. Anyway, I built a fire & fried the steaks in our mess kits. I believe we could have eaten two more & we did eat all the bread.

On the noon break today we got to rummaging around in a bombed-out men's clothing store. We found a bunch of straw hats — mostly the old-fashioned stiff straw sailors. Just fooling around we began trying them on. About that time a fellow came up, said he was a photographer for Reuter's wire service & if we'd line up & put the hats on he'd like to use the picture.

[13] Pfc. Francis Buffone. Ironically, Pfc Buffone was the only mine casualty suffered by the Battalion during the entire war.

[14] Speedy Dymond says about his narrow escape: "I might not be here today had not one of the officers come along once when he did. We were maintaining Tucker Bridge at Carentan. Apparently the gun that was shelling was low on ammunition as they concentrated at 10:00 A.M. and 2:00 and 4:00 P.M. Those were our heaviest traffic times. The day I will never forget an officer told us suddenly to leave. We had no more than thrown our shovels down and hit the dirt on the other side when an 88 hit the bridge exactly where we had been working."

We did, feeling like fools & probably looking like thugs. Wrote J. about it so if the picture *should* be used in the States she'd know to look for it.[15]

Some of the boys bitch about some of the officers, but I think we're pretty well off. Of course, I haven't seen an old army officer or a West Point man since I left Fort Ord, but there aren't enough of them to go around & in a crash program like this officers have got to be made. The Col. was R.O.T.C. but he was also an engineer in civil life. Capt. Gamble[16] is OCS, but he was Tac officer at Belvoir for a year before coming to the 291st. I think he knows the score. Lt. Edelstein is OCS, but he was an engineer in civil life, too. I've been in the army long enough I can smell a good officer from a bad one a mile away. We're pretty well off, I think.

Mail call. Three letters & one from home. Thank God they have all heard since D-day now. That sweat is over for them. With her usual interest J. is armchair-generaling the whole peninsular war! She doesn't like this second front. Says either we shouldn't have gone into Italy at all or we should have followed through with Churchill's idea. Says this is a political trap. I sometimes worry she may talk too much.

Friday, July 7, 1944

Haven't seen the sun for days. Cloudy & rainy all the time. The clothing in my barracks bag has mildewed. Doesn't spring ever come to this part of Europe?

Went into a cathedral in Carentan today. It had been bombed but not completely destroyed. Part of the roof was left & all the side walls. Everything was covered with dust & rubble, but the altar & paintings & statues hadn't been wrecked.

---

15 Associated Press picked the picture up from Reuter's and it appeared on the front page of practically every metropolitan daily in the United States.

16 Captain James H. Gamble, Company A Commander.

It was beautiful. Our 180 I.Q. genius, who can't push a wheelbarrow without fouling up, knows a lot of history. He said this cathedral was built in the 12th century. It's a pity beautiful old things must be destroyed, but that's war for you.

This is pure rumor but it's all over the outfit. For a long time everybody's been saying that the Kraut artillery fire on the road & bridge is too damned good not to be observed & that the observers had to be some of the civilians in Carentan. Some of those "bad" Frenchmen the army pamphlet warned us about.

Anyway, this is what we heard today. Some infantry details were sent in to flush them out. They found two French women with walkie-talkies. The way we heard it, the detail "liberated" them permanently & immediately. If it's true, guess they had "consorted" too long with some Kraut officers. Sort of makes you sick at your stomach, though, both the collaboration and the execution. S & S has had a lot of stories about how delighted the French people have been to be liberated and what a great welcome they have given us. Personally, I haven't seen it. The French people I've seen around Carentan go on about their own affairs & don't pay any attention to us. You wouldn't think there was a war going on all around them, the way they act. We've heard the Krauts let these people in Normandy pretty well alone — they needed their milk & butter. So maybe being "liberated" hasn't been so wonderful for some of them.

I was rummaging around in the back yard of a bombed-out house today & in an old shed found about a dozen potatoes & some onions. Stuffed them in my pockets & tonight cooked them for our supper. I used Hinkel's mess kit & mine, too. Fried the potatoes first until they were almost soft, then sliced up the onions in them. Hinkel said they were the best fried potatoes he had ever tasted. Tried to get some more bread at the bakery but the fellow said he was sold out. My guess is the officers have found the place.

We had plenty of cider to wash it down with. One thing there is plenty of here is cider. We have found it in big vats that hold two or three hundred gallons. We're getting to be cider-drenched. In fact, some of us are beginning to be cider-shocked.

Beginning to rain. Just heard the mail hadn't come up.

Saturday, July 8, 1944

Lieutenant Edelstein found a French tar mixer today & we've got it to working, so now we can really get some place fixing these potholey streets.

Crazy thing happened today. I had to go across the river for some equipment & Villines drove me over in his air-compressor truck.[17] We got over all right, got the equipment & when we got back to the bridge a shell or two was falling. Villines gunned the truck for all it was worth & we shot across wide open.

Back on this side a bloody little one-star general waved us down. Villines had on his stripes but I was wearing fatigues & didn't have any chevrons showing. We're supposed to have them on everything, but it's too much trouble & the officers look the other way. Anyway, this little tin Jesus Christ took me for a Pvt. so he chewed Villines out for all he was worth for not maintaining the speed limit over the bridge. Speed limit hell! With 88s falling? If he'd taken as much fire as this outfit has on that bridge he'd gun across, too. Been good enough for him if a shell had landed right in the middle just as he crossed. I, for one, wouldn't have minded cleaning up after that hit & I'd have liked to pick up the pieces left of him.

Anyway, with my bare arm I didn't get any of his cussing, which I would have if I'd had stripes on. But you keep your mouth shut when a general is talking. Villines took it, just kept

17 Sgt. R. F. Villines, H/S platoon, motor pool.

saying, yes sir, yes sir. When the damn fool finally let us go he just shook his head & grinned. Said, "Sometimes I worry about this war with jackasses like that wearing stars." Sometimes I do, too.

No mail came up tonight. It's a little early to expect a reply but I'm beginning to sweat it out. I got up the courage to write Janice (at the marshaling area in England) if she thought she could live on a farm. She's strictly a city gal & besides she has a good job she may not want to give up. But for a long time I have known that when this war is over that's what I want — a small farm down home. In fact, I know just the one I want — the Old Place, where I grew up. Dad will sell it to me cheap, I'm sure. For anyway six months I've been dreaming about it. I'm almost sure she would be willing but just not quite dead sure. I'm asking a lot of her. She's never said what she thought our future ought to be, except to be willing to help save for it. I think she has been waiting for me to say. She has mentioned wanting a home several times. And she has this big thing about a real fireplace. I believe she'll be willing to try the farm but I'll be glad when I know for sure.

Sunday, July 9, 1944

Feel pretty blue tonight. Hinkel was hurt today, down on that damned road. So was Street. Somebody was bound to be hurt sooner or later. There's too much hot lead flying around for it not to happen.

I'm still working details in Carentan, so I wasn't there, but Billington told me about it. Said the 88s started zipping in & they all hit the ditch. Hinkel landed on top of Billington & wasn't down far enough & a piece of hot iron got him in the fanny. It's not a bad wound, but he's had to go to the hospital. Sent word for me to take care of his stuff till he gets back & of course I will. Don't know any of the details about Street, but hear he wasn't too seriously hurt, either.

I am going to miss Paul. Hope he does all right & gets back fast. From what we've heard about hospitals & replacement depots, though, it may be a long time. Everybody says stay away from the Medics — stay away from hospitals. You have to work your way back through the repple depple system & sometimes you don't make it back to your own outfit.

The Lieut. called me in & sort of grinned & said, "The platoon's yours if you want it." Back in England when McCarty left us for H/S Company I had to take it as "acting" for six weeks & I guess the Lieut was remembering I took it only on that basis — till he could find somebody. Nothing was done about it until I figured he didn't mean to do anything about it & went to see him & told him he'd have to bust me, but I was through with the job. I suggested Hinkel, then, & we got him.

Well, same old deal. Told the Lieut. again I couldn't take it. We talked about it a little & then I suggested Pigg, at least as "acting" till we knew whether Hinkel will get back pretty soon. He said O.K. Pigg it would be. I think Pigg will do all right.

Paul is the only man in the outfit I ever really let my hair down with — the only one I ever talked to seriously. But we roomed together for so long & got to know each other so well that both of us told each other things & talked about things we wouldn't have with anybody else. We talked a lot about our plans after the war, how we wanted to live, what we wanted to do, etc.

A good many of the boys have stopped by my tent tonight. They know I feel bad about Paul. Then Jeff came with a bottle of cognac. Said, "I thought you might need some medicine tonight."

I did & appreciated his thoughtfulness.

Tuesday, July 11, 1944

Pigg has been made "acting" platoon Sgt. until it's known
how long Hinkel will be away. Billington makes buck Sgt. &
takes over 3rd squad. Black Mac moves up to line Cpl. in 1st
squad — assistant squad leader. Good deal all the way around.
Billington will do fine as a squad leader. Billington hates army
regulations worse than anybody I ever saw, but he'll do to go
down the river with.

If I don't get a chance to bathe & change clothes pretty soon
I'm going to have to bury the ones I'm wearing. Don't think
the stink will ever come out of them. All I've had is a wash out
of my helmet — what we call a whore's bath — and it would be
a waste of clean clothes to put them on after no more bath than
that.

Bunch of us been sitting around talking tonight. Griping
mostly. When the mail doesn't come up & the food's bad there's
more bitching & everybody gets a little edgier. Then, too, there
are a lot of rumors that we are pinned down on this peninsula
— can't get moving. From all the troops & supplies that have
been pouring in you wonder why we don't get on the ball.
Tonight somebody said, "What the hell's holding us up?"

"A bunch of Krauts, you goon!"

Somebody else said, "Not enough troops over here yet."

I said, "S & S says there are over a million now."

"Well, there you are. What are we waiting for?"

"Another million."

It was the opinion of one guy it was the weather. "It's been
lousy ever since we got here. Hell, we got to have air cover to
break out. And they sure can't fly in this soup."

Somebody else said, "Naw, it's the terrain. It's rugged getting
through these swamps & hedgerows. Tanks can't work in 'em."

Then somebody said he heard two reporters talking today &
they said it was Montgomery holding everything up. He was

too cautious. Then there was an argument for half an hour about whether Gen. Montgomery should have been put in command of all the ground forces.[18] Generally agreed finally it had to be done because of an American in Supreme Command.

Somebody said, "Well, I'd sure like to do something besides fill potholes in these crummy roads for a change."

Somebody else, "What the hell's the difference? You're gonna be filling potholes from here to the Rhine anyway."

"Hell, no, they'll quit before then."

"Wanta bet?"

"Sure, I'll bet you. Bet you five bucks they quit before we get to the Siegfried Line. They're not gonna want us on *their* sacred soil."

Then there was another half hour of arguing & betting when the war would end. Most think by the end of the summer, *if* we get moving soon. Some said by October. A few thought November. But I guess we all believe, or hope anyway, it will be over by Christmas. One guy said he had promised his wife to deliver her Christmas present in person this year. There was some kidding about whether he *could* after being out of practice so long. He seemed right confident, whether because he's not been much out of practice or just has faith in himself. He said she promised it would be a boy.

This began the talk about women — where it usually ends up. In a war sex talk gets to be an obsession with men & we're no different than any other G.I.s Some of the boys are bragging already. I think they're cider-shocked.

Some of us had our shoes & socks off & we got to comparing the color of our feet. Nearly all of us have athlete's foot. I picked mine up as far back as the shower room at Swift. The

18 General Bernard L. Montgomery, Commander of the British 21st Army Group, had been named commander of all Allied ground forces for the Normandy assault only. It was not generally known, however, that this was a temporary assignment.

Medics paint your feet with purple gentian. As far as I can tell it might as well be cider for all the good it does. Black Mac said, "Hell, they use it for everything. You got athlete's foot, they paint your feet with it. You got a sore throat, they paint your throat. You got a scratch on your hand, they paint your hand. I know one guy had a bellyache & damned if they didn't paint his stomach."

Anyway we counted six different shades of purple on our feet.

Then some music began coming over the loudspeaker system from the field on the other side of the hedge & we all got quiet & just lay back & listened. It was beautiful. They played "Smoke Gets in Your Eyes," & "What a Difference a Day Makes," & "Sweet & Lovely," & a lot of others that were sweet & a little sad. Music like that makes you think of home & where you were & all the things you could do when you were hearing those songs all the time. The very last song they played got me all choked up. It was "Sentimental Journey." That's our song — mine & J's. She says it ought to be played at our wedding.

When the music was over everybody drifted away to hit the sack, another day gone & surely another day closer home.

Thursday, July 13, 1944

Pigg & I went back to that meat market today & bought some more steaks. Had some onions left over from those I found the other day, so I smothered the steaks in onions. They tasted fine. The boys say I make a good short order cook — and that's funny. Back home I never even fried an egg, but I've watched Mama cook enough to remember what she does to make food taste good. Some of the boys couldn't boil water, though.

Pigg had a bottle to go with our steak & onions — some good wine. It washed down fine.

My tent is fixed up rather cozy these days. Don't have a room-mate but I have Paul's shelter half & all his blankets & yesterday several of us were working on a side road & we found a dozen blankets the Infantry boys had thrown away. They'll be sorry, for the nights are still chilly here, but since they'd thrown them away we picked them up. I took three & that gives me seven in all. I sleep with four under me, folded, which makes eight thicknesses & three over me & sleep warm, thank God.

Music over the loudspeaker again tonight. Mostly hillbilly & westerns tonight. Somebody is singing, "Low and Lonely Over You," right now. Used to hear that on the Grand Ole Opry back home. Seems a thousand years ago — or more like something I just dreamed & it never happened.

Mail call. Eight letters and one from home. J. says something is wrong with her right hand, that it's sometimes stiff in the morning & sore. Says she hopes it isn't arthritis for she needs her hands badly. I hope it isn't, either. This is the first time she's ever mentioned anything wrong with her — not even a cold — and it makes me uneasy. But she'll have the good sense to see a doctor if it keeps bothering her.

La Raye
Thursday, July 20, 1944

Moved here the 18th. This is inland, west of Carentan. The outfit is working on the main road that runs north & south through the peninsula & most of us are wondering if they haven't got us mixed up with the dogfaces. Have had some of the worst artillery fire since we landed. Have heard the Krauts figure we're getting ready to take the offensive & have pulled up some of their best stuff to stop us.

First day on this road they started smashing the stuff up & down & we had to hit the ditches a dozen times. By God, I *hate* artillery fire — the damned 88s & the screaming meemies that sound like all the witches in hell let loose. They mortally do wear down your nerves. Our tar mixer took a direct hit today

& if we hadn't been so damned scared it would have been funny. The tar flew in all directions. I got plastered with the stuff & when it was over Billington said, "Sgt. Giles, you look just like Br'er Rabbit & the Tar Baby." I know I did. I also knew I had a hell of a time getting it off.

Since the Krauts don't know the difference between daylight & dark I have myself about the fanciest foxhole I've ever had. It's good & deep & I've laid logs over it very close together, then packed the dirt back over tight. It would take a direct hit to get me.

Bunch of us tonight got to talking about the different ways you feel when you're scared as hell. I've heard you never hear the one that gets you, but you could get damned bad hurt by those you can hear. Sometimes they come in with a wild whistle. The meemies make a wild, screaming noise. None of them sound good & you just by God hit the dirt mighty quick.

Pigg said he sweated all the time. Said he could feel the sweat pop out all over his face & start running down under his arms & his shirt would get so wet it stuck to his back.

Cornes said he got hot & cold all at the same time. Said he got so hot he felt like he had fever & at the same time he was so cold he was shivering.

One said he had a hard time keeping from filling his pants. LaCoste said he just got weak all over & sick at his stomach. Said he felt like his knees were made of tallow & wouldn't hold him up. Black Mac said he clamps his teeth together so tight his jaws ache for an hour afterwards.

I think I do all the same things. I know I sweat & shake & feel a little sick, but the worst thing with me is that my heart pounds so hard I feel like I'm going to choke to death.

Then we got to talking about what we were most afraid of having happen to us. Being hit in the face, blinded, losing an arm or leg, or getting hit in the privates. I don't want any part of it, but I believe my worst fear is being captured. I'd rather be killed than captured. I've read & heard too much about the way the Krauts treat prisoners. I *know* I'm not made of the stuff to stand being tortured.

The others have gone now but Pigg stayed & chewed the fat a while longer. Brought a bottle of Calvados which we took down considerably. I appreciated it.

Been gun cleaning today & something was fouled up with 1st squad's .30 cal. Wouldn't fire but once & had to be hand fed. Finally I found what was wrong. Somebody had put the belt feed pawl in backwards. Any of the boys can fire a machine gun & they have all had classes in dismantling & assembly. Seems I wasn't a very good teacher. Well, there *are* a hell of a lot of parts to remember & some of them, like this pawl, can be put in backward.

Friday, July 21, 1944

I unappreciated that Calvados this morning! First I've tried & man, it's a certain derailer. Two drinks & you're sitting on top of the world. Two more & you've slid off. It's liquid lightning. And here I was drinking it like bourbon. If it doesn't strangle you to death going down, it'll probably eat holes in your guts when it gets down. I've had a hell of a headache most of the day from what I drank last night.

Funny, but it made my mind as clear as a bell. At the same time it was like being in another world. Remember going to bed & lying there watching the artillery flashes through the chinks of my foxhole roof & the tracers & thinking how beautiful they were. Looked as if the whole sky was lit up by the biggest thunderstorm & lightning in the world & the tracers red & crossing & recrossing. Kept trying to think what they looked like & couldn't. Next thing I knew it was morning & my mouth felt like it was lined with cotton & my head was splitting.

Keep hearing rumors of an offensive very soon. Hope they're true. This slogging through these hedgerows & swamps has been rugged on the Infantry boys. I never see a line of them going up that I don't think, poor bastards. And, my God, am I ever glad I didn't go to Infantry OCS now. Ambulance after ambulance comes down this road. A hell of a lot of boys are being hurt — more than you'd think this army could take & keep going. S & S doesn't give the casualties, but they are plenty — they are plenty.[19] It does something to you to watch them go by. You know they're full of guys like yourself who maybe will never see again, or walk again, or have hands to use again. You feel guilty for thinking, thank God it isn't me, but you feel it just the same, and at the same time you just wish to God there was something you could do.

Mail call. Three letters & the one I've been waiting for. She thinks a farm would be fine & is excited about it. I don't know what I would have done if she'd said she didn't like the idea. Try to live in Louisville, I guess. But I would hate it & I imagine she knows it. I was *almost* sure what she would say, but not quite. Now I can really dream.

She says Nash[20] is beginning to call Libby nearly every night & she thinks things are getting serious. Says but at least he is from Kentucky & if they decide to marry the four of us will be living in the same state & can be together often. Well, I hope they get a better break than we did & if they decide they're that much in love can be married before he leaves. We didn't have the chance.

[19] In his book, *A Soldier's Story,* General Omar N. Bradley says he never hated anything worse than to keep throwing his men through the swamps and hedgerows; but high land had to be reached before an offensive could be mounted.

[20] 1/Lt. Nash Hancock, Finchville, Kentucky. At this time he was stationed at Davis-Monthon Air Base, Tucson, Arizona. Ironically when Libby and Nash were married he was sent in the final phases of the war to Santa Fe, New Mexico. They liked it so well they made it their home and have lived 1500 miles from us for nineteen years.

La Platrière
near Ste. Mère Eglise
Saturday, July 22, 1944

I think I have the name of this village spelled right but am not sure. We really fracture the names of these French places trying to pronounce them. This one is the "platter." Isigny was "I seen ya." Ste. Mère Eglise is Saint Mare Eggles.

The wildest thing happened to us last night & not a damned bit funny though we've laughed about it today. I was on a detail working on a bridge. There were parts of two squads of us. The Krauts were lobbing in a few shells once in a while, not very near but close enough to keep us jumpy. Suddenly the guards started shooting off the gas signal. It confused us & we didn't believe it at first, then the Lieut. yelled, "Gas attack! Gas masks, everybody!"

The gas masks had been piled with the rifles on the bank & there was the wildest scramble to find them in the dark you ever saw & much confusion with rifles going off & everybody yelling & falling all over everybody else. A wonder somebody didn't get killed. I didn't get mixed up in it for I didn't even have a gas mask. Lost it in one of the moves we've made & hadn't yet got around to replacing it.

I stumbled over one when most of the confusion was over & put it on. About that time here came LaCoste yelling he'd lost his gas mask, anybody seen it, anybody found an extra one, who the hell had his gas mask, somebody help him find his gas mask. I knew I had it, so gave it to him. Then I took off my jacket & kept my nose & mouth buried in it. As if that would do any good. You do the damndest things, but anything is better than nothing.

Then the Lieut yelled, "Let's get the hell out of here!"

We were good & ready so we piled into the truck & the driver gunned it & shot us away like a bat out of hell.

But it was so dark & I guess he was so scared he got turned around & at a crossroads instead of turning back toward the bivouac area he took off down a little road in the wrong direction. Everybody knew it but him & began yanking off their gas masks & yelling, "Hey, you're headed the wrong way!"

"Hell, he's driving us right into the Kraut lines!"

"Hey, stop this truck. Let's get the hell out of here!"

The Lieut. must have come to his senses, anyway, for suddenly the truck stopped & the driver began to maneuver to turn it around. Then we heard that wild, screeching noise of a shell coming in. We flattened on the truck bed as best we could. The boys were still yelling, "Get us the hell off this damned road. Get going! Get going!"

The shell landed off to our right, in a field, & there was the burst & the bright light. Then another one whistled in, & another. They were coming in from all sides, as if the Krauts could see us & had them pinpointed for us. They really had us bracketed & I *knew* they had us this time.

Some of the boys began climbing out the back of the truck, but I was too scared to move. The driver had stalled the engine, then trying to get it started had flooded it & was just grinding away, everybody yelling at him.

LaCoste was lying beside me all huddled up, looking like a monster from Mars with his gas mask on. He hadn't opened his mouth, but suddenly he jerked the thing off & began mumbling to himself. In between explosions, when I could think & hear, I wondered what the hell he was doing — praying or cussing. It was really wild, I tell you. I was *terrified*. When I'd open my eyes it looked to me like all hell had busted loose — the sky was full of the stuff & they were hitting all around us. There's no way to describe the noise — it just deafens you & when they hit it feels like the whole earth just heaves & rises under you.

All at once the engine started. The boys began piling back in the truck, everybody pulling & helping each other. The Lieut. said, "Everybody in?" We said yes, let's get the hell out of this place.

And then — the damned barrage quit. Just quit, like that, not another shell. It was so quiet you could hear the frogs croaking & your own heart pounding. Nobody said a word for a little while. I could hear somebody getting his breath in long sucks & wondered who it was & was surprised when I figured it was me. Somebody else was sort of crying & sobbing. Then somebody spoke up & said, "Boy, I like to had a s——t hemorrhage, I tell you."

Somebody else said, "I ain't sure but what I did. Anybody smell anything?"

I couldn't talk for a while. I just sat there & shook. That was the worst we've ever had & even if a shell doesn't get me I think I'm going to die of heart failure in the middle of one of these things.

I guided on the North Star all the way back to the area. I was scared the driver would get lost again. Just before we got back I had enough breath to ask LaCoste what he was mumbling to himself back there. He said, "I was saying the Act of Contrition just as fast as I could." I had forgotten he is Catholic.

I figure I aged ten years last night. That kind of thing will put gray in your hair fast.

Today we've heard there wasn't any gas at all. Some phosphorus shells had set off the detectors. We've talked some about whether the Krauts would dare to use gas in this war & haven't much believed they would because of what they know our Chemical Warfare boys could do to their cities. To be on the safe side, though, I'm going to part with six bucks to get me a gas mask. Don't want any more of last night.

Monday, July 24, 1944

Damn, we must not be living right. Last night Bedcheck Charley hit us hard. They say it was meant for the 2nd Armored just up ahead of us — but we got it instead.

It was just dark. Some of the boys had gone to bed but most of us were still sitting around — had some cider & a little wine — shooting the breeze. Heard the planes & somebody said, "Here comes old Bedcheck right on time."

Next thing we knew we heard this rattling noise, like the worst hail storm you ever heard, then bombs began hitting all over the place & the dirt started flying & we had it right on our tails. We scattered, but fast. I made a flying landing in my own trench but about six more guys piled in on top of me. Barely could get my breath, but I didn't need much, I was so scared. Think maybe I was holding it, anyway.

It's funny how quiet you stay, as if they could hear you if you even whispered. Just scrooch there, screw your eyes up tight, & sweat. Not a sound but the bombs. Between bursts I swear I could hear my watch ticking. My arm was stretched way up over my head & usually I have to hold the watch to my ear to hear it. But it sounded like an alarm clock last night.

One thing about being bombed — it doesn't last as long as being shelled. When it was over & everybody crawled off of me, we were so shook we didn't say much of anything for a few minutes. Then Billington said, "I told Orville and I told Wilbur the damned thing would never get off the ground — but, by God, I was wrong." That brought a shaky kind of laugh.

Then I told Black Mac, who'd landed on top of me, the next time he used my back for an airstrip I'd appreciate it if he'd let his wheels down — that belly landing of his almost broke my ribs. He said, "Hell, you're so skinny it was like landing on gravel. I almost broke two of my own ribs on your damned tailbone!"

We checked around in the dark to see if everybody was O.K. There had been Billington, Mac, Speedy, LaCoste & me sitting together. Then Miller spoke up.[21] He had been passing & had headed for the first trench. He's our Mormon who doesn't drink or smoke & has saved my life more than once with his cigarette rations.

Nobody hurt. Billington went off to see if any of his boys had got it. We stood around another few minutes talking about it, then everybody decided to hell with it — better hit the sack. After I got inside my tent I draped a blanket over me & lit a cigarette. The shakes hit you after it's all over & I had them again. After a few drags, though, I suddenly felt sleepy. Crazy as it sounds I slept sound all night. But there's a big let-down after something like that & in me it takes the form of tiredness to the point of weakness & then sleepiness.

Raining today, sort of slow, cold drizzle. Hasn't done a durn thing but drizzle since we got to France, when it hasn't been pouring. And it stays cold. Spring must come late in this part of the world. But I remember one of Ernie Pyle's columns. He said it always rained during wars, that it rained all through the Civil War & all through World War I & now it's raining all through this war. I believe it.

Still rumors of an offensive soon. It's a funny thing about rumors in the army. Nobody knows how they start, but there's usually a grain of truth in them. I remember back in the States, three months before it happened there'd be a rumor a cadre was being formed & even where it was going. A bunch of us would talk it over, decide whether it would be a good deal or not. If we thought it would, we'd decide to make it & start working on it. Love & I made Crowder that way, then Love & Hinkel & I made McCoy in Wisconsin, & Swift the same way.

Sometimes in England we'd know we were due to move long

21 Cpl. Abraham Miller, 2nd platoon.

before we moved. It's like the grapevine back home. A whole rumor may not be true, but nine times out of ten there's *some* truth in it.

No mail for the last two nights. Wish somebody would get on the ball.

And mark down!

Tuesday, July 25, 1944

This is it! Today is *the* day! We are breaking through the Kraut lines — breaking out of this bottleneck. The offensive has begun. We have seen and heard a lot today.

After four straight days of cloud & mist & drizzle, today is almost clear & man, you never saw such air coverage as the boys are giving us. When we first heard the planes & turned to look, just as far as you could see the sky was full of them — they just didn't quit, wave after wave after wave coming in, as far back as you could see. You couldn't begin to guess how many there were, but it looked to us as if they stretched clear back to England. There wasn't any end to them — the sky was black with them. They flew over & over us — a long slow drone at first & then the constant thundering roar & when they flew on, the bombs rained down & down. Then the sky was full beyond. God, but they were beautiful. There was something about them that made you have chills up & down your spine & raised the hair on your neck. There were so many — & it was such a spectacle. What a clobbering the Krauts took — what a hell of a clobbering. *This* is what we've been waiting for. This is the music we've been wanting to hear. And the words to the music are, "We're starting down the road toward home."

When the Air Corps got through, the artillery opened up on them & if every gun in this army wasn't firing you couldn't tell it from the sound. What a barrage they laid down! For a solid hour — then 2nd Armored began moving. Tanks, dogfaces, everything moving & fast.

An Armored column on the move is one of the most awesome sights I ever hope to see — those big, rumbling monster-looking tanks, tank destroyers, halftracks, etc. A tank always makes me think of some prehistoric animal — like a dinosaur or something. Then all that grinding, growling noise. You feel like they're eager to fight & that nothing can stop them. But the Krauts may have just as many, & of course a tank *can* be stopped. Just the same they look formidable & fearsome & you're glad we have so many.

It has been a great, great day! Everybody's slaphappy tonight — and a little drunk — predicting that now we have the Krauts on the run the war will be over in a month or two. I don't know, but this sure does make it look better.[22]

Mail call. Three letters from J. She has got my first two letters from France. There was also a letter from home. They know I'm here, too. Wish Mama would take it a little easier, but I don't suppose she can help it. There was also a box of cookies. Those good kind J. sent last in England. These were a little mashed but every crumb got eaten by Mac & LaCoste & me. She & Mama both seem to think if I don't get killed I'll starve to death & damned if I don't sometimes think they're right. She hasn't said anything more about her hand. It must be better.

Pulled Sgt. of the Guard tonight. We three Weapon Sgts. get it oftener than anybody & it's right we should. We don't have to work as hard as some of the boys. I try to do what I can

---

22 Speedy Dymond says: "I remember all those planes of ours dropping the bombs on St. Lô and St. Gilles. It was a welcome sight to us all, but the work on the roads and bridges afterward was plenty tough. Still we were better off, out of that peninsula. I suppose we just missed the action at Mortain by a hair. It was still hot and smoking when we rode in."

for them, anyway. Will always feel they're my kids, since I took them through basic.[23]

[23] Bob Billington says: "Sgt. Giles was always ready to help us any way he could. Sharpen an axe, tighten a sledge hammer head, snitch a good tool to re-place some old make-shift, temper a new axe for any of us. I'm afraid we didn't give him enough credit for the ways he made our jobs easier. Took it too much for granted." Sgt. Giles took it for granted, too. He made his first stripe as Tool Corporal.

From St. Lô to Marle-sur-Seine

St. Gilles, near St. Lô
Monday, July 31, 1944

WHERE we are now looks like the craters of the moon. This is where the real breakout took place & that saturation bombing & all the artillery fire really did the work on this country. There are pits & holes big enough to lose a house in. And burned out tanks, trucks, halftracks, all sorts of vehicles. Everything has been flattened. The road is all chewed to pieces, too. Nothing but cold mix to work with, but we've sure got plenty of rubble for filling.

Somebody saw a Kraut truck in St. Lô he thought was in good shape & the Lieut. thought we could use it. He sent me over with a driver to get it, but it was no good. They'd drained the oil out & left the motor running to burn it out.

That's a town that is absolutely, totally, completely flattened. The worst I've seen. It got it from the air, from our artillery, then when we took it, it got it from the Kraut artillery. It's nothing but a pile of rubble.

Saw Ernie Pyle while I was there, but didn't get to meet him. I'd heard he was traveling with 9th Inf. & nearly got clobbered with those short bombs on the 25th. He's a little, scrawny guy,

short & rather stooped, older than I'd expected him to be & just
as dirty & disordered as any G.I. Would like to have met him,
not to be written up, but just to shake hands with him for
I've read his columns for years & always enjoyed them. Even
before we got to France I thought he did the best job of reporting the war of any of the reporters and now I *know* it.

Funny, I told one of the fellows I saw Ernie Pyle today. He
looked at me like I was crazy & said, "Who the hell is Ernie
Pyle?" Well, there are a few in the outfit who don't even read
S & S.

I've just been reading in S & S about the short bombs that
were dropped on our own troops the 25th. Hell of a thing to
happen & I guess some of the pilots have felt pretty sick about
it. But everybody makes mistakes & they couldn't help the
drift. They did one grand job of giving air support that day.[1]

Mail call. Four letters. In the one for July 11, J. says the picture of us in the straw hats was on the front page of the
Courier. Said she nearly choked on her coffee when she opened
the paper that morning & I practically jumped out at her. I
can imagine. The picture got there a lot quicker than my letter telling about it. Several of the boys that were in it have
heard from their folks, too. We've seen it as it appeared in
the New York *Daily News*. Look just like I thought we would
— a bunch of thugs. Me, standing nearest the camera — I look
like a big ape. Well, there's nothing I can do about this mug
of mine.

Jeff came in loaded tonight — Calvados & chickens. Looks as

[1] In the tremendous air coverage of the Normandy breakout, some bombs un-
fortunately fell short of the target area. 9th and 30th Infantry Divisions were
both badly hurt by them. *Stars & Stripes* said that wind caused the smoke bombs
which marked the target area to drift. General Bradley said the planes came in
vertically instead of parallel to the road that marked the safety line and that
some pilots mistook a road nearer the troops for the safety road. Air Marshal
Leigh-Mallory said it was impossible to send the planes over parallel to the road.
It would have taken too long. His only alternative was to send them in vertically.

if we'll eat & drink well tonight. That boy is a real expert at "liberating."

Wednesday, Aug. 2, 1944

Had a *big* day today! Saw Sammie.[2] I first saw a truck from his outfit & asked the driver if he knew him. He said he knew him well & would bring him over to see me in the afternoon. He did & we got to be together for an hour & a half.

He's not exactly the kid I saw last. Nothing wrong, he's well, but twenty months overseas shows on him. He was in North Africa & Sicily, then England & came here a few weeks ago. He's with a medical outfit & Vince was with the same outfit.[3] Sammie told me how Vince got killed. It was at Kasserine Pass in North Africa. They were strafed with machine guns by low-flying planes. I knew Vince had been killed but not how.

Kasserine Pass is where my old outfit, the 19th, which I was with at Fort Ord almost got wiped out. If I hadn't made the cadre to Crowder, I probably would not be living today.

There are several fellows from around home in Sammie's outfit & I have asked for a pass tomorrow to go over & see them. They are only five miles from here. The Lieut. said it could be arranged.

Don't think I was ever so glad to see anybody in my life as I was to see Sammie today. First person from home I've seen since leaving the States. Sammie said he was so excited when the driver told him his cousin was close by he pitched in & unloaded that truck all by himself so he could get started over here quicker.

He is some younger than I am but I always liked Sammie a lot & we had a lot of fun together when we were kids. Used to sneak off from hoeing corn or suckering tobacco & go down to

2 Sammie Giles, Knifley, Kentucky, Henry Giles' cousin.
3 Vince Giles, Knifley, Kentucky, a cousin of both Sammie and Henry Giles.

the river to swim. Dry off with our shirts & sneak back & mostly got by with it. Both of us used to pile on a horse to go after the cows at night. Then get in trouble for *running* the cows to the barn. Nearest we could come to being cowboys. All that seems a lifetime ago, and durned near is.

I told Sammie about trying to find him in England & he said he got my letter & tried to find me, too. Asked him why the hell he didn't answer the letters & he just grinned & said he never was much of a hand for writing.

No mail tonight. J. is down home spending a week with the folks right now. She was to go Aug. 1st. Hope she has a good time.

Thursday, Aug. 3, 1944

Had a fine day with Sammie & the other fellows from near home. Saw Jim Walker Burton & Buck Hardin. Sure was good to talk to them & to hear their news from home. By the time we got it all put together we had a pretty good picture of what it's like back there. One thing is sure. All the fellows our age have gone to war.

Dewey[4] is in the Pacific & so are Walter Scott & William & Joe Spires. I already knew Dallas Badger was there. Saw him in Paso Robles in California just before he shipped out. The boys said Buck Watson was over here some place, & Aldous Jones, but they didn't know where & hadn't seen them. Wish I could run into them.[5]

Had chow with Sammie's outfit & made a pig of myself. Be-

4 Dewey Giles, Knifley, Kentucky, brother of Sammie.

5 These were all men of the same community as Henry Giles. Buck Watson was with the 418th Engineers Trucking Company and drove a truck later on the Red Ball Express. Aldous Jones was with the 1183rd Military Police Company of the 438th Troop Carrier Wing, 9th Air Force. He was later stationed at Melun at the same time Henry was on detached duty there. He never did see either of them, nor his cousin again, until after the war.

lieve me, a medical outfit really eats well, a hell of a lot better than we do.

Told Sammie about J. & showed him her picture. He seemed a little surprised. Said he thought I was headed to be an old bachelor. Told him I thought I was, too, till I met her. He told me about Dewey's bad luck. He was engaged to a girl from Pineville. Home on furlough before he shipped out, he bought her a bedroom suite (wonder what was on his mind when he did *that??*). Anyway, he hadn't been overseas two months till she married another guy — bedroom furniture & all. We couldn't help laughing about it.

I had all day so didn't have to hurry & Sammie had the day, too. We really had a good visit. I can go a long time on it. Made me feel fine.

Saturday, Aug. 5, 1944

Here is a story that was in S & S yesterday. In the assault on St. Lô, the commanding officer of an Inf. Bn. promised to take his men into St. Lô personally on a certain day. He didn't make it. A Sgt. came along & stared at his body, then said, "All right, boys, grab hold. The Major promised to take us in. We'll take him." And they did.

And here's a real weirdy that's going the rounds about the false gas attack. Seems the panic spread down the whole front & was triggered off by one convoy. It is said that a Graves Registration detail was working that night with some very ripe Krauts. They put on their gas masks. Along came a convoy of trucks. The drivers saw some men with masks on & not knowing why thought there must be some gas & put theirs on. Each outfit they passed from then on, seeing their gas masks, got panicky, put theirs on & then began firing the rifle signals for gas attack. But here's the payoff. The Graves Registration detail was supposed to be looking for the body of the German

prizefighter, Max Schmeling, whom rumor had it had been
killed several days before & whose body was in that particular
bunch. This story I don't believe. It could happen, I suppose,
but it sounds more sensible to me that phosphorus shells set off
the detectors.

This story I can vouch for. The Lieut. fired Jeff Elliott as his
driver the other day. The boys say Jeff was late one time too
many.

[Jeff Elliott says: I sort of wondered after I saw Omaha
Beach if I would ever leave the continent alive. Thought that
if I was going to have any life at all I had better get at it because it could be very short. We had had our baptism of fire
at the Tucker bridge at Carentan.

I was at the bridge just after Sgt. Hinkel got hit. The gun
that had been firing on that bridge must have been a long way
off because the trajectory was flat. The shells would hit in the
field & skip across smoking. It was one of those shells that hit a
building & hit Paul Hinkel. I was driving for Lieut. Edelstein
at the time.

We got inland near St. Gilles, close to St. Lô, & I had been
goofing off driving German tanks & anything else I could find
that would run. I had a nice MK-5 that ran good. One day
Col. Pergrin came out to the road where the boys were working
& Lt. Edelstein asked him if he would like a ride in a Kraut
tank. He said yes, so I took him for a ride around a field that I
had been over & knew was safe. He seemed to enjoy it. I then
said I would show him what it would really do. Drove fast
into a bomb crater. The barrel of the damn 88 stuck out front
& when we zoomed into the crater about 4 ft. of the gun barrel
buried itself in the opposite bank. We were stuck tighter than
hell. With that the Col. got disgusted & left.

Next day I got the tank out but then along came an Ordnance outfit with a tank retriever. They asked if there were any tanks around that would run & damned if Goombah didn't give them *my* tank! Dern him, anyway. Never could have any fun.

Next thing I found was a nice V8 German halftrack. It was out of gas but that didn't take long to fix. Had a nice road down through the woods all laid out & had a lot of fun down there with this halftrack. Until one day Edelstein wanted me to drive him some place & I was out zooming my halftrack down that road. He took Willy Willis of H/S platoon to drive him. When I got back the jeep was gone. When *Edelstein* got back, he fired me.]

near Marigny
Sunday, Aug. 6, 1944

We've been milling around in a few little villages, but came here last night. Today I had time for a good wash even though it was in my helmet. Was stripped down & in a big way washing all over when I looked up & not more than fifty feet away two women were walking goggling at me. I followed my first impulse, which was to dive into my tent & it was the worst thing I could have done. Ought to have casually draped a shirt around myself. What they got when I made that nose dive was a good southern view of my rear end going north. It took me several minutes to recover. Me, mother-naked in the broad daylight for women to gaze upon is something I'm not used to.

This is real Calvados country here & the outfit floats one day & hangs onto their heads the next. And if what McDonald tells me is true I have got to take back my brag that I never black out when drinking.

We got through with a job yesterday & are having a day off before starting the next one. A very good time, says we, for hanging one on. This is not social drinking we do. You belt it

down fast & get your jolt fast. I knew I was feeling mighty fine
when several of us decided to wash a few clothes. We are bivouacked in a field & on the other side of the fence row there's
a pond & a sort of wash place with some tubs on a bench, etc.

We took the bottles along thinking to ease the pain of doing
the laundry. That's the last I remember! But Mac says there
were a couple of women there doing their washing. He said I
took a liking to the one at the bench & began chasing her —
round & round the bench. He said I was so wobbly I was barely
on my feet & the woman, laughing fit to kill herself, was having
no trouble staying out of my way. First around one end, then
around the other. Mac said he stood there & laughed till his
sides hurt with stitches. Said he didn't know what the hell I
could have done if she'd stood still, for I was barely on my feet.
Finally he & the other boys decided I'd better sleep it off &
started to take me home. Said my knees buckled about the time
they got me to the fence row. I must have had one moment of
lucidity for I do have a vague memory of crawling on my hands
& knees down the fence row to my tent & thinking, Giles get
up & walk, & not being able to do it.

Woke up late in the afternoon with it slept off but my
mouth felt like a herd of cows had been driven through it.
Well — this is not how my little blue book told me to behave!
I'd better have more respect for that stuff. Apparently it makes
you crazy.

Flash: The woman did my laundry. Mac brought it in, a hell
of a lot cleaner than I'd have got it.

Drinking & sex & war — they all go together. Doesn't matter
if you should or shouldn't, you do. It's got nothing to do with
the kind of guy you were back home or want to be when you go
back. And that's the jinx — you may not go back. Your life ex-
pectancy is durned short. What's here & right now is living &
all you may have of it. It would shock the hell out of the people

in the States if they knew what went on. Everybody's little boy over here is supposed to be as pure as the driven snow. Nuts! Anything that will take the edge off & let you forget for a little while, even an hour or two, there's a war on & tomorrow Graves Registration may be putting a tag on you, is welcome.

As for sex — the word we use most in the army, with practically every breath we draw, is the word most of us saw first scribbled on privy walls & the bigger boys at school snickeringly told us what it meant. War and sex and drinking — they go together like ham, eggs and coffee.

Just the same, nobody in this outfit misses his job because of his drinking. We pick our times. We know we have time to hang one on before we begin. Offer Mac a drink when he's going to have guard & he'll say, "Nope. Pulled guard tonight."

Offer Billington a drink when he's going to take his boys out on a job & he'll say, "Gimme a raincheck, willya? I gotta work."

And, by God, offer me one when I've got a job coming up & I don't take it. But we sure belt it down when we can.

Mortain
Wednesday, Aug. 9, 1944

Things are moving rather fast these days. We have been shifting around, making mostly one-night stands. Trouble is we do most of the moving at night, catching what sleep we can in the trucks. Jobs mostly roadmending, not lasting too long, then move on. The front is fluid and advancing. But maybe we moved a little too fast today. The Krauts began an offensive against this place the other day & here we are. Artillery fire again. I'm beginning to believe the army thinks this little outfit of Engineers is pretty expendable.

Everything is smashed to hell here. The Krauts threw all they had into the place trying to break through, but S & S says

30th Inf. stopped them cold. Many wrecked German vehicles all around. You can sure tell it was rough going. We have acquired a few of the Kraut vehicles ourselves. Mostly trucks the mechanics can fix so they'll operate again.[6]

It isn't official yet, but it might as well be — everybody knows it. The American forces have been split in two armies, the First & Third & Gen. Patton is commanding the 3rd. We are with the 1st. Patton has taken off like a bat out of hell into Brittany. We were in the 3rd back in the States. Wonder a little why we weren't assigned to them here, but they didn't ask us anything about it.

Mac & Speedy & LaCoste are sitting here now. Mac is cleaning his rifle. Speedy is trying to fix one of his leggins. He tore some latchets loose on it this morning. LaCoste is shaving.

Mac is scrubbing away at the bolt of his gun & grumbling. "*Why* in the hell didn't they make these bolts out of something that won't rust?"

Speedy hardly ever cusses & you rarely see him show much temper. Just now, looking at the leggin, he says, "Who do you suppose thought of making it regulations for us to wear these things?"

"Some pencil pusher in Washington," I said, "Why?"

"I'd just like to lace one around his fat neck is all."

LaCoste has finished shaving very carefully around his little moustache. He says, "Well, you can't dump *them* in the Atlantic."

Speedy gives a sigh. "No. To my sorrow I have learned you can't buck the system."

Then we got to talking about Patton. "Glory boy," Mac says, "just a headline hunter."

---

[6] The Battle of Falaise Gap began on August 7, with a very strong German counterattack. They penetrated into the outskirts of Mortain the same day, then were slowly pushed back.

Speedy said, "It'll take a lot of glory to make people forget that slapping episode in Sicily."

LaCoste says, "Pistol-packin' Papa — that's Patton. Making like a cowboy."

Well, from what I've read about him he is hot-tempered — he shoots off his mouth too much & he does have this gimmick with those pearl-handled pistols slung in their holsters. He likes a good press & goes for it. But he gets things done, too. He likes action.

Mac says, "I got all I want right here where we are."

Amen.

Chow time about then, which ended the discussion.

Later: Pigg somehow got hold of enough wine to give several of us in Hq squad a quart each. I appreciate it. Don't know what kind it is — the label is gone — but it's the best wine I ever tasted. Half the quart is gone already.

Washed more clothes this afternoon when I got in off a detail. Meant to take a bath but there were too many women doing their laundry. These people beat the hell out of me. With tanks rumbling through the streets & shells still falling all around they go ahead like nothing was happening. Women doing their washing, cleaning, cooking — men working in the fields. I've wondered why they don't leave. Then I got to thinking if it was back home, say, maybe I wouldn't get very far away either. Where would you go? Home is the only place you know or want to be. So maybe three walls & part of a roof is better than a whole house in some strange place.

Mail call. Three letters, and I'll be damned. Libby & Nash did get married. In Tucson. J's aunt lives there & she helped with the wedding. J. didn't go. Seems she gave Libby the money to go. Nash has about six weeks before he goes overseas, so they decided to make the most of it. J. says Libby will come home when he leaves. Short honeymoon they'll have, but I wish them the best. Wish he didn't have to go overseas, but J. says he asked for it. Been stuck in the States as flying instructor so long she said he'd got ashamed to walk down the streets without an overseas stripe on his arm. Pulled wires to get sent over. I didn't pull any wires to get sent over, but I know how he felt. A little like a 4F.

Sleepy. This wine is really blurring the edges & I'm writing from southwest to northeast.

Wednesday, Aug. 16, 1944

Been too busy the last week to write here. All I could do to write my letters & had to miss two days writing to J. This battle has made a hell of a lot of road repairing & bridge work necessary. Not over yet but the Krauts are being pushed back, according to S & S. We'd never know anything if it wasn't for S & S. It's our Bible.

This has been one of the meanest stretches of roadwork we've had. The traffic is heavy & the dust fogs up & we're hot & sweaty & it settles on us & turns to mud. The worst thing, though, is the stink. The hot weather soon bloats all the dead cows & horses & there must be a million of them. You breathe that stink all day & you get to feeling like it's in your clothes & your hair & your mouth & even the food gets to tasting like it.

There are a bunch of dead Germans lying around, too, and they don't help.

Yesterday we had a break and a bunch of the fellows went to Mont St. Michel. I would have liked to go but my knees have been giving me fits the last four or five days, hurting at night till I've been losing sleep. Figured the best thing I could do was give them a break. Sometimes I wonder if they're going to last out the war on me.

The boys said the abbey was very beautiful, but Billington

told me they had to do a hell of a lot of walking and climbing stairs, etc. It's just as well I didn't go.

Later: Keenan[7] just came by & stopped to chew the fat for a while. Don't see much of him any more. Back in England we were together all the time, but he was in the platoon then. Was transferred to H/S Company to be assistant construction supervisor, on account of his railroad experience, and when a man leaves the Company you just don't see him as much.

He brought a bottle of cognac, which was a little fiery but settled down smooth. Wanted to know what I'd heard from Hinkel & it's not a word. The boy could be dead for all we know. I ask every hospital outfit we run into about him & nobody knows a thing. I would have thought he'd have written me, if he was able. It could be he was worse hurt than we thought, but it could be the mail is just snafu.

After a few drinks Keenan & I got to talking about old times back in England & laughing about some of our sprees there. He & I sure stuck our necks out one night in Shepton Mallett. We were on pass together & it was almost time for us to head for the trucks to go back to camp. About that time somebody told us that a couple of the boys had been picked up by the MPs. They were the eightballs who'd gone AWOL sometime earlier & had just got out of the brig. Seemed a pity for them to get thrown right back in, so I said, "Let's go get them."

We were much in our cups ourselves. Keenan said, "Hell, we're too drunk. They'll throw *us* in the brig."

I said, "We're drunk, but we're not that drunk, Bill. Now, let's straighten up & go get those boys."

We did. At the MP office a kid 2nd Lt. was at the desk. We marched in briskly, brought up to smart attention. Then I nearly went through the floor. Keenan was throwing the guy a British salute — palm out, upper forehead & all. I thought sure

7 Sgt. Ellis W. Keenan, H/S Company.

the fool had given us dead away. But the Lt. didn't notice it. We asked him to release the boys to us, promised to report them, promised to get them safely to camp, promised to keep them out of trouble, etc. And got by with it. He turned them over to us. Two more grateful enlisted men you never saw. Turned out they weren't half as drunk as Bill & I were. We had split a quart of Scotch. But these two particular boys will never grow up. If they live to be a hundred, they'll still be pulling fool kid stunts.

Then Keenan got to kidding me about Cherry. This was at Shepton Mallett, too, and again Bill & I were on pass together. He went his way & I went mine after a time. I was comfortably full of beer, all by myself, idling down the sidewalk by the park. Not looking for anything particularly, unless it just came to pass. It did, under the trees. She was pretty, friendly, & accepted a cigarette, one of my "Lucky Stripes." After a few moments of chat she was willing to walk in the park. It was dark & we were alone. But she only wanted to hold hands & talk. Being a gentleman (ahem!) we held hands & sat on a park bench & *she* talked — for about an hour. Time for me to catch the trucks to camp, then. She said it was time for her to go home, too.

We walked out of the park & down the street to the intersection. There we were blitzed by a full squad of MPs & a more rapturous greeting a girl never got. "Cherry! You're home!"

"Cherry, where have you been?"

"Cherry, we were worried about you!"

"Cherry, we missed you!"

I said "Cheez," and left her, an unpicked cherry, to their tender mercies. Told Bill about it later & he said she was probably squad property & I was lucky not to get hauled off to the brig.

My, my, the things Keenan & I have pulled together.

He got to laughing at my fresh "baldy" hair clip. Said I looked like an escaped criminal. I know — but it's cool & easy to keep clean. Besides, nobody cares how I look. Lieut. Hayes has been threatening to take a picture of me & send it to J. But said he didn't have the heart to disillusion her. He is our censor, so of course he knows quite a bit about our girls & wives. Don't think he reads my letters any more. He called me in one day in England, after we'd been there a couple of months, and told me he was putting me on my honor. He had never had to censor out a word. He said I could write more freely & personally now if I wanted to, for he wouldn't be reading my letters any more.

We heard of another invasion in the south of France today — somewhere near Marseilles. That should take some of the heat off us up here.

No mail tonight.

Thursday, Aug. 17, 1944

Have just had all the props knocked out from under me by a letter from J. written Aug. 9th. Her hand got bad while she was visiting the folks. She went to a doctor as soon as she got back to Louisville. The hand has been X-rayed & she has to have an operation. Says it's a bursa at the base of the third finger — very swollen & painful.

Of course she says not to worry. The operation is simple — she'll only be in the hospital a couple of days. But she may not be able to write for a little longer, since it's her right hand. It's all over by now. She was to go to the hospital the 11th. I hope to God she was right & it has turned out all right. I won't rest easy, though, until I hear. What a hell of a break — to have to spend the rest of her vacation in the hospital & nursing her hand. She has to give up her visit to Arkansas with her folks. I keep thinking of her in Louisville all alone. Nobody with her. Libby in Tucson, etc. I know she has friends, but that's not the same. And not a damned thing I can do but sweat. I can't even expect to hear for God knows how long. This is the first time I've had to worry about her, and I'm already panicky. How much more guts *she's* got!

Monday, Aug. 21, 1944

Don't know the name of this village. We move around road mending, building by-passes, fixing bridges, and I'm not even sure some of these little places have a name. We spend three-fourths of our time loading up, moving, finding the bivouac area, trying to feed ourselves. There's a hell of a lot more "house-keeping" in an army than there is fighting.

No mail — no mail — no mail. Nothing since the 17th. I'm very uneasy.

Well, the news is a little better at least. The battle is over & according to S & S more than 70,000 Krauts were killed or captured & most of the equipment of 19 divisions has been taken or ruined. From what we saw around Mortain I'd say that's right.

I talked with one kid from 30th Inf. who was in the battle & had been pulled back. He still looked dazed. He said the Krauts were all over that valley where they were. And these were Adolf's crack troops. No Russian or Polish prisoners doing this fighting. S & S says it was an all-out offensive, planned to split the Allied forces in two. But they're on the run again now & everything is beginning to look pretty good.

Later: Stopped there to clean up a little & shave, then felt hungry. There's a farm not far away so I went over there & "erfed" a little & was able to buy a dozen eggs. About that time Love came by. I scrambled the eggs with some onions &

we ate them. I had a bottle of Calvados with which we washed them down.

Asked him if he'd been abusing any of the French highways. That's an old and corny joke. One night in Shepton Mallet, too full of beer, Love suddenly had to take a leak & couldn't wait to find a rest room. He cut loose in the gutter. A couple of English bobbies picked him up for "abusing the King's highway." We razzed him good about getting arrested for pissing on the King's highway.

Love & I have been together all the way — from the old 19th Engrs. in California. He enlisted one month before I did, but I caught up with him at Fort Ord. We made NCO at the same time. Made all the same cadres, Crowder, McCoy, Swift. But when he wants to sound off he still calls me "rookie" because of his extra month. A real swell fellow.

We talk about England nowadays as if it was the States. But we were there so long we got to feel almost at home. I still miss the pubs & wish we could have brought a few along with us. And what wouldn't I give for a "mess" of those good fish & chips, washed down with some of that fine English beer. Those were good days & we didn't have sense enough to know it. We bitched about everything. I'd like to play a game of darts again & listen to a bunch of those crocky old World War I veterans in the Home Guards telling about the blitz & how "you just carried on, you know."

Thursday, Aug. 24, 1944

Still no mail. And for once, no razzing from the fellows. Usually when mail slows up for a guy the whole outfit is on his tail kidding him. But they know about J's hand. Not a day passes some of them don't ask, "Have you heard yet?" "Is she all right?" "It's a damned shame. Maybe you'll hear tomorrow."

Black Mac took a whole hour to talk to me tonight. "Now, look, Sarge. It was a simple operation. She can't write yet because her hand is still too sore. It doesn't mean there's anything wrong. She just can't use it for a while."

I keep thinking about infection. Mac says, "Look, they have sulfa — they've got everything. You're just rushing the cadence, boy. You're expecting to hear too soon."

I know. I know. I know damned good & well the first time she can use that hand the first thing she'll do is write. At the same time, I just want to *know!* Well, I just have to sweat.

We heard over the radio yesterday that Paris had been liberated. It's happened a hell of a lot sooner than I would have guessed. And I think the boys betting the war would end when Paris was liberated are going to have to pay off. It's not. My own hopes are like a seesaw. One day I think there is a good chance it may be over by winter. Next day I feel certain it won't. The news one day looks good. Next day, not so good. Right now I'd guess we'll be lucky if it's over by Christmas.

Bunch of the fellows were sitting around playing poker & just shooting the breeze when Pigg came up & said it was supposed to be straight dope — we'd be pulling out & heading straight for Paris soon.

Much wild speculation & talk. "Me for Paris. I'm gonna get me a three-day pass & I'm not gonna do a damn thing but eat, drink & be merry."

"Ooh-la-la! Paree, here I come! Wine, women & song! That's for me!"

"Those Paris women. Just waiting for us American soldiers! Mmmmmh, man, let me at 'em."

I nearly got clobbered for predicting we'd never get close enough to Paris for a pass & if we did it would be "off limits." Three men hit me at the same time.

Boulancourt
Saturday, Aug, 26, 1944

We made a long convoy here yesterday & today — 190 miles. Just one Company in convoy is a pretty impressive sight. Usually the Capt's command car leads — 1/Sgt next — then squad trucks by platoons — kitchen truck, equipment trucks, all our vehicles. It takes a hell of a lot of them to move just one Company and when you think of *all* the companies of all the Battalions of all the Divisions over here, by God, just the supply must be the biggest headache the top brass have.

We're not too far from Paris & I was wrong. Much putting in for passes all at once, everybody excited, everybody happy. It has suddenly turned into a damned good war. The Krauts are on the run, no artillery fire, & the outfit on the outskirts of Paris! The boys remind me of kids waiting to go to a circus.

Gen. Eisenhower has issued a statement through S & S that Paris is to be used as a rest area for all troops. Rest? One guy says, "Who the hell wants to *rest* in Paris?" Says he is going to the best hotel he can find, take a long, soaking bath in a tub, sleep (with feminine company naturally) in a fine, soft bed, with, of course, plenty to drink to make it tops. Well, good luck to him. It's been a long, hard haul & this outfit deserves anything it can find in Paris.

Saw a little tobacco growing today as we came along. First I've seen since my furlough home last June (1943). Made me homesick. I've worked so hard in tobacco all my life I never thought I'd want to see another patch of it. But that one today made me wish all I had to do was sucker it & cut it & split it & stick it.

Arlie Wall just came by & told me the mail didn't get up. I didn't think it would. We made too long a move. So there'll be several more days of sweating.

The three of us have had gun cleaning details at work today.[8] Arlie skinned his hand pretty bad. For some reason it reminded us of that time I lit into him back at Swift. I was platoon Sgt. then. The boys had just finished basic & there'd been a beer bust. A rookie beer bust was something to avoid as far as I was concerned, so I just drank mine at the PX. Got in early & went to bed. The kids came in pretty mellow, feeling fine. Somebody had the idea it would be fun to dump the Sgt. out of his bunk. It made me madder than hell & I set out to find who did it. For some reason I thought Arlie knew. Backed him in a corner & tried to make him talk. He wouldn't. Just kept standing there laughing & shaking his head. I swung on him. He got out of the way & the boys pulled me off. A good thing, too. I was mad enough to beat the hell out of him & hitting a man of lower rank is a courtmartial offense. It's the only time I ever did it — the only time I was ever tempted to.

Anyway, next day I apologized to him & told him he had a right to report me & I'd take what was coming. He just laughed & said, "Hell, Sgt. Giles, forget it. You know I'm not going to report you."

They dumped Flaherty[9] the same night. He somehow fell out on top of his mess kit, & mashed it up. Flaherty has always been a hearty eater & durned if the only thing about getting dumped that worried him was his mashed-up mess kit. He grumbled around & worked for an hour trying to get it straightened out.

We're roadmending here. The war has gone off & left us, thank God. It's a good feeling not to be under fire & I can take a lot of it. But we'll probably catch up with it all too soon.

Wednesday, Aug. 30, 1944

Mail still hasn't caught up with us. Thirteen days now since

---

[8] That is, the three Weapons Sergeants.
[9] Cpl. John J. Flaherty, Jr. 1st platoon.

I last heard. It's all I can think about. Very much on my mind all the time.

Some of the boys have been to Paris & they report it's ooh-la-la. Just what we've heard — everything — and all to be had. I'm broke. Have to sweat out payday & hope we don't move out of range. I just plain left myself too blasted short with those double allotments — but don't want to do anything about them now. The news is so good the war *could* be over in a couple of months.

Pigg asked me to take a little work detail today on a small culvert. Took Hall, Hernandez, Rog & LaCoste.[10] Not much of a job. Just shouldering up the approach & filling a few potholes. We got through the middle of the afternoon & I've done a washing since, written letters & read S & S.

We have run into some very good champagne here. The natives tell us this is real champagne country around here & seem very proud of it. "The best," they say, "the best in the world." Well, I don't really like even the best champagne in the world, but it's an improvement over Calvados. What I wouldn't give for a fifth of good 100 proof Kentucky bourbon right now. My idea of luxury is never to run short of bourbon again in my life.

Near Melun on the Seine
Friday, Sept. 1, 1944

Tonight I believe I am at my all time low. 2nd platoon is on detached duty here & I'm not likely to get any mail now until we get back to the Company. I've been beefing & bitching a lot I know, but right now my personal worries are more important to me than the war. It doesn't seem very important to me to maintain this damned bridge across the Seine. There's nothing, absolutely nothing, I wouldn't give for a letter tonight & I might as well cry for the moon.

10 Pvt. Arnold K. Hall; Pfc Louis Hernandez; Pvt. Rog — all 2nd platoon.

Don't know where the rest of the Company went. We got shuffled like a deck of cards.

Well, Giles, quit beating your chest.

Our surroundings are rather unique tonight. We are quartered in a big chateau up on the hill from the river — & needless to say out in the country from the city. Somebody said it belongs to the Rothschilds. It is big enough to cover several acres. We came in & there was a big flight of marble stairs going up, tall mirrors along the hall, some pictures on the walls & dark red curtains of some kind of heavy material at the windows. We dumped our stuff & went wandering around. It hasn't been bombed, but most of the furniture had been moved out. There were some tables & chairs left & a piano. The place is so big everybody that wants one can have a room to himself — and I do. Much as I like the fellows, once in a while I want to be by myself. And in my present mood I'm not good company for anybody.

After chow I tried my hand at the piano. Any musical instrument fascinates me. The white keys defeated me, but I found I could get the chords & pick out the tune of "My Old Kentucky Home" on the black keys. Nobody appreciated that phenomenon but me, however. I was soon told that as a pianist, I qualified more as a tuner.

Dark about that time. I climbed up the stairs to the room I'd picked, pulled the curtains for blackout & lit a candle. Tried to write Janice. Then it hit me how damned lonesome I was — & not for anybody in 2nd platoon. Homesick, I guess, is a better word. Just sick & tired of the bloody war & all the moving around & never having a decent bed or a decent meal. How dirty I am & how dirty I have to stay & never time to do anything for yourself. Let's go, let's go, all the time — somebody always bellering. Load up, move on. Another stretch of road, another damned bridge. No knowing when it will end, or if it will ever end & if it does maybe having to go to the Pacific next.

It's mostly no letters. Fifteen days, now. I know the minute I hear I'll feel better & things will look brighter.

Wednesday, Sept. 6th

Still maintaining the bridge here in Melun. Main Red Ball highway goes through here. Believe me, those boys are in a hurry & if you don't get out of the way fast they'd just as soon knock you over as not. Well, it's getting to be a long haul from the beaches in Normandy to the front & they have to get in a hell of a hurry to keep the stuff moving.

Melun is a rather pretty town. Built in three sections, one across the river, one on this side, & a third one on the island in the river. They say that's the old town. There's a cathedral there which you get a good view of from the bridge — if you have time to look.

Most of the boys go in town every night & some of them report contact made. "Who was she?"

"Hell, I don't know."

"She got a friend?"

"Didn't ask."

"Well, you dirty sonofabitch!"

And so it goes. Anything to drink is very short here, though. Too many other outfits around. After work tonight Holbrook & LaCoste & I walked into a little village near the chateau to see if we could find something there. All we could hear, everywhere we went, was, "Boche. Boche." The Germans had taken it all. Finally we saw an old man with a bottle of wine & some cider. Tried to buy it, but instead of selling it he took us home with him & we helped him drink it. Didn't stay very long. LaCoste said the old man told him the big Kraut brass had their headquarters all around in this area — some of them in our

chateau. He said they took everything that had any value. Just
stripped the places clean & sent the stuff to their homes in Germany. Well, if they don't give up before we get into Germany
I imagine a bunch of American G.I.s will show them what some
real stripping is.

Mail call just now! And *ten,* count them, *ten* letters from
Janice. Also one from Hinkel & one from home. Needless
to say I feel just about 1000% better. The letters from J.
took up right where she left off, except for the five days she
was in the hospital & they are all in order for once. I could
have cried over the first one, though. It was written the day
she got home from the hospital & with her *left* hand. She got
someone to address the envelope for her. Next day she had a
typewriter sent out from the office & all the others are type-
written. Says she is pecking them out with her left hand. Everything is fine, but she can't use the hand much yet. God, what
a wonderful relief.

I think I'm the happiest man in the outfit tonight — just
plain walking on air. Some of the boys are almost as glad for
me. "Giles heard from his girl." "She's all right." What good
joes they are. Pigg said, "Well, now maybe you'll act like a human being again." I know. I pull in my shell like a turtle
when things like this happen. No fun to be with. No good to
be around. Black Mac came in my room with a big grin.
"Heard you got ten letters."

I fanned them out to show him. He said, "I told you. Now,
what the hell were you beating your brains out for?"

So I told him. I told him I'd get to thinking maybe I'd
never hear again. Maybe she had died. And it just shriveled my
soul. I had got to where I wanted to start *walking* back home.
He nodded & said he knew.

Then I let him read Hinkel's letter. He has been in a hospital
in England & is in a replacement depot now. He wanted me to

do everything I could, see everybody I could, to help him get back to the outfit. Mac & I talked about it & decided we'd both talk to Capt. Gamble & see what we could do. It may not be much, but I know how I would want to get back if I was ever separated from the Company. All this time I've been asking hospital units about him & no wonder they didn't know. He was in England.

Pigg just came in & said we'd be going back to the Company in a day or two. That will be a good deal. My pay is overdue.

From Marle-sur-Seine to Luxembourg

Marle-sur-Seine

Saturday, Sept. 9, 1944

MOVED here yesterday & the Company is all together again. We are bivouacked in an orchard within walking distance of the village. Job here is to build a timber bridge across the Seine. Any bridge is work, but a timber bridge is a piece of cake compared to a Bailey.

Marle is a rather pretty village, but it sure would be nice to see a frame house again. Everything in France seems to be stone or brick. And so old. Seems they're a hundred years behind in their ways, too.

All across France I've noticed the farms & buildings. They build their stables right onto the house, usually next to the kitchen. Then the floor of the stable is made so that the urine from the cows can drain down into a tank. They use it as fertilizer on their fields. I thought manure smelled bad enough but it's perfume compared to fermented urine. The manure piles are usually right beside the front door. Wonder why they think they have to have it all so handy? And if they don't know it isn't very sanitary.

But people who build "pissoirs" in the open on the streets are people I don't even pretend to understand. That really gets you to see a man walk into one of those things, not even a door on them, & cut loose with women passing right beside him. I've always read the French are the most cultivated people in the world. A pissoir cultivated? Not in my book.

After we got in yesterday & got settled down, Wall & LaCoste & I walked into the village, looking as usual for some wine or cider or anything to drink. Met a Frenchman on the corner & LaCoste started talking to him. I thought he was asking the fellow where we could buy some wine, but he turned around in a minute & said the man wanted us to go home with him for supper. I said, "All three of us?" Paul said something else to the man & he nodded his head up & down half a dozen times & pointed to each of us. Brother, a free meal! A homecooked meal! What a deal.

And his wife really gave us a fine dinner. She was a wonderful cook & served the meal in courses. First we had sliced tomatoes with some kind of good dressing on them. Then came a rabbit casserole, with mashed potatoes & green beans. For dessert she gave us apple dumplings or tarts with sauce. Wine to drink before & all through the meal.

I felt as awkward as a fool sitting at a table again, with a nice white tablecloth, trying to use a knife & fork & trying not to eat too fast or act "unmannerly" in any way. Hope I did all right. But it doesn't take long to forget your table manners in the army.

Wall & I don't have enough French to talk much & I can't understand it at all unless they go very slow. But LaCoste is right at home. He said these people told him they had suffered much under the Boche & they were very happy the Americans had come. Said they wanted to do all they could for American soldiers. They did all right by three of us. When we left we asked LaCoste if he remembered to thank them for us. Said he did.

Tonight was a different story. Black Mac, Holbrook & myself went scavenging for some eggs to cook. We know about a dozen words of French between us, but "erfs" is one we learned very early. Mac goes around "erfing" like a crazy pup but he gets results. People may be afraid not to sell to him for fear he'll bite. Anyway we rounded up 21, which was just enough for the three of us. We bought some potatoes & onions, too. Fried the potatoes first, until they were nearly soft, then put in the onions, then last scrambled the eggs. Mighty, mighty fine eating.

One letter tonight, Aug. 24th. Says she is using her hand more all the time, exercising it, playing the piano to stretch it. Wonder what the hell that means? [1]

She sent a snapshot of Libby & Nash taken on their wedding day. First time I've seen a picture of Nash. A very handsome guy. They both look happy, and why wouldn't they? Wish I could have left J. my wife. Some guys don't feel that way, but I do. Besides the better memories & closer tie, it would make some things so much more simple. My allotment savings, for instance, & my insurance. As my wife, if anything happens to me, they would go to her. And I'd rather she had them. I feel that I have done enough, my part, for the folks. All I ever made, since I was old enough to work, they have got part of. And they have always got an allotment since I joined the army. I don't feel I owe them any more, with Dad still living & no older than he is. If I should cash in my chips I'd like to know Janice had it a little easier.

[1] The operation was considerably more serious than I had allowed Henry to know. The bursa was quite extensive and the surgeon had to shorten the muscles at the base of the finger in the palm of the hand. The hand was left, at first, with a reach of less than five inches. By diligent exercise a fairly useful reach was eventually attained, but to this day the hand lacks a full inch of having the reach of the left hand.

Tuesday, Sept. 12, 1944

Have drawn my pay but have decided *not* to go to Paris. It would take every penny I've got to have a real good time, then I'd be broke until next payday. Fellows who *have* been think I'm nuts or something. But I'm short enough every month the way it is. Maybe later I can get back for a rest furlough & have a week or more there.

The boys are having some dances here. I went last night. They're wild & woolly but the French girls can take it, I guess. They seem to enjoy it all. Sgt. Love caught my eye & motioned me outside. He had a bottle of wine, so we went over & leaned on a stone wall & began to take it down.

Got to talking about the old days in the old army & laughing about the difference in this new army's idea of fun. In this crash army the great worry seems to be the boys' morale. Nobody gave a damn about our morale. There weren't any USOs or Red Cross canteens, or Company dances. You slogged all week, got cleaned up for the weekend, got your pass & went to town. You also got your fun your own way & nobody gave a damn as long as you didn't pick up a VD & got back to camp for work.

I've never had much truck with the official "morale lifters" of this war. When I want my morale lifted I know exactly how to go about it, just as I did in the old days, and it sure as hell is *not* at a Company dance. Love said sometimes he got the notion this isn't an army at all any more — it's just a wild conglomeration. Well, soldiering in peace times & soldiering in war times are two different things. And the old army & this war army are two different things. We decided a bottle was about the most consoling thing for us old hands.

He asked about Janice. He was with the Company up around Soissons when I was sweating the worst over her hand, but somebody had told him. I said she was fine, now. Kidding, he asked if I was going to invite him to the wedding. Told him he'd have to get out the same time I did, catch the same boat home if he made it — for it was going to be the first item of business. He said, "I'll beat you home, rookie. How about meeting you in Louisville?"

I said, "Fine. If you can do that, you can be my best man."

He said Jeff Elliott showed up & visited the Company for a little while & not in the best shape. He's riding motorcycle for Group[2] & he'd had a wreck & was all banged up. He stayed around until his motorcycle was fixed, then took off again. I've missed old Jeff, but am glad he's having himself a good war.

I've been working on the bridge the last couple of days. We're not trying to break any records & it's not too bad.

Wednesday, Sept. 13, 1944

Didn't work on the bridge today. Did gun inspection & cleaning. Finished early & went into Marle. I'd forgotten my lighter & wanting a cigarette asked the first Frenchman that passed for a match. He surprised me by speaking passable English. We got to talking. He wanted to know if I was one of the men working on the bridge. Told him I was. One thing led to another, then he invited me to his home for a "bite to eat." Well, I'm always ready for that. Turned out to be waffles with real butter & homemade peach preserves. Nothing ever tasted better.

The old man's name is LeClair. His family consists of himself, his wife, his daughter-in-law, Marie, & her 12 year old son. The old man is a violinist. Said he was educated at the Sorbonne. At one time he was an instructor of music in Paris & was also the conductor of an orchestra.

They have had a rugged time. The son (Marie's husband) is a prisoner of war. Since 1940. They don't know where he is.

2 1111th Engineer Combat Group, under whose command the 291st came.

Haven't heard from him for years. Don't even know whether he is alive or not. They're living in a patched up old house & there's been very little work for the old man. He takes private pupils, but not many people can afford music lessons these days, he says.

They all speak a little English, but the old man speaks it best. I noticed one thing. When they talk about the "Boche" their faces show their hate. They really hate them & when they start talking about them they can't find the English words so they start spitting out French so fast I can't follow them.

The old man has taught the boy violin & they played for me for about an hour. You can tell they are real musicians. Told him I played guitar, mandolin, banjo, but had never tried a violin. He thought he knew where he could borrow a mandolin. Said I must come back & play for them. I had to laugh. My hillbilly repertoire would probably give them heart failure.

Been reading S & S since I got back to the area. Looks as though 1st Army has won the race to be the first across the border & set foot on German soil. Some elements of 3rd Armored crossed over about 10 miles south of Aachen on the 11th. Guess that's put a crimp in Patton's boys. Old Blood & Guts would have given his right arm to be the first across, I'd bet.

There is also an article in S & S about a point system that's to be used for demobilization. I wonder if they're not a little premature. The news is good generally but we haven't won the war yet. The point system is based on longevity of service (that's where I shine), time overseas, number of dependents, battle campaigns, etc. If I counted correctly I have 70 points. They don't say what's essential for demobilization. Say that's top secret yet.

Bunch of us have been talking about it. LaCoste said, moaning, "Jeeeesus Christ, I ain't got enough points to *ever* get out of this army. I just as well start looking for me a home in France right now."

Schommer said, "Well, Frenchie, there would be one consolation. You speak the language. Mightn't be too bad a deal."

LaCoste says, "I want to get me back where they really talk French — back home."

Black Mac says, "Wonder why they got to give points for dependents? Kids. What's that got to do with winning the war?"

Pigg says, lazy, "Reckon you could count bastards?"

Somebody else spoke up. "I ain't even got any of them . . . that I know of."

Which brought on a good laugh. We'll just have to wait & see, I suppose, how this point deal works out.

No mail for me tonight. Am anxious to know if Nash has left for overseas yet. About now was when they thought he'd be going.

The password tonight indicates what time of year it's getting to be. "World Series." I've lost interest in the pennant race. The Cincinnati Reds are way behind.

Friday, Sept. 12, 1944

Bridge finished & we're taking it easy till the next job. Rumors are we'll be moving in the next few days.

Was back visiting with the LeClairs tonight. Took them some cognac I was able to buy. The daughter-in-law gave me a scarf to send J. Don't know what the material is, but it's some kind of silk & it's a pretty blue color. Hated to take it, in a way, they're so bad off, but was afraid if I didn't it might offend them. "Mama" LeClair had baked a cake so we had cake & cognac together. The old man played again. It's all classical music & I don't know from nothing about it, but I could listen to him play anything all night. He can really make that violin sing.

He wasn't able to find a mandolin. We had a nice evening.

Two letters today. Libby & Nash were spending a week, partly with his folks, who live about twenty miles from Louisville, and partly with J. Janice's mother & sister & her husband had been there, too. Glad they could go since she had to miss her trip to Arkansas.

Nash definitely headed overseas. In fact, he & Libby were on their way to Topeka where he'll get his final orders. Libby to go home when he leaves.

Sunday, Sept. 17, 1944

There are so many kids hanging around the area I don't know whether I can write or not. One just now fell into my tent & knocked it down. Don't believe I ever saw children any handsomer than the French children are. I've not seen a real ugly one yet. There's one little black fellow in the bunch today. Cute little beggar. But they're all that — beggars. They want candy, gum, cigarettes for "Papah." The last we don't have. For some reason we're having a hell of a shortage of cigarettes right now ourselves. Hard for us to have enough for ourselves, much less give any away.

We're all suckers for these kids, though. Give them what we can. One of the boys took a picture of several of us this morning, with two of the cutest you ever saw.

Later: Had a nice surprise. The LeClairs, all of them, walked out to the area to see me. They came to invite me to dinner tomorrow night & also "Mama" LeClair brought a handkerchief for me to send J. Said she had embroidered her initial in one corner. Because she took the trouble I know J. will like it. I'll have to wait until I find a box to send the scarf, but I can put the handkerchief in a letter.[3]

I wished I had had something to give them — especially some tobacco for the old man. He smokes a pipe & I know he's short. But I'll swear we're almost down to taking butts again & I didn't even have a sack of Duke's to give him.

Monday, Sept. 18, 1944

Went to the LeClairs' this afternoon. Couldn't go for dinner tonight because the outfit is pulling out early in the morning & I drew Sgt. of the Guard tonight. But I wanted them to know not to expect me, also wanted to thank them for being so nice to me, & to tell them goodbye.

They fixed some sandwiches anyway & the old man insisted on going out & buying some wine. He wouldn't let me pay for it. Then he played for me one more time. These people have been wonderful to me & I have enjoyed knowing them. I don't believe I will ever forget them. I don't know why they have liked me, but "Mama" LeClair even cried a little when I left & wanted my picture. Didn't have one, naturally. I have their address, however, & promised to send one as soon as I can. They all, even the old man & the boy, kissed me goodbye (on both cheeks, of course). I think I must have reminded them in some way of their son.

Well, that's war. You make friends, you leave them. I hope their son makes it back some day. They live in that hope.

[3] The scarf never reached me, but I still have the handkerchief. The material was natural silk pongee, hand hemstitched, with the initial exquisitely worked in tiny blue forget-me-nots.

From Luxembourg to Liége

Steinfort, Luxembourg
Thursday, Sept. 21, 1944

WE ARE near the town of Steinfort, but it's right on the border & we are bivouacked on the Belgian side. Job here is another timber trestle & the orders are, don't spare the horses.

Made another long convoy up here. From Marle we came through the country where a lot of World War I was fought — the Marne valley, the Argonne Forest & we crossed the Meuse (Mooze to us) at Verdun. It was a hell of a terrain to fight in & in those days the strategy was to dig in & stay dug in — strictly entrenched warfare. One thing you can say about this war — it's probably the most mobile war ever fought.

From the Argonne on the country was very hilly, you could almost call it mountainous, & thickly wooded. They say you can still see some of the old trenches around the Marne. From the road we couldn't, of course, & we were highballing right along with no time to stop.

Only Company A is here. Think the Battalion went into Belgium. The first night's bivouac we were still in France, but yesterday we left France & crossed into Belgium. By walking a little way down the road to a couple of taverns, we are in Luxembourg. Anyway, we could brag we had been in three countries in one day.

Today, we've worked like hell. Lieut. Edelstein sighted in the bridge & I helped him with the transit & stakes this morning. By george, he's *good*. When he gets through, you don't come out with any errors to correct. But when he gets through the hard work begins. Looks as if the work will be round the clock, with another & bigger bridge ahead of us, we hear.

Second platoon was off tonight, so several of us, Bossert[1] & Cornes, Billington, Pigg, etc., explored one of the taverns. Walked in & the guy behind the bar said, "Hello Joe."

Billington said, "Where the hell did you learn to speak English?"

The guy said, "I was born in Chicago."

Billington said, "What are you doing over here?"

The fellow said, "I married the business. Doing fine, too. Got me a Buick car, a good Frigidaire, everything O.K. Have a beer, boys?"

We did. Several. And pretty good beer, too. Walking back we wondered about it. How anybody born in the U.S. could just walk out like that, spend the rest of his life in Europe, no matter how good a deal he had. Guess we're too homesick for it to make much sense.

Then the subject changed. We never stay on one very long. Bossert got to bitching about First Sarge riding us today. Made me start laughing, remembering the time at Swift when Bossert got fed up with him & really let off steam, saying what he'd do to that blankety-blank so & so if he fooled around with him. Suddenly somebody noticed First Sarge was standing where he was hearing every word of it. We got Bossert shushed, but, my God, he had the shakes.

Asked him, as we walked along, if he remembered it. He

1 Cpl. Harry Bossert, 2nd squad, 2nd platoon.

said, "Remember it! God, I'll *never* forget it. It scared the hell out of me. For a week I expected any minute to get a court-martial."

There never was a thing done about it. First Sarge just ignored it. If Bossert had spouted off to his face, he couldn't have — but the way it was he could let him blow steam & get it out of his system.

Wish to hell I had a smoke. Haven't even got the makings. Don't understand to save my life why we're so short. Wrote J. tonight & asked her to send me some if she could & not to bother trying to find Luckies. I'd take anything she can find, for we've been smoking Chelsea, Raleigh's, Twenty-Grand, Kentucky Winners & rolling our own with anything that would make a cigarette.

On a rest stop during the convoy, Billington & I spotted a hospital & went in thinking for sure they would have something to smoke. Saw the chaplain & he said they were out of everything but a few cigars. He rummaged around & found nine. We gave them out, three to a squad truck. They only made the cigar smokers happy but at least a few men had a good smoke.

Last night when we got in everybody wanted a smoke damned bad. Pigg said he had a vague memory of putting a sack of Duke's in his B. bag. He had plenty of help emptying it out. We found it, right at the bottom. The tobacco was molded but nobody minded. That one little bag made a slim cigarette each for Hq. squad & tasted wonderful, mold & all.

Mail hasn't caught up yet & I'm too tired to think any more tonight.

Ettelbruck
Monday, Sept. 25, 1944

Finished the bridge at Steinfort & came here to Ettelbruck yesterday. This is in Luxembourg proper & by God right on the German border. A bridge across the Our River here, an I-beam job, but Company C has come in to help.

If we didn't establish some kind of record on that fixed job at Steinfort in three days, I'm a monkey's uncle. It was fast, man, *fast*.[2]

This is 4th Armored territory, but you sure know Germany's not far away. All the roadsigns, the signs over the stores, the street signs, are in German & in fact the people speak German. They don't appear to be unfriendly, but the look of all the German signs & hearing the Kraut language sort of gives me a crawly feeling.

Luxembourg is a beautiful country, though, the most beautiful we have seen. Full of mountains & old castles & rivers, although no river looks pretty to this outfit any more. Just the sight of one is enough to drag out a groan. But Luxembourg is a sort of picturebook looking country — a little the way I've always pictured Switzerland looking.

We are bivouacked in an open field in the edge of the town. It's a beautiful town — the streets are cobblestone, there is a cathedral & up on the mountainside is either a castle or a monastery. I've been buying postcards of the prettiest places we've been — Mont St. Michel, Marle, the chateau at Melun, etc. & I sure do want to try to find some here. When censorship is lifted enough I can send them to J.

Played poker tonight, Pigg winning. Then Billington & I worked a while on the crossword puzzle in the New York *Daily News*. Between us we can usually work them, but it ain't easy!

The mail came in last night behind us & was given out this morning. I hit the jackpot with 17 letters. King[3] was away somewhere & Love had mail call. Thought he'd have some fun.

---

2 It was the second best time for a fixed timber bridge built on the Continent during the war.

3 Cpl. John A. King, Clerk, Company A.

He bunched the 17 letters together. When he got to them he fanned them out, squinted his eyes as if he couldn't make out the name, licked his thumb & finally droned, "Sgt. Giles." He went through the same act with each letter until the fellows got enough of it & yelled, "To hell with Sgt. Giles, get to the rest of us!" There are those in the outfit who think Sgt. Giles is the luckiest man of them all with his mail & Sgt. Giles is one of them. I *know* how lucky I am. If there is mail at all, I usually get some.

Libby is at home with J. now & Nash is on his way but they don't know where yet. Wherever it is, he'll be flying bombers & brother, I don't envy him. It takes guts to sit up there & ride through that flak & I'm damned sure I don't have that kind. I've watched them plow through when it was as thick as a carpet under them & you couldn't see how any of them could make it. And some didn't. I've never watched one of our planes fall that it didn't make me sick at my stomach. The worst is when they spin down in flames. Somebody is being fried to a crackling & he hasn't got a chance. I don't begrudge a single one of those boys his easy life between missions, for when they fly it's rough.

Sunday, Oct. 1, 1944
Somebody located the local "bootlegger" & the booze has been flowing & the work on the bridge, which is a stinker, has gone better. I've not worked on this bridge. We're so near the German border & front that even with 4th Armored all around somebody with bars on his shoulders decided we needed our own air security — so I've been with my gun most of the time.

Some of the wildest things can happen. I didn't have Sgt. of the Guard last night. Think Loftis did. Anyway it was set up & security posted. Then a work detail had to go out to repair a culvert. They either didn't know the password or had forgotten or something went snafu. Anyway, some kid got excited, thought they were Krauts & started shooting off his rifle. Today we heard practically the entire artillery of 4th Armored was alerted.

And there's a weird story about one of the artillery gun crews. Seems they have their own private dame. One of the boys swears it's the truth. Says she visits them every two or three days & they "queue" up. Asked him why he didn't join the line. He said, much astonished, "Hell, them artillery boys'd murder you!" He's a sort of mild fellow, quiet type, doesn't talk much & just the way he said it sent us into convulsions.

I've not heard of anybody making any time with these Luxembourg women. We got a real lecture on nonfraternization before we came here & were told it would be strictly enforced. Cost an EM 65 bucks if he's caught — an NCO $30 a stripe. That's something of a hindrance when there's *one* officer with an eagle eye & goes strictly by the book. Not enough to stop these boys if they really want to get going, but enough to make a guy feel his way.

Went to mass with LaCoste & another boy this morning. First time I ever went to a Catholic service. We wondered if they would let us in with our guns, but we are under arms at all times & had to take them in with us. Nobody blinked an eye.

I couldn't make heads or tails of the service, but didn't expect to. LaCoste had told me it would be in Latin. But he & the other guy were kneeling & getting up all the time. I started by kneeling when they did but got lost in the shuffle, so just sat it out. The church was beautiful. Many beautiful statues & one of Mary that was more than lifesize with candles burning before it. Many beautiful paintings on the wall. LaCoste said they were the stations of the cross. It was nice to sit & look at the altar & the stained glass windows & the paintings & all the people in their Sunday clothes, the children & all — just as if there wasn't any war. This front is so quiet you could almost believe there isn't — but there's that M1 slung across your shoulder & that puptent you're sleeping in & First Sarge bellering & the bridges & roads & you know the Krauts haven't given up.

We'll be moving on soon & most of us will be glad. It's beginning to turn a little cool for dogtents & maybe if we get back to France, or into Belgium we can go into houses. And durned if it wouldn't be nice to hear some French spoken again. It was just beginning to make a little sense to me — but this German! Sounds to me as if they just grunt & cough.

Been reading S & S since chow. Big shortage of gasoline & general snafu in supplies. Seems our big sweep across the country is coming to a halt. Schommer & I have been talking about it, wondering if it would make a difference in when the war would end. Everything has been going so swell & we've been so sure it was almost over that for things to slow up now sort of throws us. Just the other day S & S said Antwerp had been taken & it was the best deep water port on the channel. Looks to me as if they could shorten the supply lines by using Antwerp. Doesn't make sense to keep hauling the stuff from the Peninsula, but that's what they are doing & it's a hell of a long way back.[4]

News like this makes you feel low — then, too, there's not been much mail lately. Something is snafu in getting it up to us. I am very anxious to know where Nash was sent. The girls are praying it won't be to the Pacific. I don't think it very likely.

---

[4] The British took Antwerp on September 4. In his haste to move rapidly into Holland, however, General Montgomery did not take the Scheldt Estuary. The Germans were strongly entrenched on islands in the Estuary and the port was useless to the Allies until the Estuary was cleaned out. This was not done until the middle of November. General Bradley felt that General Eisenhower was anxious to leave General Montgomery much freedom in his movements, but this turned out to be a very costly decision at this particular time. Had the port been available as early as September, the war in the winter of 1944 might have been quite different.

His take-off point was Topeka & it seems to me if he had been headed west it would have been somewhere nearer the west coast.

Salmchâteau, Belgium
Sunday, Oct. 8, 1944

Left Ettelbruck on the 5th, went to Bastogne, came here to-day. The bridge in Ettelbruck finally went up — a 130 ft. 12 in. I-beam job. Nasty bit of business, though I didn't have to work on it.

Only 2nd & part of 3rd platoons are here. Rest of the Company has gone, we hear, to Hockai. This is a small place not far from Vielsalm. We have a bridge to repair here. And good deal — we're in a house, a big, gray, stone, barny place, but with enough room for us to spread out. Rather chilly & damp & it smells musty as all stone houses do, but it's better than a pup-tent outside. The room I'm in has got the wildest wallpaper you ever saw — roses & vines & leaves crawling in all directions. It's a good thing I'm too tired most nights to look at it, for I never did like fancy wallpaper. Sometimes at home Mama would pick a flowery pattern for the living room & it would al-most drive me nuts. I'd try not to, but in spite of myself I'd find myself hypnotized by a vine of flowers & it was like work-ing your way through a maze trying to find where it began & ended. I'd just have to get up & leave the room.

This deal will be no sweat & we're all glad of it. It's a nice town & the people are friendly. *And* the beer flows freely, some cognac, too, which is always a good deal.

Saw Jeff Elliott a little while in Bastogne. Sure was glad to see him. It's been nearly three months. He brought me up to date on what he's been doing — mostly riding motorcycle for Group, but he's driving for Lieut. Hayes now.

I like that boy. He's good for you — gives you a laugh a

minute. I sometimes wonder, though, what he's like under all the wisecracks. He's nobody's fool, but he doesn't let his guard down much. But, neither do I. The first thing the army teaches you is if you've got any brains it's best to keep it to yourself. You get along better if you play it strictly G.I.

Mail finally came up & there were six letters. They still don't know where Nash is, but they do know for sure he's on his way. Libby had been hearing from him daily from some unknown place, but his letters have stopped. She'll have to sweat a while now. J. sent 50 Airmail stamps. She tickles me. The minute she gets a V-mail, which she hates, she sends a bunch of stamps. Well, she knows I'm out of stamps & broke when she gets a V-mail.

[Jeff Elliott says: "After Edelstein fired me I went down to motor pool & did the dirty work around there for a few days.

Then Smoky Conover[5] came in one day & said an ME109 had strafed him down the road & into a house. Smoky was the motorcycle rider. He also said an awful case of piles had come on him & he just couldn't ride that damned motorcycle any more.

A call came down from Group to send our motorcycle & rider to Group to ride messenger service. Sgt. Lincoln[6] asked me if I could ride. I said, "Hell, yes, I was brought up on one of the damned things." (Never was near one before). He said, "Get your things, you're going to Group for a month."

I loaded up & climbed on. Stalled the damned thing 18 times before I went 10 feet. He said, "Get the hell off it, you fool, you never even saw a motorcycle before."

I said, "One more time. Just let me try one more time."

I got it going, gunned it & spun out of that area & out of sight. I didn't see him again for about five weeks & by then I

5 T/4 Smoky Conover, H/S platoon.
6 S/Sgt. Kenneth Lincoln, head of motor pool, Company A.

could ride hell out of a motorcycle. When I did see him, he said, "I thought I'd seen the last of you." I told him he had & got the rest of my things & went back to Group.

Didn't see any of the outfit again until near Braines, France, southeast of Paris. I had been with Group a long time then & wanted to go back & visit with the Company. Was going around a long curve, about 65 mph. There were heavy woods on the left so I couldn't see all the way round the curve. Suddenly I spotted a Frenchman on a bicycle up ahead. He looked back over his shoulder to see what I was & as he looked he swerved into the middle of the road. I laid the motorcycle over onto its left crash bars & hit him flat with the wheels toward him. He went over the top of me, breaking the windshield as he went.

Me, the bicycle & motorcycle, went sliding on down the road at 65 mph. I wore an awful lot of hide off my knee, hip & elbow. Finally got loose from all the machinery & began to roll like a bear cub. Then finally I stopped rolling, after about an hour it seemed. The motorcycle went off the left side of the road & hit a telephone pole. It was still running. I got up & limped over & shut it off. Then I lay down beside it & passed out. I came to strangling. Some Frenchman was pouring Calvados down my throat.

The bicycle was a wreck & the guy I hit was cut from his wrist to his elbow. Wonder I didn't kill him.

I went on to Company & did odd jobs for a couple of weeks until the motorcycle was fixed, then I went back on it & on down into Luxembourg. My sores wouldn't heal but I was afraid to go to the hospital for fear I would lose the outfit & the job. It was too good a job to lose. I was my own boss, more or less, & could find my own booze, women, & if I wanted a side trip to Paris, I took it. I was having myself a hell of a good war. Of course I was a rolling target for every trigger happy guy in the American or German army & I was damned lucky not to get myself killed.

Then in September my free, happy life ended. I was drafted to drive Lt. Hayes. You know the rest.]

Wednesday, Oct. 11, 1944

Somebody with bars on his shoulders decided we'd better not repair the bridge here after all — better build a new one — a timber trestle. Well, it suits the hell out of us. We're having a very pleasant war right now. I'd just as soon stay here all winter.

Met a woman yesterday, on the bridge, who thought I looked lean & hollow evidently. She took me home with her & fed me & a better meal I never ate. The wine also flowed. As I ate she talked — broken English & spitfire French. But I got the gist of it. Her husband is in forced service in the German army. She said when the Krauts came through here in 1940 they made a clean sweep. All the men who wouldn't collaborate were hauled away. For a long time she didn't know what had happened to him. Thought perhaps he'd been executed. Then she heard from him & he was in an Inf. Div. in the German army. She said they always put their prisoners of war in the Inf. She said Salmchâteau was Belgian but there were places that weren't. I asked her which places, but she wouldn't say. She just said many like the Germans the best. I wonder why? You'd think they'd be glad to see the last of them. Don't see how it could have been easy for any of them under German occupation, but she said there were many with German sympathies.[7]

[7] The Ardennes section of Belgium had changed hands four times since 1870. Originally Belgian, it had been annexed by Germany in 1870 on a line roughly running from Aachen, through Eupen, Malmédy, Spa, Saint Hubert and south to the French border. For forty-nine years the area was part of Germany. It was

About that time the family came home — Papa, Mama, kid brothers & sisters & her own kids, all over the place. Joy & happiness. Papa broke out more wine & then more until I finally came home like Cousin Corie, weaving through the weeds.[8] They said come back, come again, bring your friends. I don't think there's any doubt where their sympathies lie & they're not afraid to show it.

Billington & Pigg just came in. Pigg says Billington has found him a girl with green hair. He swears it. Billington says it's not really green, it's just sort of chartreuse.

[Bob Billington says: I still have a picture of Alice, the girl with the green hair. Not a bad looker. We built a temporary bridge at Salmchâteau, then a fixed bridge.

All the girls in the town hung around the bridge, Alice too. She began finally trying to speak a little English. Did very well, too — said "trom" for train & things like that, but we could talk together. She was embarrassed no end by the green hair. Told me they had dyed her hair & put glasses on her to keep the Krauts from conscripting her for brothel service or a labor camp. Her hair came out green and about that time along came the Yanks. She came from a nice family who had a nice home & we had a number of good times there.

Alice found a girl for one of the other boys. This girl's old man ran the saloon at Salmchâteau. Alice & I could understand each other, but this fellow couldn't talk French at all & the girl couldn't speak a word of English. I used to have to do

---

ceded to Belgium in 1921 following World War I. In 1940, Hitler overran it and annexed it again. Then in 1944 the Allies moved in.

8 Among the dozens of Kentucky mountain songs Henry Giles knew and sang was one about Cousin Corie, who made the finest mash liquor. Her downfall was that she only sold what she didn't drink herself. She came to an untimely end. "The last time I seen Cousin Corie, she was weaving through the weeds, a revenue officer behind her, gonna grab her for her deeds."

their talking for them. He would say the most goshawful things right in front of her & I would have to try to translate for him. Once he said, in English naturally, "My Gawd, Bob, look at those buck teeth! She could eat corn off the cob through a keyhole."

I floundered around & it came out garbled French that she had beautiful hair & beautiful white teeth. Found out later they could understand us a lot better than we realized for I soon learned that Flemish & basic English are a lot alike. It had its embarrassments, for you know what kind of language we used on those bridges. I thought of all the times we had cut loose in front of them.

Then this other guy picked up a couple of girls, also on the bridge, who lived four or five miles away, up in the hills. We couldn't finger a jeep to go see them, so we walked up one night. The girl I drew was Gabrielle, and she had a brother about my age. He and I got to know each other pretty well & finally we got to going deer hunting with him. We had to ring Coupe in on the deal, for he could steal a jeep where we couldn't, and we had to have a jeep for the deer hunting.

Edelstein liked to hunt, too, so we took him along several times. Jeep no problem when the Lieut. went.

Gabrielle was a beautiful girl & her family fed us several times. My, oh, my, what a hungry bunch we were along about then. And how good a homecooked meal did taste.

Alice was a good correspondent for a few years. She sent needlework to me in Germany and after I got back to the U.S. Some of it was beautiful and I gave it to my mother at holiday times. She finally got married, so that was that.]

Friday, Oct. 13, 1944

It's a black Friday, all right. For a long time we have been hearing rumors about a big blackmarket gang operating in &

around Paris. Today it was in S & S. They say it's mostly AWOLS & that there are about 17,000 of them running loose highjacking & stealing stuff to sell to the French. Everything from cigarettes to gas to food, tires, jeeps, all the stuff we need so bad.

But there are some SOS people in on it, too.[9] And that burns the hell out of us. As if they didn't have the softest jobs of anybody, sitting on their fat asses in their big plush headquarters in Paris, they have to go stealing from their own troops.

There is one whole railway battalion involved. One damn major has sent home over $30,000. It's the dirtiest, lowdown thing I ever heard of. They're up for courtmartial & I hope to hell they all get life at hard labor. They *ought* to be shot. Here we have been taking "butts" on each other for weeks for smokes, short of gas for the vehicles, short on everything, & they've been stealing us blind & selling it. If that's not treason, I don't know what is. If they could hear *this* outfit saying what they'd do to them if they could get their hands on them, they'd be glad for a nice, safe guardhouse with good strong bars to hide in. Brother, what a war!

LaCoste & I did right well at the bridge today & got taken home for a homecooked meal. We'd just as soon never finish this bridge. It's been built with women & kids running out our ears. I counted them today, when there were fewer than usual hanging around, and there were 15 women and 23 kids. Are the Yanks ever popular in this town! It would be a pretty stupid guy who couldn't find whatever he was looking for here.

But, alas, all good things have to come to an end. We're just about through. The town is going to have a dedication ceremony for the bridge & we hear the Col. is coming for it. First time we've had a town honor us in such a way.

[9] Service of Supply.

Monday, Oct. 16, 1944

This writing is going to look like henscratching for I'm pretty drunk but wanted to put down a little about the bridge dedication today. The whole town turned out for it & there were flags, a band, a priest to bless the bridge & speeches, etc. The mayor made a speech, & Col. Pergrin made a speech. Then somebody turned the faucet on a hell of a lot of cognac & everybody in the outfit got drunk. *It has been wild.* Civilians & G.I.s all, happy as if we had good sense. Much chasing around, much singing, much joy.

LaCoste & I were supposed to go to a Belgian home for dinner, but never did make it. The invitation came while we were sober. When we remembered it, we were in no shape to go & had forgotten where they said they lived anyway. If I can remember tomorrow, will try to go around & apologize. But I don't think they much looked for us under the circumstances.

This does it for today. Now I'll lay me down to sleep.

By God, not quite! Just at that point Hinkel walked in! Same old jerk. Put his hands on his hips & looked at me, bottle by my side, & said, "Drunk last night, drunk the night before, drunk again tomorrow night. Haven't you done a damned thing but get drunk since the last time I saw you?" Told him I'd done a hell of a lot more & not as much of that as I would have liked.

He was glad to get what was left of my bottle. Am I *ever* glad to see him again. Had given up hope of his making it back to the outfit. Almost like seeing a long-lost brother again.

Tuesday, Oct. 17, 1944

Having a day off today & it's welcome. They let us sleep late this morning & I've done nothing all day but loaf with Hinkel. For a change the weather is beautiful. Sun is shining & it's warmer than it has been. Fine day for being lazy.

Hinkel wanted to know everything that's been happening

to us & I brought him up to date as best I could. Don't know when I've had more fun or laughed more than in remembering what this bunch have done all across the country — Marigny, where the Calvados began to flow — Marle, where the natives adopted us — Luxembourg, where they didn't — *and* Salm-château, which has been one of the best. He said we sounded like the Dead End kids. It has been an advance to remember & wouldn't do to write home about — but there has also been a hell of a lot of work & many times, long dry stretches with no compensations of any kind. This outfit takes its fun where it finds it, but it can also work the tails off any other Engineering outfit in the army.

Hinkel is glad to get back, but he's a little uneasy about what kind of a job he'll draw. He'd rather be with the platoon, of course, but there's no chance of that. When he was gone so long, Pigg was made S/Sgt. & got the job permanently. Hinkel is actually in the spot of being an extra S/Sgt. they'll have to find a job for. They will, but it may not be what he'd like.

Only flaw in the day today is that I have got one hell of a cold. Head as big as a waterbucket, nose running, coughing & some fever, I'm sure. Throat pretty sore. My ears are beginning to bother me, so stopped up I can't hear well & hurting a little. Hinkel thinks I ought to go on sick call, but I'll be damned if I do. I don't want to be sent to the hospital.

Mail call. Six letters tonight & one had quite a surprise in it. Janice has begun writing a book. Says it's probably a silly idea but she's been wanting to try her hand at it for several years. Well, I don't think it's silly. From her letters I'd bet anything she writes would be good. She says if I don't mind after we're married she would like to go into it more seriously, but this first book is a sort of story of her & Libby's life together. I sure as hell don't mind & she'll get all the encouragement I can give her. She says Libby has her old job back & there are a lot of nights when she's on the swing shift or night shift when J. is alone. That's when she's writing.[10]

Had to stop there & I never felt as sorry for anybody in my life. A fellow came in with a letter he just got — an anonymous letter.[11] He wanted me to read it & tell him what I thought about it. It said his wife was running around, going steady with some stateside soldier. Said it had been going on for six months & it was the reason she wanted to move from her folks' home — so this fellow could be with her more.

I asked him if his wife had said anything about moving. He said that was what shook him so bad — he had a letter from her not long ago & she said she was thinking about moving into an apartment with a girl friend. Reason she gave was she would be closer to her work.

Well, I don't know. I didn't say so, but it did look a little as if there was some fire where there was that much smoke. We talked about it a little. He said he didn't *want* to doubt her & had never thought he would, but he didn't see how he could just put it out of his mind. He hated to write & ask her about it, for if it's just someone trying to make trouble, no use getting her all upset, too. I said, "What about just sending her the letter? Not say anything about it one way or the other. Then it wouldn't be you accusing her." So he may do that. But he may write some friends at home to check around a little.

If it was me, I *know* I'd have to find out. For when you get a thing like that riding you, hell you've *got* to know. You can't just live with it. It'll eat your guts out.

The letter was signed, "A Friend." Fine friend to tear a man all to pieces like that. I'd be willing to bet it's some woman,

---

10 Libby was a very minor chemist at National Synthetic Rubber Company.

11 The man is identified, but at this late date there seems no point in revealing his identity.

too — probably somebody jealous of his wife or mad at her about something. What in the hell good did it do to write him about it? What can he do about it from here? If she'd kept her damn mouth shut, even if it's true, it might have blown over & he never would have known it.

I don't know why a thing like this has to happen to such a decent guy. It sure has jolted him. There are some in the outfit it would be sauce for the goose — but not this kid.

And I could kick myself clear back to England. It's got me moody & blue. You just don't like to hear about such things. It really shakes you, for you know he's believed in his wife just as much as you believe in your girl. It's all too easy to imagine what hell it would be if *you* got it in the neck.

After he left, several of the other fellows drifted in. Everybody is sore as hell about it for him. Wishing they could do something, help in some way. Mac said, "What I'd like to do is get my hands around the neck of the bitch who wrote him." We all think it's a woman. Men don't do things that way. If one of his friends in civilian life was going to wise him up, he'd have had the guts to sign his name. At least we figure it that way.

Most of us think it's true. It just adds up too well. Pigg said, "I'll bet she took this flyboy away from the damned bitch & that's what she's so sore about." And that figures, too. She had to hate this girl to blab like that. She was wanting to get her into trouble. And didn't give a damn how much heartache she caused this kid. It's got the whole outfit shook.

Just now it felt like there was water in my right ear. Turned my head over & a lot of pus ran out. Not good. Not a bit good.

Wednesday, Oct. 18, 1944
Both my ears hurting now & damned bad. I don't know how

much more I'm going to be able to take. Not sleeping much with them.

Don't know where we are either. Moved today. Think we're in Germany but was hurting too bad to pay any attention. Remember hearing one of the fellows say, when we went through some town & I think it was Aachen, what the hell were we doing there — it was just taken a few days ago.[12]

Wherever we are it's in the middle of the most godawful damned forest I ever saw. The worst bivouac we've had yet. The woods are so thick if the sun decided to shine some day it couldn't get through. The fog rolls in & these damn pine trees do nothing but drip. The mud is a foot deep & there's no dry place anywhere. We used three cans of gasoline to get us a fire tonight so we could dry out a little. We piled limbs, brush, anything we could find in the mud for our bedrolls & then they just sank on down in the slush. Besides which, it's getting too damned cold to be out in puptents. Ice in the puddles this morning. All told it's very snafu & very little future in it.[13]

Field Hospital
Friday, Oct. 20, 1944

Couldn't take any more of the pain, so went on sick call this morning. Haven't slept much for a week & none at all the last two nights. Last night my ears hurt so damned bad I passed some urine in an empty cartridge & made Hinkel pour it in them. He didn't want to, for they are both draining now & he was afraid it would infect them. I said, "Hell, why do you think they're draining? They're already infected. Pour it in." I

[12] He was actually in Hockai Woods, near Eupen, still in Belgium.

[13] Bob Billington had this to say about the Hockai Woods: "Wet? Mud? Miserable? Land of Goshen! We finally got some shacks built by hook or crook. Made ours of logs and some stolen roofing. Cornes had a palace built of sections from some old Kraut barracks. I stayed with the local padre for a time. Still have his card. Boy, was that ever a hole! We didn't move out until November, either."

knew it would be warm & salty & might ease the pain a little. It didn't. But Hinkel said if I didn't go on sick call today he was going to report me himself. Said I was acting like a damned fool. I knew he was right. The way they hurt it feels like the eardrums are going to burst.

If there's anything longer than a night when you're hurting too bad to sleep I don't know what it is. I hated to keep moving around for Hinkel didn't need to stay awake, too, but couldn't much help it. Just lie there damned near crying with the pain & wait — look at your watch every five minutes — pray for daylight & know it's five hours yet, or four hours, & when you get it worked down to one, every minute is an hour long. Everybody asleep but you — everything still except the drip from the damned pine trees. Blankets cold & damp & the mud oozing through. Shivering & hurting like hell. Then finally a few sounds — somebody coughing, something clinking, somebody's boots squishing in the mud as he goes to the latrine, somebody yawning, grunting, then voices talking. Morning! It's over — the damned long night. I'll probably wish I hadn't, but I was *ready* to go on sick call by the time daylight came today.

I'm already fouled up, though. The Bn. medical officer didn't think I'd have to go to base hospital. He thought they would treat my ears here, give me something to ease the pain & let me come on back. So I didn't go back to my tent for anything. Came off without my billfold, my writing kit or pen, my shaving kit, my last letters — everything. But the medical officer here at the field hospital took one look & said base hospital for you, son. So, I'm on my way. But there will at least be some sleep for me tonight. They've already given me something to ease the pain & for the first time in a week I'm not hurting. What I hate most is having to work my way back to the outfit through the damned replacement depot system.[14] But I'll just have to sweat it out.

Base Hospital, Paris
Wednesday, Oct. 25th

In Paris, finally, but never thought it would be this way. Left the field hospital yesterday morning. They gave me some stuff to take on the trip & I was dopey most of the time. Got here this morning.

Have been checked in & put in pajamas, but no doctor has seen me yet. The pajamas feel strange as hell. Haven't slept in anything but shorts & a shirt since I joined the army & haven't taken all my clothes off since we got to France. Feel naked as a jaybird.

The hospital is all right. In a building & warm, and *such* beds! Don't know whether I can sleep in a bed, now. Guess I'll have to sprinkle the blankets to make them damp & stuff my shoes under the mattress to give it a few humps before it'll feel natural.

I'm not worried about my stuff for Hinkel will take care of it, but I just wish I had it with me for convenience. The Red Cross has plenty of paper & envelopes & pencils & maybe I can borrow a razor. But I don't have that first centime with me to buy a thing with.

Have written J. I'm in the hospital but told her not to say

---

14 The replacement depot system was a thorn in the flesh of the Army from its beginning, according to both Generals Eisenhower and Bradley in their books. It was slow and cumbersome in shifting replacements to the front, and old, seasoned troops hated the depots for their callousness and inefficiency in returning them quickly to their own outfits. No way was ever devised that much eased the situation. The troops so hated the system that men who should have been in hospitals refused as long as possible to go on sick call. Why General Eisenhower never shook this system up and made it operate efficiently remains incomprehensible to this day.

anything about it to the folks yet. I might be lucky & get back to the outfit pretty soon & Mama wouldn't have to know.

Later: Ear specialist has just been in, taken a look. Didn't say anything. Just grunted. Nurse came in a minute ago with some pills & hung my chart up. I took a look at it & this is what it says: "Otitis Media — Chronic — Bilat — Sup." Whatever that means. Chronic, I know & I would guess "Sup" means suppurating.

Friday, Oct. 27, 1944

I'm allowed to be up & dressed now & can go over to the Red Cross canteen. They have a radio & some magazines & papers. A little time can be passed that way.

Ears still on the blink. Still hurt when the medicine wears off & I still can't hear. When I get in a room where a lot of people are talking all I can hear is a roar & buzz. Like a swarm of bees.

Thought I'd found a *Courier-Journal* at the Red Cross. It was, but only the Society section of the Sunday paper several weeks ago. Read every word of it just the same — just because it was a Louisville paper. Then I found the want-ad section & read every word of that. Looked for a crossword but no luck. Crazy, wasn't it? To sit & read about dances & club meetings & people wanting jobs & apartments & such. They were Kentucky people, though.

They get the S & S here, too, & that's good. And the chow is not bad. No mail, of course, & there won't be.

Been thinking a lot about the fellows. Hope they've moved out of that damned mudhole.

Sunday, Oct. 30, 1944

My ears are getting better. The buzzing & crackling has almost stopped & I haven't had to take anything for pain today. Don't believe they are draining as much, either. So, I'm feeling pretty hopeful. Doctor said wait another day or two before he decided. And I *will* have to sweat out the replacement depot. I know it was foolish but I asked him why he couldn't just discharge me from the hospital & let me catch a ride back to the Company. He just shook his head. But getting out of the hospital is the first step back & I'm anxious to get started.

Been reading most of the day. They have a lot of old magazines at the Red Cross — *Life, Time, Sat-Eve. Post, New Yorker,* etc. They have a few books. Found one, *Bushido,* which I've been reading. Terrible story of the Japs in Manchuria.

Get BBC on the radio & it sometimes has good music. Keep thinking about the fellows, wondering if they're still in that damned forest. Sure hope they have moved, for it wasn't fit for a hog.

Been reading S & S. Not much action anywhere along the front right now. Guess they're all bogged down in this supply shortage as well as the mud.

From Liége to the
Battle of the Bulge

[THE SECTION of the *Journal* which follows shows why officers and men alike were so unhappy about the replacement depot system.

In the beginning the system came under the command of Lieutenant General J. H. C. Lee, who is characterized in all military histories of World War II as a "brilliant logistician." He was chief logistician for all U.S. forces.

General Lee did show some concern about the system. It was his idea to begin improvement of morale by changing the name! In his book, *A Soldier's Story*, General Omar N. Bradley says he thought this a nonsensical effort to solve with words a problem that could be eased by the assignment of better officers to these replacement depots, that what men in them needed was to be properly taken care of and some interest shown in their welfare.

The most inhumane neglect in these depots was the mail, the soldier's most hungering need. If this one service could have been provided most men could have better borne the long, futile, idle days of waiting. It is inconceivable to me that men with the ingenuity displayed so frequently in the American forces, from SHAEF to the G.I. himself, could not have devised and maintained a chain of communication between Commands and depots which would have dispatched mail swiftly to men in hospitals and replacement depots, and reclaimed hospital-released men to their own outfits promptly. It was never done, however, and to the end of the war the depots seemed to operate in a vacuum of ignorance and indifference.]

Replacement Depot, Liége
Wednesday, Nov. 1, 1944

THE next day after I last wrote here a different doctor came by to check my ears, looked at my chart, then signed me out. Came here yesterday & feel pretty good about my chances of getting back to the Company before too long. It's less than 40 kilometers to where I left the outfit, so it shouldn't take too long. Spoke to an officer about it when I got here & he said it was anybody's guess — it might be a week, two weeks, three weeks, nobody could tell. Anyway, I'm out of the hospital & started back & that's something.

But this is not going to be any piece of cake. The Krauts are throwing quite a few buzz bombs into the area & they are *very* unpleasant. You hear this put-put noise like a motor boat way down the river & you start stiffening. It gets louder & louder & then it goes over with a deep growling roar, the ground shakes, & you almost hold your breath for fear the damned thing will konk out right on top of you. It's a world of relief when it has passed on. Then you hear a thud & you know it's hit & maybe some poor bastard has got it — but it's not you. Not this time.

Mail is going to be a big sweat. One fellow I talked to this morning said he had been here since *August* & hadn't got that first letter yet. I guess I could stand it that long, if I had to, but I don't see how.

My ears are doing O.K. Except the right one is still draining a little. No pain, though. Hope these boys get on the ball & get me back to the outfit soon.

We're in tents, out in the edge of the city, but the tents are pyramidals & we have stoves. Not as bad as puptents in this weather. Nothing about the weather in Belgium has changed while I was in France. Still cold & rainy.

There's only one other fellow & myself in our tent. And this is really weird. My tentmate's name is Henry Giles! Doubt there's any relation, however. He's as black as the ace of spades. Comes from Alabama. He's with an artillery outfit & was hurt right here in Liége in September. His outfit has moved on long ago, of course, & he doesn't know where they are. There are no new replacements in this depot. All are strictly old troops, hurt or sick, out of hospital.

Jeff Elliott ran into another Henry Giles, in England. He was driving that Dodge truck of his downtown in Bath one day, missed the street he was supposed to turn on, pulled up, slammed the truck into reverse, shot back & crashed into a car. He got out to see what damage had been done & as is usual in such cases to take the driver's name & address. Henry Giles — Bath. Jeff took a second gander & said, "You're sure as hell not the Henry Giles I know." We must come by the dozens but this is the first black one I've seen.

There's a Red Cross here, so I'm able to get paper & envelopes & I found a pencil stub in the dayroom which I'm hanging onto. Poor J. All these V-mails & free mails. But I have no way to buy stamps. It sure was stupid of me to come off without my things. Don't even have J's picture, no money, no razor, or anything. Believe me, if this ever happens to me again I'll lug everything I own along with me.

Saturday, Nov. 4, 1944

Yesterday the other Henry Giles & I worked all day cutting wood for our stove. Should be enough to last us a while but I don't know, it's awfully cold. We use it up fast. I pulled guard last night & nearly froze.

Was surprised today. They let me sign for a partial pay

the day I got here & today I got it — about $3.00. Also was issued regular rations. I bought some Airmail stamps & a razor. In the rations were seven packs of cigarettes. I thought I'd seen every offbrand cigarette made but I got a new kind today. Fleetwood. They burn like a twig & taste like rabbit tobacco,[1] but they do smoke. First cigarettes I've had since finishing the pack I had on me when I went on sick call, except for the few offered me when somebody would light up. Too proud to ask "butts" from strangers.

I'm writing in the dayroom. Very quiet. Most of the fellows are writing letters, some are just sitting. All of them I've talked to are O.K. but there are two I hit it off with better than the others. One is Cpl. Hessler, who is 4th Armored artillery & we were in Luxembourg when they were. Never did run into him, but there is something in common to talk about. The other is Pvt. White, 30th Infantry. He is from eastern Kentucky. But they sure don't take the place of the boys in the outfit. I think about them a lot, most of the time in fact, wondering where they are, if they've moved, what they're doing.

Some of the boys here have been here for two or three months. I'll go nuts if I have to stay that long. They say there are around 500 in this replacement depot.

The buzz bombs are still pretty bad — two or three dozen a day. One landed in the area today — not more than half a mile away. Really shook us up. I'm strictly allergic to these damned things. They make me as nervous as a whore in church.

There's a mail call every day but it's mostly for the men who work here — very little for any of the rest of us. None for me yet. I go each time, but don't have much hope.

1 Rabbit tobacco is a dried weed known in Kentucky as Life Everlasting.

Sunday, Nov. 5, 1944

Nothing. Nothing at all. We eat, draw a little work detail once in a while, read, sleep. Drag through the days. Every day just the same. I'm getting so desperate for mail I could cry. Decided to tell Janice to write this place for *one* week, but if she gets a letter saying I'm back with the Company earlier she's not to write here at all.[2]

I asked the Lieut. today why the CO here couldn't assign me back to the Company & let me go. He looked at me as if I'd lost my mind. Said, "We don't even know where your outfit is."

I told him where they *were* & he just shrugged. Said they could have gone back to England by now. *That's* highly likely, I'd say. Man, everything we've heard about these places is really so. They can drive you crazy.

There is a fellow sitting here in the dayroom with me now writing to his wife. Said he hadn't had a letter for six weeks but he wrote every day just the same. No use her doing without mail, too. So do I, but I know my letters are very dull.

Radio is playing "Goodbye Broadway, Hello France." Wonder how long it will be before we can reverse that.

No mail.

Tuesday, Nov. 7, 1944

Am writing this at night by the firelight in our tent. Abe Lincoln style, guess you could call it. We can't have candles in the tents because of the blackout.

Raining again tonight & very cold. Thank God our tent doesn't leak. We're snug inside & the rain just sounds slow &

2 When I received this letter I began making copies of my daily letters. The original was sent to the Company address, the copy to the replacement depot. This was continued until I learned Henry was back with the Company. Out of more than sixty letters thus written, he received two in the replacement depot — on the second round, at that.

soft outside. Somebody in the next tent has a radio turned on. We can hear it. With the right person, in the right place, a tent in the rain with soft music would be heaven. Funny, but the last letter I had from Janice (which I left in my B. bag) she was telling me how her folks used to camp out a lot & go fishing when she was a little girl. Well, quit dreaming, Giles. She's not here & it'll be a hell of a long time before you can go on a camping trip with her.

Wrote a letter today for White. He can't read or write. He asked me if I would write his girl for him. Told me what he wanted to say & I added a few things I thought would be all right. When I read it back to him he said it was the best letter that had ever been written for him. All I can say is he must have had some real duds doing his writing for him. But then two other fellows who had listened came over & asked if I'd write their girls, too. I thought they were kidding, but they weren't. So I was kept pretty busy for a while. My day to write letters, I'd say. Had already written J. twice.

Today is election day back home. Don't think President Roosevelt will have much trouble being re-elected. Which reminds me how I found out J. is a Democrat. It was when she was down home last summer visiting the folks. The campaign was swinging along & she & the folks were listening to the radio one night when Dewey began to speak. Mama said J. fidgeted for a while, then said, "Wouldn't you just as soon turn the radio off, now?"

Teasing, Dad said, "Why? Don't you like Mr. Dewey?"

Janice said flatly, "No, sir, I don't. I'm sorry if he is your candidate, but I'm a dyed-in-the-wool Democrat."

They all had a good laugh, then, because I suppose Gileses have been Democrats since Thomas Jefferson. Just one more nice thing about her. Come to think of it, her religion doesn't matter to me & I don't think I'd care if she was French, British, or Chinese, but I might have a hard time living with a Republican.

Thursday, Nov. 9, 1944

Just been reading the election returns in S & S. It all went satisfactorily as far as I'm concerned. Seems the betting was 17 to 1 on Roosevelt. Would have liked to have a little money on him at those odds.

Ran into a fellow today from Owensboro, Kentucky. Said this was his second trip overseas & his second Purple Heart. He was wounded in North Africa & the wound wouldn't heal in that climate so they sent him home. Soon as he was well enough he was shipped to England & he made the Normandy invasion with 1st Inf. Those boys made the assault landings in No. Africa, Sicily, Italy & Normandy. This fellow lived through two of them. He was wounded the second time in Aachen. Two times around. I think that's too goddamned much. He deserved a stateside break if anybody ever did.

Am writing in the dayroom where quite a few others are writing also. Been wondering why so many keep asking how to spell "suspicion." Suddenly it struck me the movie scheduled for tonight is "Above Suspicion." Everybody's so hard up for anything to write they're filling in with movie titles. Well, it would take a real brain to think of anything interesting to write from a replacement depot.

My right ear is acting up again a little. Not hurting yet, but buzzing & popping & I can't hear out of it very well. But I'll be damned if I ever go on sick call again. I'll sweat out anything first.

Last night I was watching a buzz bomb going over. At night you can see the red tail flare & they look even more scary than in the daytime. Like some red-tailed dragon or infernal machine — which last is exactly what they are.

No mail.

Saturday, Nov. 11, 1944

Fellow that was leaving today gave me a big pad of paper so I can quit using loose sheets for this writing. Been writing oftener than I did with the outfit, but there's very little else to do. Also write J. twice a day.

Saturday. It was always the day back in the states when we all got passes, went to town & painted it red. Just another day, now. Have to look at the calendar to know what day of the week or month it is. You couldn't tell by anything that happens.

Rain again today & *very* cold. We have used most of the wood we cut the other day for it's so cold we have to keep a big fire going. We have a gravel floor in the tent, though, so we're not in the mud & that's something. Days like today I think about the outfit & wonder if they're still in that mud & misery. Hope to God not.

Think about them a lot anyway. When you're not with them, even their faults fade away & you remember only the best things. Like all the good passes with Black Mac & Hinkel & Keenan & Wall & Loftis. All good guys to go on pass with. Been thinking of some of the stunts we've pulled — some of the good roaring drunks we've had together — and some of the girls, good, bad & indifferent we picked up. Back together shook into convulsions comparing notes. "I made out all right."

"Not too bad."

And Keenan one night. "Hell, mine was so drunk she passed out on me!"

Even got to thinking about First Sarge the other night, remembering the Saturday night before we pulled out of Swift for POE. Only married men whose wives were in Austin could go on pass that night. I went to see him & told him for all he knew I had a date with some other man's wife who needed comforting. He grinned & gave me a pass. He can beller like a bull, but he's a swell fellow just the same.

Remember on the Louisiana maneuvers how Billington complained that he liked hog meat to eat but he didn't like hogs to sleep with. They were everywhere — got in our tents at night, came grunting around the kitchens & were a general nuisance. Remember that when we went back to Swift from the maneuvers we bivouacked one night in Texas, think it was Huntsville, on the campus of a girls' school. Either they didn't know we were there or didn't care, for they didn't pull their shades that night & they put on a real show for us going to bed. We all wished for field glasses so we could see better.

All the good times in England, too. It was Pigg who found the phonograph so I could play the record Janice made for me last Christmas. I'd looked all over Bath for one. Finally Pigg put the whole work detail to looking & he, himself, finally found one in a little restaurant. The whole squad went along to listen to the record.

When I pulled that fool rookie stunt & missed the trucks back to camp from Bath, had to walk the whole fifteen miles & didn't get in until daylight, was restricted to quarters for two weeks, there wasn't a night somebody didn't bring me part of a bottle back from pass.

And when my ears were hurting so bad, several tried to give me an extra blanket or two, willing to sleep colder themselves, so I could be warmer.

It's the best damned outfit in the army. Not a one who wouldn't do anything in the world for you, and for each other. Give you anything they've got — from their last pair of dry socks to their last franc or Airmail stamp. Nobody finds a bottle & hides it — brings it straight to share. Nobody gets a package from home & hoards it. Usually the guy who gets the package has only one piece of candy, like everyone else, or one cookie or piece of cake. On cigarettes — as short as they are — nobody goes off & lights up by himself. He lights up, puffs it down a piece, then gives the butt to somebody. Goes short himself. It's a grand, grand outfit. I miss them like hell.

My ear is still buzzing & is stopped up pretty bad. Not hurting, though.

Been watching the other fellows trying to write their letters. They sit for a long time in a kind of deep study, just staring straight ahead. Then they'll think of something to say & their faces will brighten. Often they'll grin. They scratch away for a few moments. Then they're stuck again & sink back into that deep study. One sentence at a time is the way you write a letter here. I'm stuck with White's letters to his girl & the other two guys. But I hit on the idea of writing the same letter to all three girls, except for a personal line or two. Thank goodness, none of them want to write every day.

Found a book I hadn't read today, *Low Man on the Totem Pole*. Have wondered where that expression came from. It's pretty good. Full of laughs. The "library" here is a laugh itself. Looks to me as if they could work out *something* for a man to do in these places to keep him from getting dryrot. And I don't see why they can't move us faster. There isn't a new man in this depot. Every man here has been in combat & either wounded or made sick by it. If S & S is right & replacements are so damned short we're all needed back with our outfits. There's a hell of a lot that's snafu about this whole damned system.

The rain has turned to snow now. Very wet, big flakes. This

is the first snow of the winter. It's pretty but it just makes life more miserable if you're out in dogtents or up front.

Thursday, Nov. 16, 1944

Today we were moved into a building — much better quarters. This is a big, gray stone building that must have been a school or monastery. It has two wings & a central section that make a sort of courtyard out front. Five stories tall. The other Henry Giles & I are still rooming together. We're on the second floor of the east wing. Everything bare & barny — whatever was here moved out bag & baggage, when Liége was taken in September, I imagine. But we have cots & our stove & at least we're in out of the weather. We can black out the windows & have a candle at night, too, which makes it more cheerful. Now that we're in out of the weather maybe my ear will quit bothering me.

Being inside makes me feel a little easier about the buzz bombs, too. Even if this building took a direct hit it's so big your chances would still be pretty good.

Sent Christmas cards today to home, to J's mother & sister, & to Libby. Can't think yet what to do about a gift for Janice. I *may* get another partial pay, but don't know for sure. Will have to decide something pretty soon.

Wish I'd get some mail. So many things I'd like to know. How J. is doing with her book. Where Nash was sent. If J. decided to spend Thanksgiving down home. Said she was if Libby went to the Hancocks'. Otherwise she didn't want to leave her. Wish I knew if everybody at home is all right. Wish, wish, wish, that's all I do. I'm ashamed of myself for crying the blues so much but this is no piece of cake to sweat out. As a last wish, I wish I had about a quart of cognac. I'd by damn drink every drop of it by myself.

Monday, Nov. 20, 1944

A month today since I went on sick call & started down this damn road away from the outfit. I'll have to be unconscious or dead if I ever do it again.

Decided yesterday I'd better not risk being able to buy J. a Christmas gift. Wrote Mama to draw $100 from my savings & send it to her. Used my last Airmail stamp on the letter in the hope it will reach her in time for her to get the money to J. before Christmas. It's the best I can do.

Also wrote Hinkel to get on the ball & get me the hell out of here.

Tuesday, Nov. 21, 1944

Thought I was leaving today & got in a real flurry. While we were in a movie some names were called over the public address system to report to the office. Giles was called & even spelled out. I broke all records getting there but the other Giles had beat me. No mistake about it for I double-checked. His Company had come for him.

And *that* gave me the best idea I've had in a long time. I'm going to do something about this goddamned mess myself. I applied for a 5-hour pass for tomorrow. I'm going to wander around the whole damn 5 hours & look for a vehicle from the outfit. If I see one I can send word to the Lieut. to come *get* me. I'm scared if I stay here much longer I'll be reassigned to some other outfit & besides I'm fed up with this kind of foul-up. You can't even talk to these damn fools. They just say, "You'll have to sweat it out, buddy." I'm going to get out of this place some way, some how, I swear it.

Thanksgiving Day
Nov. 23, 1944

No passes yesterday but I have my name in & I mean to drive them nuts till I get one.

They gave us a good Thanksgiving dinner today, though — real turkey, not the canned stuff, dressing, everything else that was good. Once or twice a year you get fed like a king. Took three hours in the chow line to get it, but it was worth it.

No mail. Have been thinking all day of home & wondering if J. is down there. Hope so. Hope they are having a wonderful Thanksgiving.[3]

Thursday, Nov. 30, 1944

Have written nothing here for a week & didn't mean to write until I got that pass. Today I got it. Hitched a ride over east of the city where the main highway from Aachen comes in & stood there the rest of the time looking for any 291st vehicle. No luck. I must have seen vehicles from every outfit in Belgium but none from the Bn. Will try again tomorrow & keep on trying until I see one. Sometime, somebody from the outfit is going to have to drive into Liége.

It was cold out there, but I kept from freezing by walking around & sometimes went in a little restaurant that was near & got warm. Very little money but I had enough for a couple of beers.

Sunday, Dec. 3, 1944

Had a pass again the 1st, with no better luck than before. Tried for another pass today but there's some kind of damned foul-up. They were ready to give it to me but on checking

[3] I was with Henry's people for Thanksgiving, but it was not a particularly happy time. We were worried about his ears and the first of his unhappiness in the replacement depot was beginning to show through. We comforted ourselves with the thought he was at least "in out of the weather."

the roster it was learned I was on *restriction!* What for, I don't know, but I sure mean to find out. I haven't done a damned thing to be restricted for. Have been very careful to get back on time from the other passes & there's nothing else I could be restricted for. Just damn all these depot people to hell anyway!

Since the other Henry Giles left, Hessler & White have moved in with me. My room was a little larger & the three of us make out very well. We're together most & I didn't want having to break in a new roommate.

Tuesday, Dec. 5, 1944

Got some action on the restriction today. Went clear to the CO to get it. It was a mistake. Probably some little clerk with too much beer in him just checked the wrong name on the roster. Anyway, the restriction is lifted.

During this time I've been doing nothing but reading, writing letters, playing checkers or poker, passing the time some way or other. A long time ago Janice wrote that when I got back she wanted to run through my letters & learn everywhere I had been & what I was doing at that time. When we get to 20 October 1944, we'll look at no more until I get back to the Company. Even in peacetime I don't want to be reminded of these days.

For some reason the buzz bombs are letting up a little. Only three have gone over today. Now, I'm all in favor of that.[4]

Friday, Dec. 8, 1944

Haven't been able to get another pass yet. Worst days I've had so far. Absolutely nothing to do but a little guard duty

---

[4] The Germans were preparing to mount their offensive and in order to cause a greater sense of security in the American forces, the V–1 barrage was ordered eased on December 1st.

once in a while. I've heard guys in the outfit say — and have said it myself — that when they get home they don't want to do a thing for a month but rest & eat & sleep. I can tell them that a week of it is about all you can take. After that it can drive you nuts.

I've read every book they have here, all the magazines, all the papers, all the comic books, worked every crossword puzzle I could find, played checkers until I never want to see a checkerboard again, stared out these windows, walked a hundred miles in that courtyard, hunted up jobs to do, done everything I could think of until I've run out. Sometimes I look at the other fellows & wonder if I'm beginning to look like a zombie, too. No reason I shouldn't.

Wrote Hinkel again & told him if he had to go clear to the Col. to do it, *get me out of here.* But I don't think they even mail our letters. Think they must burn them. I believe if a man should stay the duration & six in one of these damned hell holes he wouldn't get a single piece of mail.

Monday, Dec. 11, 1944

Had a pass again today & looked for a vehicle from the Battalion again. Didn't see any. So I've decided to try something different. I'm going to try to *find* the outfit. If I can get a pass tomorrow I'm going to begin hitching rides & see if I can't run across them.

The weather is lousy — very cold & a mixture of sleet & drizzle all day. But I felt a hell of a lot better out in it trying to do something than I would have sitting here in the warm & dry doing nothing.

Tuesday, Dec. 12, 1944

Nothing. No passes.

Wednesday, Dec. 13th

Ditto.

Thursday, Dec. 14th

Ditto.

Friday, Dec. 15, 1944

Got a pass today. Had three or four good rides & got into Germany but was stopped in the outskirts of Aachen.[5] An MP there said I couldn't go any farther. And he didn't know anything about the outfit. Said he hadn't seen any of their vehicles at all, at any time. I didn't have time to do anything but head back to Liége. Got a short ride to Monzen & that was a lucky break for while I was waiting for another lift I saw a fellow that was transferred out of the Bn. some time ago & he said he thought the outfit was near Verviers. I'll try there tomorrow, or as soon as I can.

Along about this time last year, in England, Hinkel & I were wondering if we'd be home for Christmas this year. My Christmas packages had come & between the folks & Janice I had every good thing to eat & wonderful presents. We had mail regularly & good quarters, but we were bitching just because we were out of the States. We didn't know how good we had it.

Hessler & White & I have decided if we're all still here (and I don't mean to be if I can help it) we're going to have a Christmas tree, come hell or high water. If we can't do any better we mean to steal a piece of the hedge out front. We decided to begin saving stuff to decorate with. Each of us should get several cans of hash before Christmas & we can cut the tin into strips, and our "D" bars are wrapped in tinfoil so we can use

[5] It is to be remembered that Henry Giles was under the impression that when he left the outfit to go to hospital they were near Aachen.

that for tinsel. *If* we get a partial pay before Christmas we can buy a little beer, too. Hell, we've got to do something.

Found a dirty old Airmail envelope on the floor today & used it for my letter to J. Have been using all Free & V-mail lately. Told her about our plans for our tree.[6]

[On December 15, 1944, the Ardennes front of the American First Army stretched eighty-five miles on a very thinly held line from Monschau on the north to Echternach, Luxembourg on the south. Only 75,000 troops, some battle weary and resting, others green and new, held the line. They were elements of six divisions; 4th Infantry, farthest south at Echternach; 9th Armored (one Combat Command) next; the battle-weary 28th Infantry next; the new 106th Infantry Division (latest division in Europe) next in the snowy Eifel mountains and across the Losheim Gap (the historic gateway through which German troops had poured in 1870, in 1914, and again in 1940); farthest north was the 99th Infantry, with elements of 2nd Armored attacking through them toward the Roer River.

It was a very quiet front and had been very quiet since October. In fact, it was called the "ghost" front because nothing ever happened on it.

On December 15, 1944, three full German armies were massed all along the Ardennes front, the "ghost front," with twenty divisions, 250,000 men, 1900 pieces of heavy artillery, 970 tanks and assault guns. This was Operation "Wacht am Rhein," Adolf Hitler's plan for taking the offensive again, smashing the western front, and perhaps ending the war in the West.

[6] This letter reached me on Christmas Eve. The envelope had been badly crumpled but he had straightened it as best he could. It had evidently been much walked over, for there were dirty shoe prints on it. The news the letter contained, the pitiful determination to have a Christmas tree, almost undid me. I think I cried the hardest over this one letter than any I received. We were so safe and warm and well off. I was trying so dreadfully hard to get some kind of mail through to him. I even sent a cablegram to the replacement depot address. It never reached him, either.

As Henry Giles' Journal continues, this is its background
. . . the German offensive which became known as the Battle
of the Bulge.]

Saturday, Dec. 16, 1944

Got a pass today & headed out in the direction of Verviers but
didn't get very far. Hell of a lot of traffic coming this way but
not very much going the other. Got a few short rides is all.
Finally ran out of time & had to give it up & start back. But I was
lucky again. This time I got a ride with some Ordnance boys
who told me part of the Battalion is in Malmédy. These boys
were through there just two days ago & talked with some of the
fellows. Said they were running a sawmill there. So this is
straight dope. I've been going in the opposite direction all the
time. Tomorrow I ought to make it. Malmédy is closer than
the other places, too.

Sunday, Dec. 17, 1944

Had a pass & started out pretty early but never did make it to
any place. Got a ride with a Lieut. in his jeep, but you never
saw such a line of vehicles headed north in your life. The Lieut.
was trying to get to St. Vith. None of us could figure why
there was so much traffic. One MP told us he had heard there
was going to be an offensive up north. Finally the Lieut. lost
his patience & told his driver to find a side road & get on it.

The driver turned off & drove us down into the hills, but he
got lost & the road was nothing but snow & slush & mud, & the
Lieut. got afraid we'd get bogged down, so in disgust he told the
driver to turn around & get back on the main highway. We
came out at a different place & an MP stopped us there & told us
all hell had busted loose, the Krauts were attacking & the whole
country was crawling with them, they were headed for Liége

& we'd better get back there as fast as we could. He was shaking like a leaf & it was plain whether it was true or not he believed it. The driver gunned the jeep & we shot back into the suburbs. Here, I got out & walked on in.

When I got back here there was much excitement with a lot of rumors & some garbled radio reports about a German counterattack. The rumors vary. Some are so wild they say the Krauts are in the edge of Liége right now & there's fighting going on. Others say it's nothing but a weak counterattack & already under control. You don't know what to believe & nobody really knows the score here.

It's a very uneasy time, however. It's no secret that this whole end of Belgium is just one huge supply dump since the port at Antwerp was opened, Liége in particular. One of the rumors is that the Krauts want Liége to get those supplies.

Everybody in this place has got the shakes, bad. And wishing we were with our own outfits. Hessler & White & I have been talking about it. White's outfit, 30th Inf. are up north some place. Hessler doesn't know where his is, but he said to me, "Hell, if your outfit is in Malmédy they'll be overrun before the Krauts get to Liége. You're better off here."

But I feel like I'm in jail waiting for the place to burn down. I'd rather be with them. Wish I could have got there today. Ought to have got out & walked when the Lieut. turned back — but hell, I was lost, too. Maybe it's just a big scare & maybe the news will be better tomorrow.

The Battle of the Bulge —
Henry Giles

Monday night, Dec. 18, 1944

LATE yesterday afternoon we were called together & told as much of the situation as is known here. The Krauts *are* attacking in a very strong offensive & they have penetrated as far as Malmédy & Stavelot & it is believed they are heading for Liége. *That* kind of news gives you the real jitters. To think they're headed right at you & in strength enough to overrun everything in their way so far. Gave me the shakes so bad I found myself lighting a cigarette & wondering why I was so awkward at it, looked down & found I already had one going.

Somebody asked the Capt. just how *much* strength they had. He said he didn't know. Nobody knew, but it was a hell of a lot & they were moving fast & all over the place. He said those of us in this replacement depot would be used in the ground defense of Liége, at least until reinforcements could get here. He said they were on their way but it might take time & until they got here every ablebodied man in Liége would be used to man roadblocks & outposts. He asked for gunners, so I stepped up & was handed a .30 cal. machine gun. I'd have felt better if it had been a .50 cal. but he said they didn't have any.

They loaded a bunch of us on trucks & hauled us out, dropping two or three off at each outpost, until two other guys & myself were left & we were taken to a roadblock out on the main road west. The Krauts are expected to come from that direction & the south. The Lieut. told us to position our own guns & to stay till relieved. He said every position was a "hold fast." In other words, get killed but don't fall back. Said they'd try to relieve us in the morning.

The roadblock was nothing but some mines across a paved road & some logs & not even a damn bush to hide behind. I sort of took over, being a Weapons Sgt. & got the guns in position, to either side of the roadblock & one a little farther back, but God, it was a naked position. A .30 cal. can mow down a line of infantry but against a tank it wouldn't be much better than a rifle.

Cold, my Lord! Snow & ice & slush underfoot & a drizzle of sleet falling. The sleet fell down your neck even with your collar up & you just hunched up & tried to keep the wind & the wet out the best way you could. Gloves too short & checking the guns every now & then soon got wet, then froze. Feet were soaked inside of half an hour. I don't have any overshoes & my shoes leak like a sieve.

All we could do was stamp around trying to keep some feeling in our feet & my hands got so numb if anything had happened I don't think I could have fired the gun. All tensed up, looking & listening, thinking every vehicle we heard — and what a hell of a lot of them there were — was a Kraut. Everything that moved scared the living hell out of us. Don't know whether I shook worse from cold or fear.

One of the gunners was just a kid & he got to crying. He had been in the hospital for trench foot & said his feet were still swollen & sore & were killing him & if the Krauts came he was going to get killed anyway. His name was Logan. I felt so sorry for him I told him & the other fellow, Swain, to hang on & I'd see if I couldn't find some planks or boards or rubbish of some kind for us to stand on. Rummaged around & found a sack in a ditch but that was all. Told Logan to fold it up & stand on it & get his feet out of the slush for a while — till it soaked through the sack.

About midnight a bunch of Kraut planes came over & I thought, this is it! Here's where we get it! They circled around & around & dropped flares & brother that makes you feel as naked as a jaybird. Everything lit up bright as day. I yelled at the boys to freeze — don't move. You can be seen pretty far away & if you move they've got a target. I was terrified & kept waiting for the bombs to fall — but they didn't drop any. Not in our area, anyway. Just dropped the flares, hundreds of them, circled & droned around above us, then went away. Don't know what the hell the idea was.

We could see artillery flashes to the south all night, but nothing came up this far. Could hear the guns, too. Somebody down there was getting it & that worried me. That's where the outfit is & they could all be dead or captured by now. The Lieut. thought Malmédy had been overrun. If so, I hope to hell the boys got out in time. My God, what a mess! What an everlasting mess!

Nobody came for us until nearly noon & it was a damn, long, cold miserable night & morning. Next time I'm taking a blanket.

They told us yesterday, also, no mail would go out for a while. Close security again. When this news hits the States & then my letters stop, Janice & the folks will be scared to death. J. follows 1st Army like a hawk & she knows, in general, where we are most of the time. But there's nothing I can do about that, either.

Got to sleep now for I have to go out again tomorrow night.

Wednesday, Dec. 20, 1944

I thought I'd be going back out with a machine gun but the Lieut. asked all Engineers to step up yesterday. "You're bazooka men," he said.

A bazooka is a sort of rocket launcher. It takes two men. The one in back loads. He has to wear goggles or a face mask because of the back flash. The one in front aims & pulls the trigger. I never fired a bazooka in my life, but Jennings, the man I drew to team up with, & I looked it over, decided we could handle it & helped load the truck with ammo. A bazooka team went with two machine guns. I told Jennings I'd load & it was O.K. by him. He was scared to death of that back flash.

We loaded up again but were taken to a different outpost this time. Like the other one, however, it was on a main road & not much different. I warned the other boys & we all took blankets & fared a little better than the time before, but not much. It's been snowing for two days & snowed most of the night.

Same thing as before — Kraut planes circling again most of of the night & dropping flares. But they didn't scare me as bad this time. Knew about what to expect. There was a hell of a lot more artillery last night, heavier firing. But we didn't see any Krauts. The line must be holding farther south & west.[1]

But it's a hell of a mess & it makes me madder than hell for the brass to have goofed this way. All we do is take orders, but they are supposed to know. I don't see how they could have been caught short like this. Nobody knows where the Krauts are. All we know is that this whole end of Belgium is crawling with them. And they say a whole bunch have been parachuted in dressed in American uniforms, with American vehicles, all speak English & are running around behind our lines.

[1] 82nd Airborne Division had been brought into the line at Werbomont. 30th Infantry Division had taken over the Malmédy–Stavelot–Stoumont area. The western front was slowly being stabilized, although there was still much confusion.

We have to stop every vehicle, everybody, & ask questions only a real, genuine American would know the answers to. It's real screwy & makes you jumpy as hell. Some of the questions we are told to ask, such as what is the capital of Iowa, what is Bob Hope's theme song, etc., I wouldn't know the answers to myself. They say these Krauts even have G.I. identification & have been briefed on the outfits they're supposed to belong to. I imagine a few real Americans will get taken in, but it's better to do that than let these spies get by.[2]

Friday, Dec. 22, 1944

Another 24 hours at the roadblock. Foggy, windy, snowy & the worst cold yet. But outside of nearly freezing to death, nothing happened. No sign of a Kraut yet, although the latrine rumors are wild & there isn't a day somebody hasn't heard they're in the edge of the city. No planes & flares last night.

S & S says both St. Vith & Bastogne are surrounded. Also reports 1st & 9th armies now under command of the limey general, Montgomery, on account of communications with Gen. Bradley's Hq. cut up so badly. Reports, too, Gen. Patton rushing up from the south. 1st Infantry is down from the north & I feel much better about the outfit. 30th Inf. is holding fast at Malmédy.

The Ordnance boys told me it was mostly B Company at Malmédy, but the rest of the boys were in the same general area. They were cutting timber & running sawmills. If they didn't get out & are still there, I hope to hell they haven't been cut to pieces.

I don't see how this could have happened. Looks to me as if

---

[2] One of the most amusing incidents during this scare was that Brig. Gen. Bruce Clarke, in command at St. Vith, returning from an inspection of the front was captured by jumpy MPs because he said the Chicago Cubs were in the American League. He was held five hours before he could convince his captors of his identity.

the big brass were caught asleep. For weeks we've been hearing & reading that the war was all but over. One more big push across the Rhine & we'd have it made. Just last week Gen. Montgomery issued a statement which was in S & S & he said the Germans could not possibly mount another offensive — they were too weak & bled. By george, somebody has been caught offguard & a lot of good boys are having to pay for it. The Krauts are still in there fighting. They still have plenty of tanks & troops & man, are they ever throwing them in, now. The worst is, they picked the best time they could for it. The weather is lousy — cloudy, drizzly, sleety, snowy & foggy. The Air Corps can't fly. If the sun would just come out, our boys could begin to clobber them.

The lines are holding pretty well, now, & if they can just hang on until the boys can fly, maybe this deal can still be licked.

[Many people, in fact most of the United States and allied countries, wondered just as Henry Giles and other soldiers did how the Allies could have been caught so off guard.

Both Generals Eisenhower and Bradley, in their books written after the war, state that the thinly held Ardennes front was a calculated risk. A strong offensive was soon to be mounted in the north by General Montgomery, supported by the U.S. Ninth Army. An equally strong offensive was being planned in the south for the U.S. Third and Seventh armies, geared to the British offensive.

General Montgomery is said to have been a master at the "set piece" type of battle, but he demanded mountainous reserves of supplies and troops. Generals Patton and Patch likewise needed tremendous reserves of supply and troops. First Army, holding in the center, along the mountainous and densely forested Ardennes front, was bled to supply the needs of both ends of the front.

According to John Toland, who wrote the excellent book

Battle: The Story of the Bulge, only one man, with a strong sense of history, seems to have been uneasy about the thin Ardennes front. Colonel "Monk" Dickson, Chief of Intelligence on General Courtney Hodges' First Army staff, could not forget that in 1870, 1914, and 1940, the Germans had used the Losheim Gap in the Eifel mountains to pour into the Low Countries and overrun Holland, Belgium and France. He became convinced the massing of German troops, which it was impossible for Allied Intelligence not to be aware of, was for that purpose again. It seemed too highly improbable to the generals, however, and the massing was dismissed as preparations to stop the Allied offensive soon to begin.

Even the details of Operation Greif, the American dressed, armed and vehicled German troops, were known. Captured papers had been forwarded to Allied Intelligence. For months, Otto Skorzeny, one of the most brilliant agents of the German Intelligence, had been training a brigade of picked troops in American ways and folklore, slang, history and habits. This training was so excellent that the German soldiers knew to smoke "dry," that is without wetting the lips as the Germans did; they knew Americans scratched a match toward themselves, not away, and they knew American soldiers opened only half of the end of a package of cigarettes and that they flipped the cigarette up instead of reaching inside for it. American uniforms, captured American vehicles and arms, were furnished this brigade. This information, too, was brushed aside. It was considered scare propaganda. It is true both sides used such scare tactics constantly.

The principal reason for the initial success of the German breakthrough would seem to have been overconfidence, therefore. No one could believe that after the swift advance across France and Belgium, the rout and defeat of German armies everywhere, the strength to mount a genuine offensive could be found.

Linked to this overconfidence was an underestimation of the German industrial potential. Air reconnaissance photos showed terrific damage to German industry. It was never as badly crippled as the photos showed. Somehow, some way, they always managed to keep operating and producing; and even their crippled railway systems were always able to keep material and troops moving.

Finally, it was forgotten that the man who still gave the orders in Germany was a madman, a fanatic, perfectly willing to sacrifice all of Germany rather than admit defeat. *Wacht am Rhein* was Hitler's own brain child.]

Saturday, Dec. 23, 1944

Beautiful weather today, sunny, clear & our planes are flying. They aren't going over in wave after wave as they did at St. Lô, but there are plenty of them & do they ever look wonderful! This is what we've been praying for & needing, air support. I think this deal is going to begin to fold up on the Krauts as of today. If the pretty weather will just last, they're going to be plastered, but good.

S & S says that 101st Airborne is in Bastogne, but the town is completely surrounded. Being supplied by air drops. St. Vith has been evacuated. Luxembourg is completely overrun. They sure made a wide sweep while they were at it, but the change in weather is bound to make a big difference.

Still manning outposts. They somehow got hold of some overshoes for us the other day, though, and that helps a lot. Feet get cold but not wet.

No mail, & of course still can't write.

Christmas Day

1944

Weather good again yesterday & today & the Air Corps still working overtime. They look very beautiful from where I stand. Things are looking better all the time. We haven't taken the offensive, but all the lines are holding. Bastogne has *not* fallen & during this good weather S & S says plenty of ammo & supplies have been dropped so they can hold out till Patton gets there.

Spent last night at the roadblock with my trusty bazooka again but we were told today it was the last time. Enough reinforcements here now that we are relieved. Glad we never had to fire that stovepipe. Also told today that mail will begin going out again tomorrow. Have written Janice & home.

Christmas Day! What a hell of a Christmas present it has brought us. I thought it would be bad enough to be here in this replacement depot away from the outfit but didn't think it could possibly be as bad as it's been. Don't even know whether there *is* an outfit left & God knows now when I will know. Don't know which of my friends is living or dead or if all of them are gone. Like being in a fog.

Not much of a Christmas dinner today but it was probably a hell of a lot better than the fellows had, if they had any at all.

The Christmases I've had in the army. Christmas, 1940 — in Fort Ord, California. Pulled guard on Christmas Eve. Christmas, 1941 — *inside* the Rose Bowl in Pasadena. Some kind of submarine scare had rushed the outfit to the coast. My squad slept in the women's rest room. Christmas, 1942 — Camp McCoy, Wisconsin. Snow four feet deep & thermometer 40 below. Hinkel & I lay awake most of the night listening to Christmas carols being played over the loudspeaker system. That was one cadre Hinkel & Love & I all wished we'd never made. I only left the base one time the whole four months we were there. It was too damned cold to go anywhere or do anything. My ears froze one morning on the rifle range. Believe me, we sure worked like hell to make that cadre to Swift. Texas sounded mighty good to us after Wisconsin.

Christmas, 1943 — England. Now, here. And from the way

things look, I'll probably spend another Christmas away from
home, too. If this can happen when we had the war practically
won, Lord knows when it will be over now.

My ears are bothering me again. Buzzing, crackling, popping
& draining worse. No wonder. Seems that being out in the
weather brings it on.

Tuesday, Dec. 26, 1944

Am pretty excited tonight. The clerk from Company C was
here today to pick up two fellows from his outfit. I didn't even
know there was anybody here from the Battalion but me.
Haven't run into these boys at all, but with 500 men in a place
this size you could go a year & not see them all. Besides, they
haven't been here long.

I tried to get him to sign for me, too, but he said he couldn't.
He did promise to tell the Capt. or Lieut. Edelstein where I
was, though, so they could send for me. So, my hopes are very,
very high of getting out of here soon. If they don't come for me
by the end of the week I think I'll go AWOL back to the outfit.[3]

They've been through a hell of a lot. This fellow didn't
know much about Company A. He said the Battalion was scattered over 25 miles from Malmédy to Werbomont when they
began to get hit on the 17th & 18th. Said the Col. had orders to
hold Malmédy until reinforcements could get there & he by
damn did. 30th Inf. got there on the 19th.

The worst, though, the very worst, was they got bombed
three days in a row by our own air force. And all these three
days I was watching the sky & thinking how wonderful they
could fly again & clobber the Krauts. The Col. was hurt, but not

[3] Many men, more than can ever be known, did go AWOL back to their outfits
from these replacement depots. With what results to them is not known. But
Bill Mauldin, the famous cartoonist with *Stars & Stripes,* went AWOL to his
outfit from a replacement depot in Italy. He was not traced, nor ever heard anything concerning it.

badly. Capt. Conlin of C Company was hurt so seriously he had to be evacuated. And one man, Barker of B Company was killed. It must have been pure hell. He said the town was pulverized. Didn't have time to tell me any more. But he promised to tell somebody where I am, so maybe they'll get on the ball & spring me from this damned jail.

Sure good to know most of them are O.K.

Wednesday, Dec. 27th

First Sgt. here told me this morning to report to sick call. I asked him why. Told him I was O.K. Wasn't sick. Said he didn't know why. He just had orders for Sgt. Giles to report on sick call. Well, I won't. For all I know the orders are for the Negro Giles. I can get by with it for a few days & by then I should be back with the Company.

Modave, Belgium

Friday, Dec. 29, 1944

This is a red letter day! Finally, finally, I'm back with the outfit. The 291st was relieved in Malmédy on the 26th & in moving farther west for regrouping to this place, Lieut. Edelstein sent for me last night. And just in time. I had that sick call hanging over me.

By george, it sure is good to see the fellows again. Have seen & talked with most of them. 2nd platoon got scattered to hell and gone all over the country during the worst of things. When it began, B Company was at Malmédy, though some of our 1st platoon boys were there, too. C Company was mostly around Stavelot. A Company, that is 2nd & 3rd platoons had got back to Werbomont after a narrow escape down near St. Vith. Abe Caplan's squad of 1st platoon got caught down near St. Vith. They were on detached duty & got commandeered by another Eng. outfit. Arlie was along.

Anyway, the Col. had orders to hold Malmédy, so he had most of C Company come there. Radioed for the guns, gunners & ammo from A Company & Black Mac took them over. They had their biggest battle on the 21st & on that day Holbrook was killed manning my .50 cal. at an outpost.

Pigg & Billington took some boys out from Werbomont & blew a bridge just as the Kraut tanks were coming into sight. Some H/S boys were at Trois Ponts, & some 1st platoon boys. J. B. Miller[4] blew the bridge there just as some Panzers drove up. And the Col. rescued some of the men who survived the Malmédy Massacre.

What rides me is that if I hadn't been stuck in that damned replacement depot & had been on my own gun, Holbrook might be living today. *I* might have got it, but you never think so. They told me a tree burst got him. Don't know who positioned him near some trees. Mac wouldn't have. I'm afraid he just got a gun shoved at him, was unloaded at the place & told to stick. As good a boy as he was, Holbrook wouldn't have known how to position the gun. I'm no hero & I wouldn't have enjoyed being on that gun under the circumstances, but it was my job & I don't *think* I would have been too scared to lose what sense I've got. I was doing my damn best to find the boys, but couldn't make it.

Another thing. The Col. phoned that damned replacement depot for reinforcements on the 17th. They said we were needed to defend Liége. Hell, the defense of Liége was down there at Malmédy & Stavelot & Trois Ponts & in damned good hands. One thing is sure — they all, every man of them, deserves the Bronze Star & I hope they all get it.

Hinkel had taken good care of my stuff. The only thing lost is my pen. He said he never could find it though he looked all

4 Sgt. J. B. Miller, 1st platoon.

over for it. He knew I valued it. But if it was dropped in that mudhole we were in, it would have kept sinking right on to China. I told him to forget it. I'm too happy to be back & have the rest of my stuff to grieve over the pen.

Thought there would be a lot of mail stacked up waiting for me but there isn't. King said he had been forwarding it to the hospital until Hinkel heard from me, then he sent it to the replacement depot. Thirty miles away & I didn't get that first letter! That's good organization, I'd say.

But I'm not even crying the blues over no mail. I know it will be coming now. There was one old letter of Oct. 6th in my B. bag & I've read it over at least a dozen times today. Lieut. Hayes said I'd been getting about 17 letters a day & that my Christmas packages came, they kept them a week & then opened them & ate all the goodies. Even if it was true, they were sure welcome to them. What a *good* feeling it is to be back with the boys again.

Saturday, Dec. 30, 1944

We are living in a big chateau. Belgium is full of these places and I suppose they were once the country homes of very wealthy people. They aren't even comfortable any more, much less luxurious. But I'd rather be cold & miserable with the outfit than dry & warm in Liége. At least I can shake with the cold among friends.

There is still very much of a jittery feeling all around, sort of like walking on eggs. Roadblocks are maintained, mine fields laid, special patrols the order of the day. I've been on a roadblock today with my gun. Very cold, very miserable & that business of the paratroopers gives you a hell of an uneasy feeling. Every vehicle gets a good going over before it's allowed to pass. S & S says they were supposed to assassinate Gens. Eisenhower & Bradley.[5]

Have heard today a few of the men recommended for decorations — for the Bronze Star, Capt. Gamble, Black Mac, J. B. Miller, Rondenelle, Lieut. Walters,[6] Lieut. Taylor,[7] Sgt. Geary, Walt Landry,[8] McCarty,[9] & others. In my opinion every man of the Battalion deserved one.

Hinkel is with H/S Company now — G2,[10] so I won't get to see him so much any more. He seems to like it all right. Mac just came by & asked if I still felt like a million dollars. I sure do. Only one little thing wrong — my ears aren't right, but I'll never say so.

Talked tonight, also, for a little while with the fellow who had the anonymous letter about his wife. He said he hadn't heard from her since he sent her the letter. It must have been true. He still has it on his mind very much of the time. Very blue, yet. Just wonder if he'll ever get over it.

---

[5] There was much confusion concerning a parachute drop of German troops behind Malmédy and Operation Greif. The parachute drop was a total failure and only a few jeep loads of Otto Skorzeny's specially trained men infiltrated the American lines. One group, captured, told that the ultimate objective of their mission had been the assassination of Generals Eisenhower and Bradley and that Skorzeny himself was to lead the special force to accomplish it. Because the German word *greif* means "grasp" and because Skorzeny had brought off the daring coup of rescuing Mussolini when he was captured by the Italian government; because he had also kidnapped the son of Admiral Horthy, Regent of Hungary, this kind of commando action was associated with his name. He allowed his men to believe this was his purpose in order to preserve the secrecy of their real mission. In his trial, after the war, he was able to prove that this was never his mission and that he, himself, was never behind the American lines. But at the time none of this was known and the witch hunt for paratroopers dressed as Americans was very much on.

[6] 1/Lt. Albert E. Walters, platoon commander, 1st platoon, Company A.

[7] 1/Lt. Archibald Taylor, platoon commander, 3rd platoon, Company A.

[8] T/4 Walter J. Landry, 2nd platoon.

[9] 2/Lt. Ralph J. McCarty. Lt. McCarty also received his battlefield commission following the action at Malmédy.

[10] G-2, of course, is Intelligence.

Mail call. Two wonderful letters today! For the record, it has been two months, one week and two days since the last one. I never want to have to sweat that kind of thing out again — any of it. I had the most lost feeling the whole time — as if I had been cut off from the whole world.

These were written Dec. 11 & 19th. She got the $100 in time & bought a watch with part of it, put the balance in savings. On the 19th she was scared. U.S. newspapers full of the break-through. She knew it was in the section of Belgium we are in. D-day all over again for her. Sherman sure said it — war is hell, and in more ways than one.

Nash has the cluster for his Air Medal. I think that means twenty missions — ten for the Medal, ten for the cluster. She has told me long ago in some of those lost letters where he is, of course, so doesn't mention it here. Well, in time I'll learn.

Sunday, Dec. 31, 1944

Damn — damn — damn — damn! First Sarge told me this morning the Medics wanted me on sick call. I told him flatly I didn't want to go, didn't need to go. He said I had to because they had some kind of report on me from the hospital & they can't turn it down.

I asked to see the Capt. & did & he told me the same thing. Said I'd have to go, but he said if I had to go back to the hospital he would see to it I got back to the outfit faster this time. Said after all they were pretty busy last time & my records had been finally marked "Lost to Hospital," but that if I would let him know as soon as I got out of the hospital this time, he would see to it someone came for me as quickly as possible. That's some comfort, but not much. I can't think what it can be that's brought this up.

Later: Well, I reported. Capt. Kamen[11] said they had a report

11 Capt. Paul N. Kamen, a Battalion Medical Officer.

from the hospital in Paris. I wasn't supposed to have been discharged from there & they've been trying to catch up with me ever since. Said I'd have to go back to the hospital, but not to Paris. My papers are in Liége, now. So here I go again. Same old razzle-dazzle. Leave tomorrow & it makes me sick. This time I know the ropes better, though, & I won't sit there & sweat. Guess this was the reason I was told to report on sick call back in the replacement depot. I'm glad I didn't. At least I'll have all my stuff with me this time.

Mail call, and am I ever lucky! Hit the jackpot with 27 letters from J. and four from home. These are all old but I feel a hell of a lot better about going back to the hospital. I can go a long time on this bunch of letters. Think I'll ration myself. If I have the will power I can make one letter each day do me & surely by the end of 27 days I'll be back with the Company. I always sort through a batch & read them in order. The first one in this bunch is for Sept. 13th. Good God! We were back in Marle, France, when it was written & that seems a lifetime ago.

The Battle of the Bulge—291st Company A

[FROM the following sources I have reconstructed as much as possible of the action of the 291st during the Battle of the Bulge.

1. Battalion History.

2. An article by Helena Huntington Smith, a woman war correspondent, who interviewed Lt. Col. David E. Pergrin, Battalion Commander, on January 17, 1945, and was shown over the scenes by him. The article was reprinted in *American Heritage* magazine for August, 1957, under the title "A Few Men in Soldiers Suits."

3. *Dark December,* by Robert E. Merriam, published in 1947 by Ziff-Davis Publishing Company. Mr. Merriam was Chief of the Ardennes Section of the Army Historical Division, European Theater of Operations. He was on the spot as an army historian, saw much of the action in person, had access to all army documents, reports and files, and interviewed both American and German men and commanders within a year of the close of the Battle of the Bulge.

4. *Battle: The Story of the Bulge,* by John Toland, published in 1957 by Random House. This is an excellent and well-documented book. Mr. Toland also interviewed as many of the American and German commanders and men as possible and traveled widely to obtain his material. But his book was written ten years after the end of the war and because his style is

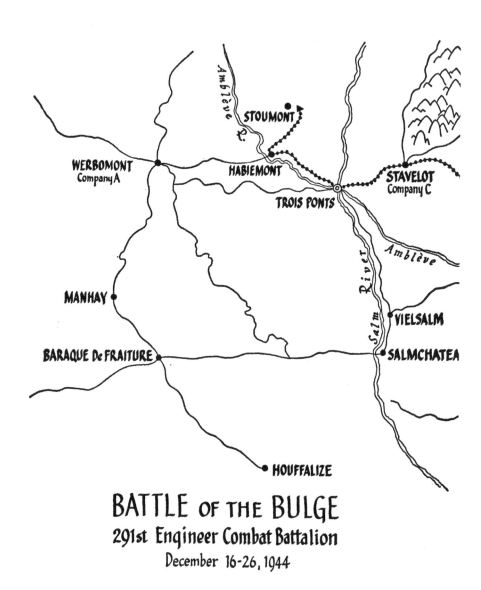

BATTLE OF THE BULGE
291st Engineer Combat Battalion
December 16-26, 1944

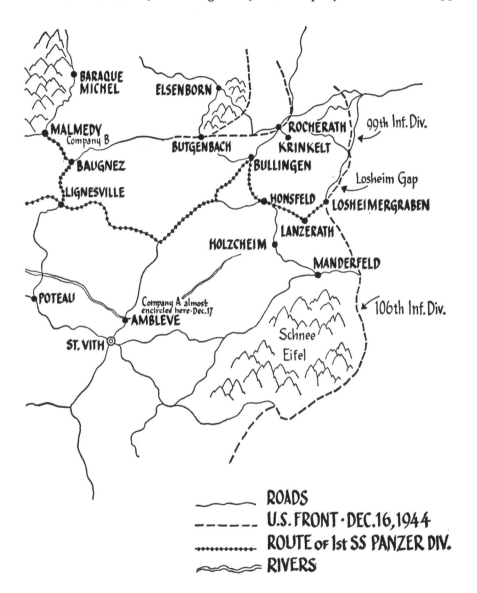

BARAQUE MICHEL

ELSENBORN

MALMEDY
Company B

ROCHERATH

99th Inf. Div.

BUTGENBACH

KRINKELT

BAUGNEZ

BULLINGEN

Losheim Gap

LIGNESVILLE

HONSFELD

LOSHEIMERGRABEN

LANZERATH

HOLZCHEIM

MANDERFELD

POTEAU

Company A almost
encircled here · Dec. 17

106th Inf. Div.

AMBLEVE

Schnee
Eifel

ST. VITH

_____ ROADS
- - - - - U.S. FRONT · DEC. 16, 1944
············ ROUTE of 1st SS PANZER DIV.
〰〰〰 RIVERS

more personal, many important events and units and persons could not be included.

5. By far the most important help we had in reconstructing this section of the book came from personal stories of several men of Company A, 291st Engineers. They were:

Lt. Col. David E. Pergrin, Battalion Commander

Sgt. R. C. Billington, 3rd squad leader, 2nd platoon

Sgt. John Coupe, H/S platoon, driver of the Company Commander's Command Car

Sgt. Abraham Caplan, 2nd squad leader, 1st platoon

T/4 Merlin Dixon, 1st squad truck driver, 1st platoon

Pvt. George J. Courvillion, 1st platoon

Pfc. Louis T. Dymond, 1st squad, 2nd platoon

T/4 Jeff Elliott, 2nd squad truck driver, 2nd platoon

Pfc. Vincent A. Fresina, 1st platoon

Capt. James H. Gamble, Commander, Company A

S/Sgt. Paul J. Hinkel, H/S Company

Cpl. John A. King, Company Clerk

Cpl. A. C. Schommer, radio operator, 2nd platoon

Cpl. Louis Kovacs, Hq. platoon truck driver, 2nd platoon

The morning of December 16, 1944, was thick with a soupy fog, the perfect weather, as predicted, for the German attack. At 5:30, all along the eighty-five mile front there was the sudden explosion of artillery fire, from rockets and mortars and 88s to the huge railroad guns, the big Berthas, whose range was so long.

Behind the terrific artillery barrage, German tanks and troops began to move swiftly. The plan called, first, for total surprise so as to create the utmost confusion and panic; second, for swift unimpeded movement in a sweep across the Meuse to Antwerp. Antwerp was to be reached within a week, the purpose to cut the Allied forces in two, roll back the wings, push to the sea and consolidate the gains with heavy reinforcements and further attacks on the northern flank.

The 6th Panzer Army, commanded by Sepp Dietrich, with four Panzer and five Infantry divisions, was given the primary job; to pour through the weak nine mile front of the Losheim Gap, roll back the 99th Infantry Division on the north, consolidate the northern shoulder, keep rolling to the Meuse, cross at three places between Huy and Liége.

The 5th Panzer Army, Baron Hasso von Manteuffel commanding, with three Panzer and four Infantry divisions, was to break his 66th Corps through the Losheim Gap also, along its southern edge, and smash the green, new 106th Infantry Division, two of whose regiments were occupying the Schnee Eifel. The Schnee Eifel was a fistlike bulge in the American front which jutted farthest into Germany. 106th Headquarters were at St. Vith, near the German border. Manteuffel, when he rolled up the two regiments in the Schnee Eifel, was to move on to capture St. Vith. The major effort of the 5th Panzer Army, however, was to swing across northern Luxembourg and roll up Bastogne and Houffalize, keep going to cross the Meuse in the neighborhood of Dinant.

Farthest south, the 7th Army, largely Infantry, General Ernst Brandenberger commanding, was to swing through Luxembourg and spread his army along the border as a southern shoulder to keep General Patton from reinforcing from the south.

On the morning of December 16, when the German offensive opened with its devastating artillery barrage and its swift blitzkrieg movement, 291st Engineer Combat Battalion Headquarters was located at Haute Bodeux. Company A was moving from Werbomont into the tiny village of Ambléve, five miles north of St. Vith; Company B was in Malmédy operating a sawmill; Company C was at La Gleize, but they were operating a sawmill at Stavelot. These were, at least, the Command Post locations. Many squads and units were on detached duty, on work details away from their platoons and companies.

By 9 A.M. the German offensive was going relatively well. The

Losheim Gap was pierced in many places, but Sepp Dietrich's 6th Panzer Army had run into unexpectedly stiff resistance in his frontal attack on the 99th Infantry south of Monschau. The 99th was the southernmost division of V Corps, which was itself on the offensive striking toward the Roer River. Through a corridor of the 99th, elements of 2nd Armored Division were moving forward. Reinforced by 2nd Armored thus, 99th was battling desperately but holding fairly well.

Manteuffel's 66th Corps was having no trouble beginning its encirclement of the Schnee Eifel where the two regiments of the green 106th Infantry were almost isolated from the rest of the line. His two Panzer Divisions striking through northern Luxembourg were heavily attacking Clervaux and the 28th Infantry, battle weary and resting, was slowly being overwhelmed.

In southern Luxembourg, the German 7th Army had bypassed Echternach and overrun Vianden.

At SHAEF, in Versailles, nothing was yet known of the offensive. Nor was General Bradley in touch with First Army Headquarters at Spa. A staff conference concerning the shortage of replacements had been called and General Bradley was on his way, by car, from his headquarters in Luxembourg City to Versailles.

By noon, Dietrich's 6th Panzer Army was not only having trouble with the 2-99 front at the twin villages of Rocherath and Krinkelt, but most of his Army was ensnarled in a massive traffic jam caused by the blowing of a bridge by retreating American forces. Only one Panzer Division, the 1st SS (Hitler's own) spearheaded by Colonel Jochem Peiper, broke free of the traffic jam near Losheimergraben in the late afternoon hours of December 16. Peiper broke free by ruthlessly shouldering other outfits off the road and by racing across a field into the open. He sacrificed six of his own tanks to clear the field of mines for the rest of the division. He raced forward, arriving at Lanzerath on the Belgian border by midnight. Here he halted to regroup.

Around nightfall, the conference on infantry replacements

was occurring at SHAEF. It was interrupted with a message saying the enemy had penetrated First Army's front in five separate places. In his book, *A Soldier's Story,* General Bradley admits to having thought it a "spoiling attack" to divert troops from Patton's Third Army on the south and Simpson's Ninth Army on the north, both of whom were scheduled to mount strong offensives within the next few days.

In his book, *Crusade in Europe,* General Eisenhower says that he pondered the news and reached the conclusion it was not a diversionary attack. He said it made no sense to him that a local attack should be made against the American weakest point. But the consensus seems to be that no one yet realized precisely the strength of the offensive, for General Eisenhower only suggested to General Bradley that he divert one armored division from General Patton to go north, and one armored division from General Simpson to head south, to assist the beleaguered First Army in the Ardennes. 10th Armored Division of General Patton's Third Army was ordered north, and 7th Armored Division of General Simpson's Ninth Army was ordered south.

At about midnight of December 16, General Courtney Hodges, Commander of First Army, reached the conclusion this was a full-scale offensive and he ordered both the 1st Infantry Division and the 30th Infantry Division of V Corps to the south. The 1st Infantry was to reinforce the 2–99 line and the 30th was to reinforce the Amblève line along the Malmédy–Stavelot–Trois Ponts–Stoumont route.]

CAPTAIN JAMES H. GAMBLE, Company A Commander: After twenty years I still recall the terrible dilemma in which Company A found itself on December 16–17, 1944. Things had been reasonably quiet, in fact too much so, and the Company was pretty much intact except for the 1st platoon, commanded by 1/Lt. Albert Walters. His unit was divided between Trois Ponts, Malmédy and Grande Halleux. Grande Halleux was a tiny crossroads near St. Vith. One has only to look at a military map to appreciate fully the significance of such deployment. I do not imply, however, that this deployment was the result of advance knowledge of the events which followed. God knows such was not the case. We were simply doing our jobs, cutting timber and operating sawmills for bridging operations.

We had established our Command Post in a schoolhouse in Werbomont. On the morning of December 16, I received orders from Col. Pergrin to proceed immediately to Amblève, set up a CP and await further orders.

This movement disturbed me greatly, and I remember discussing the situation with my remaining officers, 1/Lt. Frank R. Hayes, 1/Lt. Alvin E. Edelstein, and 1/Lt. Archibald Taylor. They were a bit upset about the move also, but I, of course, could not enlighten them. We had begun to hear rumors of troop movements north of us but had no details nor any official confirmation of such. Our move to Amblève was without incident and we established our CP there in another schoolhouse. The usual security and road patrols were posted.

Sgt. R. C. Billington: As we moved down to Amblève we went through Malmédy. It was a dark winter day and the city appeared deserted. Rubble from tree limbs was all about the streets and there was little or no traffic. A shell or two drifted in and knocked off more tree limbs. This caused much consternation and amazement. We couldn't understand it, for things had been quiet for so long.

When we reached Amblève and the CP was set up, security and road patrols were posted. My squad drew road patrol for the night.

Cpl. A. C. Schommer: I was on radio duty that night in Amblève. Sometime after midnight I received a message that was so poorly sent I thought the operator had found a jug and was imbibing. I could make no sense out of the letters that came in code. I finally put some words on paper and delivered it to the 1/Sgt. He thought it quite hilarious as any 1/Sgt. naturally would when awakened from a sound sleep. I returned to my radio and tried to get clarification. I was greeted by radio silence.

Pfc. Louis T. Dymond: I was on guard that night outside a house occupied by H/S platoon. I could hear a lot of traffic going along the hardtop road. A halftrack started to pull into the courtyard. The driver seemed surprised to see anyone and at first was reluctant to answer my questions. I found out from him that the vehicles going by were not going back for a rest as I had first assumed, but they were retreating and the Germans had broken through two green infantry regiments and some other units. I reported this, but naturally nobody could believe it.

Pfc. Vincent A. Fresina died on February 4, 1964, but his wife, Ladieruth Fresina, reported this: Vince and one or two of the boys, including George Courvillion who was his closest friend, were in a beer hall drinking beer that night. They overheard two German-speaking Belgians telling a man in the pub that the Germans had broken through and the town would soon be in German hands again. They reported this when they returned to the area, but nobody believed it because it did not seem possible.

Cpl. Schommer: At daybreak, I opened the blackout curtain and was surprised at the activity and crowds in the area. It had been very lonely and quiet when we arrived. Suddenly a group of American fighter planes appeared and seemed to concentrate on a particular area. Just as suddenly the sky was filled with anti-aircraft fire from ground guns. When the first plane was hit, I was surprised but still thought it was accidental. When three or four went down in flames, I woke the 1/Sgt. again, told him what I had seen, then held my ears for his blistering. This time, however, even he agreed something was fishy. He decided to investigate and woke his driver to take him to find out. He wasn't gone long before he was back reporting to Captain Gamble that he had run smack into a German tank. This was, of course, an impossibility to us. We were winning the war. It was only a matter of time until Germany would surrender and they didn't have enough tanks or planes left to do any offensive maneuvering, and gas they didn't have, we thought.

About this time radio silence was broken and a message, uncoded, came over the air. As I remember it said: IMMEDIATE DANGER IMMINENT RETIRE TO FORMER POSITION. You can easily see how a nervous operator would have trouble with those words, especially when all messages were supposed to be in Morse code. But a quick decision had to be made. The trucks were almost out of gas because of our move to Amblève. Arthur Van Dame and Pfc. Wheeler were dispatched to find gas. Van Dame's truck was quickly destroyed by a tank and he barely escaped. He returned to report German tanks all over the place. To get gas would be impossible. Wheeler's report was the same.

The order was given by Capt. Gamble to drain all tanks of all vehicles possible and transfer the gas into two or three trucks. All equipment except rifles, machine guns, bazookas, ammunition, and the radio, was to be abandoned. All personnel would ride in the few vehicles we could provide gas for.

The only amusing part of the whole mess to me was the fact that the one guy who really hated the Company radio and everyone connected with it, the First Sarge, had to climb up on the roof of the schoolhouse to help remove the antenna. This, of course, with German soldiers all over the place! I believe his pride was hurt, but it had to be done. It had long been First Sarge's theory that radio operators were the goldbricks of the outfit and it had also been his long threat to get us onto some real work details. He never did, though.

T/4 Jeff Elliott: We had just had chow. I was sitting in the jeep. I heard someone running, looked around and here came a Negro. He was one of the truck drivers of an artillery convoy which had just gone down the road about an hour before. He ran up to me, damned near scared white. I asked him what was the matter. He said, "All the rest of the convoy is dead and the damn Krauts nearly got me, too." He said, "Which way is the rear?"

I said, "Down that way," and pointed. He took off like a scared jackrabbit.

Pfc. Dymond: When we were told to pack up things we were out in the road waiting for further orders when an officer came by and said there was small arms fire just down the road. In the meantime, a group of colored boys had joined us and were pleading for a ride out of there. From the looks of them, they had dropped their guns and equipment and had come cross country through briars and woods. They were mighty glad to see us as they had come quite a distance in the night.

Truck driver Van Dame had been sent for gas and he met an enemy tank outfit and they shot up his truck. He escaped through a culvert under the road and went through the woods and came back in an air-compressor truck. He told Capt. Gamble not to wait or we would all be trapped.

T/4 Elliott: About that time we got three or four 88s and I
ran from the jeep into the CP. Much confusion in there as the
shells began to hit. I grabbed a pair of binoculars off the table
and looked out the back window and I could see a hell of a lot
of firing and smoke up the road toward St. Vith. Then I saw
three tanks and three or four German cars and a bunch of men
running down the road toward Amblève.

I got scared and hollered for the Capt. He took a look and
ordered the 1/Sgt. to load up and get ready to move. I loaded
the jeep (I was driving for Lt. Hayes at the time) and helped
with the rest of the loading out of the CP.

Cpl. Schommer: Did you ever see a gypsy caravan? Well, that's
what we looked like and a grimmer bunch of GIs you never saw.
When we left town a few MPs were still hiding from the Germans, an artillery outfit had already been overrun and either
killed or captured. We offered the MPs a lift but they refused,
preferring to take their chances with the Germans.

Sgt. Billington: When my squad returned from road patrol
on the morning of December 17, we found the outfit wild with
latrine rumors about a German breakthrough. These got wilder
and wilder, then finally there was proof toward the end of the
morning, so, with radio communications practically nonexistent,
we were ordered to "advance back to Werbomont."

Cpl. Schommer: The Capt. probably gave our situation much
thought because he sure surprised most of us when he announced that, as an afterthought, we had better take a power saw
along because we might need it.

Without hesitation he had the drivers head toward the woods
instead of doing what we thought was the logical thing and
leaving town by road. The trucks took the worst beatings of

their lives for a while. After several miles of fields and forests and numerous fallen trees and stone walls, we finally reached a road of sorts. Capt. Gamble knew where he was going, but the rest of us didn't and we had the uneasy feeling we might wind up in Berlin or somewhere deep in German territory. But we never saw an enemy soldier during that traveling through fields and woods. Soldiers, like deer hunters, I guess, stay on roads.

Capt. Gamble: Our move back to Werbomont was mainly by side roads, partly for security. It seemed logical to me that German armor would be on the primary roads. When we did reach what I considered safe territory, the primary roads were blocked by our own heavy traffic and it was impossible to travel on them. So we continued to make our way back by side and crossroads.

Cpl. John A. King: During our flight back to Werbomont there was the reassuring sight of seemingly endless numbers of our own tanks lined up awaiting von Rundstedt's assault. I can still recall thinking that things *couldn't* really be "so bad" after all because surely no force could penetrate such a formidable line of defense. But I also wondered angrily why our outfit hadn't been warned since it seemed that everyone else had been.

Sgt. Billington: We passed miles of 7th Armored stalled and trying to get through to St. Vith. So we had to take to another crossroad through the hills. If we hadn't, we would have gone right through Baugnez and at about the time of the infamous Malmédy Massacre. We missed it by about three miles and maybe half an hour. Lucky? You said it.

Cpl. Schommer: Until this time we had always been advancing, so retreating was a new experience. Believe me, I liked the other way best. The uncertainty, the confusion, and most of all the thought that the powerful American army was being pushed back by an army that was considered to be too weak to last long even in retreat, was hard to swallow. We told ourselves it was probably just a Nazi trick and it would be over in a few days. But we *were* retreating and we would continue to feel the power and determination of the German army for weeks to come.

After driving along secondary roads for a long, long time we finally came to a real highway fairly clear of traffic. Here we encountered our first roadblock. Two large American tanks were dug in on either side of the road with nothing visible except the barrels of the large guns. As we approached, we were stopped short and held there for a very long time while the Captain was questioned. Apparently many American units had been overrun and they were taking no chances of Germans infiltrating our lines dressed as Americans.

Finally we were cleared, but were requested to stay and reinforce the roadblock. The Captain explained that we had left most of our equipment behind and that we had other assignments. They allowed us to pass.

Sgt. Abe Caplan, 2nd squad, 1st platoon: My squad of 1st platoon and most of 3rd squad were quartered in a church auditorium in a small village in Belgium, called Grande Halleux. This village was halfway between the towns of Trois Ponts and Vielsalm.

We were operating sawmills in Vielsalm on a 24-hour basis to provide lumber for winterization of troops on the front lines. The men sawed timber in the forest outside St. Vith, bringing it to the sawmill at Vielsalm to be sawed into board lumber. The squads of 1st platoon alternated the work shifts.

The 106th Infantry Division, which had just arrived from the

states, was up on the front line in that area — in the Schnee
Eifel. Some of their equipment was not even unpacked.

In the auditorium at Grande Halleux where we were quartered, we made our bunks from the timber we sawed and up-
holstered them with straw and hay which gave us some sem-
blance of the comforts of home. A kitchen unit was set up for
our food which made living more bearable, also.

Part of the auditorium was used by the church to conduct religious services and instruction for the young children. The
teachers were priests who lived three miles away. They com-
muted by bicycle on Thursday and Sunday afternoons. Very
often one of our trucks would take them back to their church
parish. The enjoyment the children gave to us gave us a sense
of well being.

A Christmas party was being planned for them. Many of our
boys were receiving their packages from home. I, myself, received seven fruit cakes (at least five pounds each). All this
we held in store for the children.

On Sunday, December 17, I, with about eight men of my
squad in a truck drove in the early morning to the forest outside of St. Vith to haul timber which had been cut down the day
before. It was to be hauled to Vielsalm.

We knew nothing of the breakthrough, nor of the shelling of
Malmédy on December 16, but we sensed an unusual amount
of activity, movement of men and equipment of the 106th Infantry, whose headquarters were in St. Vith. We asked some of
the drivers and men on the trucks who were waiting for traffic
to move what was going on. They said the Germans were breaking through our lines around St. Vith, had captured a number
of units of the 106th. The time was by now around 11 AM.

I decided the best thing to do was to get my men back to
Grande Halleux. This was a distance of about twelve miles.
We reached Grande Halleux around 2 P.M. The platoon had

set up some roadblocks and defenses. One hour later we received orders to clear out and rejoin the Company.

We loaded the equipment in the trucks, but we left our barracks bags, clothing, everything else, behind, for we had to travel light. We did take the fruit cakes and Christmas packages which we had been holding in store for the Christmas party for the children, for we didn't know when we might have food again.

We left Grande Halleux at 4 P.M. We drove to a rendezvous with the main units of the platoon and received orders to go to Trois Ponts. We traveled on side roads in complete darkness, not being able to use lights and therefore unable to see too far ahead.

At one point the truck carrying the squad and equipment swayed. They were ordered to stop. After investigating, it was discovered that one of our left rear dual wheels was suspended in mid-air. We were on the very edge of a deep ravine. The men were instructed to get on the right side of the truck and not to move until we had secured the cable from our winch and were able to pull ourselves to a safe position on the road. It took us until dawn. When we saw our situation we realized how narrowly we had escaped death.

We met our unit and were then ordered to go to a certain road intersection in the vicinity of Marche to set up a defensive roadblock with machine guns, anti-tank mines and bazookas along with our individual weapons and rifles. Some German tank units were expected to come through that way.

We set up our defenses, moved into a house about 500 yards from the road intersection and maintained 24 hour guard on the roadblock. The occupants of the house (Belgians) a husband, wife and three children shared our fears and were reassured by our presence. We felt comforted by their presence.

The days were dull and dreary. Our mixed fears gave us

little comfort since the weather was so bad our Air Force was unable to come to our aid in bombing and strafing missions to help the ground forces stop the onslaught.

An experience of near tragedy, with a slight touch of humor, occurred when one of our men, while observing from a tree top, fell from the tree and somehow exploded a mine. But he escaped injury. The GREAT MAN must have been looking down on him to have spared his life.

We were at this roadblock five days. Coming up the road one day we saw an English tank column approaching. We stopped their forward tank, ordered its Commander to come down for interrogation. They shouted, "Don't shoot, don't shoot! We're English!"

The Commander was brought to the house for questioning. We learned he came from a town near Gloucester, which as you know had been our last "home" in England. The Commander said he and his battalion had come from Holland to aid in stopping the Nazi breakthrough. They were a very welcome sight indeed. We were assured the enemy would not be coming from the road we had so intensely guarded those long days and nights.

A most beautiful dawn broke on Christmas morning, breaking up the fog and gray clouds which had been overcasting the sky for so long. The greatest Christmas gift we could ever have received was the sight of our Air Force flying again, coming to bomb and strafe the oncoming German columns, destroying many of their tanks and other attacking units.

After New Year's we were taken from this roadblock and sent to a house outside of Spa, Belgium, where quarters were set up and the entire Battalion awaited further orders.

Capt. Gamble: We arrived in Werbomont in the late afternoon and were able to re-establish our CP in the same schoolhouse we had occupied previously. Shortly thereafter, I received a radio message from Col. Pergrin requesting all our machine guns and gunners to be dispatched to Malmédy. This was done.

Sgt. Billington: We got our old quarters back in Werbomont. 3rd platoon was quartered in the schoolhouse, but 2nd platoon was across the road in the same home we had occupied before.

That evening the Col. radioed that Malmédy was under tank and infantry attack and he asked for our machine guns and gunners. Black Mac took them over. Holbrook was one of the detail and as you know Holbrook never made it back.

Extra guards were posted even though we had just learned 82nd Airborne was on its way to the area. We began to feel our collective skins might be saved after all.

Cpl. Schommer: As soon as the radio was set up at our old CP orders began to come in. Capt. Gamble ordered roadblocks set up on several roads, mostly mines or daisy chains and demolition crews were assigned to several bridges.

Capt. Gamble: Around midnight, Col. Pergrin again radioed, this time asking for our bazookas and ammunition. These orders were carried out, and then all communications were cut off and this was the last we heard from Battalion for several days.

As Company Commander I was greatly disturbed by these events and this was certainly, at least for me, the beginning of chaos. It was days before we learned the full impact of our situation. Having a fair knowledge of the area (we had been over it all many times before) I decided that we could only retreat in some orderly fashion by interrupting what enemy movements possible and in whatever manner available to us. Let me say at this point that the judgment, bravery, and attention to duty of the men of the Company can only be attested to by the sequence of events which followed.

T/4 Elliott: I was sleeping in the front hall of the CP that night when Dennington, one of the radio operators, called me and said the Capt. wanted to see me. He, Lt. Hayes, and First Sarge and two more radio men were in the room. The Capt. said the Col. had radioed that Malmédy was still under tank and infantry attack and they needed all the bazookas we had. I was asked if I would volunteer to go to Malmédy with the bazookas.

Me? I was terrified. But I put on a hell of a good show. I told them that was what I had come over here for, to fight a war. If nobody else had the guts to take the bazookas to Malmédy, I would. I said I would get my stuff together and I would be ready to leave in ten minutes.

They sent to the other platoons for their bazookas and ammo. Lt. Hayes unloaded the jeep. Dennington went into the next room and asked for a volunteer to go with me. Red Richardson, from 3rd platoon, said he would go. Red and I didn't always see eye to eye with each other, but he had more guts than anyone I ever saw.

Then they told us radio contact had been broken and our chances of getting back were bad and we didn't have to go if we didn't want to. We said we would try it. They told us if we were fired on to leave the jeep and try to get back as best we could.

[December 17, 1944, the second day of the German offensive. In the darkness shortly after midnight 105 Junkers carrying a battle group of around 1,000 paratroopers were flying toward their drop target, Baraque Michel, a few miles north of Malmédy. They were charged with preventing reinforcements from the north reaching the beleaguered area. Sepp Dietrich, commander of the 6th Panzer Army, had blithely promised Baron von der Heydte, commander of the parachute troops, to meet him in Baraque Michel by noon of the 17th. Instead, with the exception of 1st SS Panzer Division, he was still stalled, unable to punch a hole through the 2–99 line and get moving.

Allied intelligence was messaged by an Allied agent behind the German lines at the time the Junkers took off. Destination was not definitely known, however. The planes were piloted for the most part by young, new, green men who panicked when they ran into the alerted heavy anti-aircraft fire waiting for them and out of 105 planes, only ten made their drop anywhere near the assembly area of Baraque Michel.

The others turned aside, turned back, or dumped their loads too soon and the men were scattered over parts of three countries. Toland says only 30 men gathered at the assembly area with von der Heydte. Merriam says 300. At any rate, they were too few and von der Heydte, hidden in the woods, had to watch helplessly as first, 7th Armored, then 1st Infantry and finally 30th Infantry moved in to reinforcement positions.

This parachute drop caused great confusion, however, for many of the men dropped outside the Baraque Michel area were captured and the bugaboo of large parachute drops behind the American lines began to take shape.

The parachute drop was also confused with Operation Greif, the operation calling for English-speaking German troops dressed in American uniforms, riding in captured American vehicles, armed with American identification cards and small arms to infiltrate the lines. It was believed this operation was being carried out by parachute drops.

Operation Greif, however, was a ground operation. The plan called for the vehicles to merge with retreating American troops, and for a certain group called Kommandos to move rapidly to the Meuse and hold three bridgeheads, Huy, and two others between that point and Liége, until the forward armored divisions arrived.

The rest of Operation Greif were to scatter behind the lines and create as much confusion as possible by changing roadsigns, misdirecting traffic, giving false information, generating fear and panic, and reporting back by radio on situations and conditions.

Otto Skorzeny's Operation Greif troops were attached to 6th Panzer Army and were therefore still bogged down. Toland says seven jeep loads broke free with 1st SS Panzer Division; Merriam says ten jeep loads broke free. In each jeep rode four men, one of whom spoke perfect English, the other three speaking passable English.

However many there were, they caused almost as much chaos and confusion as it was intended the entire brigade to cause. One jeep, never captured, wandered freely in the Malmédy area all day the 17th. Two jeep loads were captured, one by the British as they tried to cross the Meuse and the other by American MPs in the outskirts of Liége. The prisoners told varying stories, one of which was that Skorzeny himself was to lead a small group and assassinate Generals Eisenhower and Bradley. It did seem reasonable to believe that a full brigade of 2000 men were wandering around in American jeeps and cars behind the American lines and it sent even the High Command into the jitters.

At 4 A.M. on December 17, Kampfgruppe Peiper was on the move from Lanzerath on the Belgian border. Without difficulty he overran the village of Honsfeld in Belgium. Peiper's orders were rigid, as were those of all the commanders. Stay on your own road, keep moving, smash your armor through and leave pockets of resistance to be mopped up by following troops. Avoid fixed battles in all cases.

Peiper's road lay almost due west. He was to make for Stavelot, cross the Amblève River at that point, swing on to Trois Ponts and cross the junction of the Salm and Amblève there, swing on to Werbomont and from there to Huy where he would cross the Meuse. Once across the Meuse he would have a clean sweep to Antwerp.

Peiper disregarded his orders at one point, however. He was

running low on fuel. Knowing there was a large fuel dump at the village of Bullingen he swung north, quickly overran the village, then refueled, got back on his road and headed straight for his objectives.

In the meantime, Col. Pergrin at his headquarters in Haute Bodeux had been radioed by 1111th Engineer Combat Group to defend and hold Malmédy at all costs.

By the morning of December 17th, First Army, with headquarters at Spa, only a few miles north of Malmédy, believed that the attack was directed toward Liége with its huge supply dumps and Malmédy lay directly in the path of such an attack. General Hodges had by now, also, asked for the 82nd Airborne and the 101st Airborne Divisions to be released to his front. Both were at Rheims. The 82nd was able to leave about midmorning of the 17th, the 101st not until afternoon.

Col. Pergrin went immediately to Malmédy and with the men at his disposal, primarily Company B, and with only land mines, bazookas, machine guns and explosives, began to set up road blocks and outposts.

Early in the afternoon, Battery B of the 285th Field Artillery Observation Battalion, numbering roughly 140 men, passed through Malmédy on its way to Vielsalm.

A tiny hamlet called Baugnez, consisting of three or four houses and a cafe lay three miles southwest of Malmédy. Baugnez was, however, a crossing point of five roads. It was known to the Americans as Five Corners. At Baugnez, Battery B stopped to ask directions to Vielsalm.

Unknown to Battery B, Kampfgruppe Peiper of the 1st SS Panzer Division was now approaching Baugnez in its race to the Meuse. The young officer in charge of the Battery got his directions, his men mounted up, and the Battery was just pulling out when the lead tanks of Kampfgruppe Peiper came over the hill into sight. Without difficulty the Battery was overtaken and captured.

After surrendering, the men were herded into a field by German guards. The main German column did not even halt. But a halftrack suddenly stopped and from it a pistol was fired into the little group of prisoners. A man fell. An armored car then opened fire and the entire group was methodically mowed down by machine guns. The German guards went among them and shot those still living. The column moved on, men from the cars, halftracks and tanks taking potshots into the pile of bodies as they passed.

Several of the wounded were by some miracle overlooked by the guards. They began whispering among themselves and determined to make a break for it before any more vehicles halted to have their fun. At a signal those who *could* got to their feet and ran. Col. Pergrin who was reconnoitering in a nearby field took three in his jeep to the Battalion aid station in Malmédy.

The incident became known as the "Malmédy Massacre" and it, with the massacre at Trois Ponts, did more, perhaps, than any other incidents of the war to seal in the minds of the American troops a deep hatred of the enemy. Heretofore Americans had fought well but without any deep-seated hatred of the Germans. Henceforth they fought savagely and bitterly and, taking their cue from these incidents, sometimes they themselves "took no prisoners."

At Baugnez, having received information that Malmédy was practically deserted, Commander Peiper sent an arm of his column northeast to probe the town. He took his main column on to Stavelot, as per orders.

By nightfall, the main elements of Kampfgruppe Peiper were now rumbling toward Stavelot where one squad of Company C, 291st, were defending a roadblock.

The entrance to Stavelot from the south is down a long hill and across the Amblève River by an old stone bridge. The Company C roadblock was positioned beyond the bridge to protect it. It was not expected an attack would be made on Stavelot, since it was generally believed, from First Army headquarters down, that the primary attack would be on Malmédy and toward Liége.

It was shortly after dark when the lead tank of Peiper's column hit the mines of the Company C roadblock and was disabled. Fearing the town was too strongly defended for a night engagement, Peiper withdrew to the top of the hill where he halted for the night astraddle of the road.

During the night Stavelot was reinforced by one company of infantry and one platoon of tank destroyers under the command of Major Paul J. Sollis. They arrived in the town around 4 A.M.

Jeff Elliott and Red Richardson left Werbomont with their jeep load of bazookas and ammunition about 2 A.M.]

T/4 Elliott: Red and I took off. It was pitchblack. We opened the windshield on the jeep so we could see better. We went to Trois Ponts. We got stopped by some H/S Company guards by the railroad underpass. They had a 50 mm. set up there pointed at the underpass toward Stavelot. All of them seemed scared stiff. They said a vehicle had come from Stavelot and had turned around just the other side of the underpass. They didn't see it but they said it didn't sound like one of our vehicles.

By then I was so scared I could hardly sit still in the jeep. Red was smiling and happy as ever. They said Malmédy was gone and we'd never make it back. We decided to go on. Drove through the under pass and on toward Stavelot. We got into the outskirts of the town and saw a blue light coming toward us. I shut off the engine and coasted to a stop. Red had his M1 out through the windshield, loaded, cocked, ready to kill. I had my tommy gun across my lap and ready, but I was so damned scared I probably couldn't have shot it if I'd had to.

An American jeep came up and stopped beside us. The driver did all the talking. He wanted to know if the road to

Trois Ponts was open. I said it was. He took off. We sat there a minute getting over the shakes. Then we heard a tank on the next street above us. We took off, me in terror.

Later, we talked about what perfect English this guy had spoken and how the other three in the jeep hadn't said a word, thought maybe they were Krauts and wished we'd opened up on them. [This was undoubtedly the same jeep that had wandered around the area all day, driven through Malmédy at noon, one of the few Skorzeny Operation Greif jeeps to break free back of the American lines. The vehicle Jeff and Red heard was probably one of the reinforcing tank destroyer halftracks. No German tanks were in Stavelot that night.]

We took the short cut to Malmédy and went up over the hill. [If Jeff and Red had turned right in Stavelot, crossed the stone bridge to follow the main road to Malmédy they would have run right into Kampfgruppe Peiper who was poised on the hill waiting for daylight.]

Just then the Krauts started shelling the hell out of the road. We crept along expecting to get it any minute. Just out of Malmédy we were stopped again by a roadblock Col. Pergrin had set up. We asked where the CP was, they told us, and we went there. It was in a cellar in the center of the town. We went in and were glad-handed by the Col. himself, who poured each of us a water glass full of whiskey. We drank it.

He wanted to know how in hell we got through. Said he had no radio contact with us and figured the Company had been overrun or all killed. He didn't seem to have the shakes at all. He was sure in command of the situation. [Lt. Col. Pergrin was at this time just twenty-seven years old. A graduate engineer in civil life, he seems also to have been eminently qualified to command. It was one of those happy situations which occur all too seldom in a war — the man for the command, the command for the man.]

He asked us if we wanted to stay and fight with them or try to get back to the company. He said there was a push on at Stavelot right now and we probably couldn't get back. We said we'd try it. We had been in the area since November and as a driver I knew every side road in it. By weaving around and using every old trail I could remember we made it back to the outfit in Werbomont.

I don't know what happened to the rest of 2nd platoon. I was too busy trying to stay alive myself and too scared to find out.

S/Sgt. Paul J. Hinkel: We felt very lonely in Trois Ponts the night of December 17th. Only a part of H/S Company was there and by now we knew all hell had busted loose. By radio we had learned that Malmédy had been under attack by tank and infantry during the afternoon and night and that the Germans were moving fast. We thought it would be our turn next.

I was Sgt. of the Guard that night and I posted the usual security. We had a few machine guns, some mines and bazookas and that was about all. It was a very apprehensive and frightening night. A handful of men, either lost or headed as replacements for some other place, joined us during the night. They kept saying, "Can't we stay with you, Sarge, can't we stay with you?" I said, "Hell, yes, you can stay with us. We may need every gun we can get."

Right after dark Black Mac and the 2nd platoon machine guns and gunners passed through on their way to Malmédy. We told them from what we'd heard Malmédy was gone. But Mac said they'd have to get through somehow if they could. They went on. Nobody envied those boys their job.

Then about 3 A.M. Jeff Elliott and Red Richardson with a jeep load of bazookas and ammo came through, also headed for Malmédy. We told them radio communication with Malmédy had been broken and we thought the boys there had been overrun and the town taken. We didn't think they had a chance of getting there, much less getting back. Jeff and Red thought about it, then decided to try to make it. It sure took guts not to turn around and head back where it was still safe, but they didn't.

[December 18, third day of the German offensive. Kampf-gruppe Peiper rolled at daybreak on the morning of the 18th. A tank destroyer had been positioned on either side of the old stone bridge to reinforce Company C's roadblock. As Peiper's tanks rumbled down the hill the tank destroyers were easily demolished and the Company C roadblock was overrun. Pfc. Lorenzo Liparulo was killed and Pfc. Bernard Goldstein was badly injured. The tanks moved across the stone bridge and into the heart of the village where the American forces engaged them for a time in a brisk firefight.

Realizing within an hour, however, that the situation was hopeless, Major Sollis ordered a retreat to Malmédy over the short cut mountain road. Peiper sent some outriders in pursuit. A large gas dump was located on the mountain road, guarded by men of the Belgian underground, the White Army. They and Major Sollis' troops formed a roadblock of barrels of the gas and ignited it, effectually stopping any further pursuit on that road. The outriders turned back and joined Commander Peiper in his advance now on Trois Ponts.]

Capt. Gamble: In an endeavor to anticipate the most obvious route the German armored division was traveling, Lt. Edel-stein and I decided to prepare for demolition the timber trestle bridge across the Amblève River just east of Werbomont. This seemed to be a logical route for the advancing German armor, but little did we know that Jochem Peiper and his Panzer Division would break into Trois Ponts first.

S/Sgt. Hinkel: On the morning of December 18, a company of 51st Engineers arrived in Trois Ponts and the 1st squad of 1st platoon of our own 291st also arrived — their mission to blow the bridge across the Amblève.

The 51st had found a big gun and they placed it to guard the road. When the Krauts came into view with their tanks and infantry, the 51st gun crew went into action. They got a few tanks, which gave Sgt. Jean Miller of our own 1st squad time to finish wiring the bridge. Just as the Krauts began moving again, Sgt. Miller turned the key and bang, up went the bridge right in their faces.

T/4 Merlin Dixon: On the morning of December 18, 1st squad of 1st platoon received orders to move into Trois Ponts to guard and to set demolition charges on the bridge. Sgt. J. B. Miller was in charge.

When we arrived at our destination we found part of H/S Company there already and one company of 51st Engineers who had a Colonel with them.

We set up in the hotel lobby and began to prepare the bridge for demolition. The Krauts arrived before we had finished, but the 51st had a 57 mm. tank gun which had been abandoned. They put it at the underpass pointing toward Stavelot. When the Krauts arrived, they put the lead tank out of commission and it slewed across the road in such a position as to hold up the whole column for ten or fifteen minutes. At any rate, just as the Krauts got moving again we finished wiring the bridge, Sgt. Miller turned the key, and up went the bridge.

We had to go in cellars then, for the Krauts were all over the place. They had us completely surrounded. We couldn't get out in any direction. Those were bad days for we didn't know if we would ever make it.

S/Sgt. Hinkel: After the bridge was blown the main German column turned and left, but they left a bunch to hold Trois Ponts. We had to hide out in cellars. The Germans massacred a bunch of innocent women, men and children, for befriending the Americans.

We didn't get out of those cellars for five days. Not until the 82nd Airborne came in and routed out the Krauts.

T/4 Dixon: It was on the third day of our hiding from Krauts in Trois Ponts that we heard rumors the 82nd Airborne was to be dropped in. So we sent a messenger out by jeep to report that we were in Trois Ponts completely trapped. That night the Colonel of the 51st sent out night patrols to see what was going on.

We heard, finally, the 82nd had been moved to Werbomont by truck from Reims, France, but it was on the fifth day of our ordeal in Trois Ponts before they reached us and 1st squad and the 51st Engineers were relieved. Five days of being trapped by the Germans was right nerve-wracking, and we were very glad finally to be able to move back to Company headquarters.

It wasn't long after that until we were back clearing roads and repairing and building bridges again.

That was the most exciting thing that happened to me during the Battle of the Bulge. But as I said, I was just 1st squad's truck driver and all I did was what I was told to do. Sgt. Miller deserved most of the credit for blowing the bridge.

S/Sgt. Hinkel: It was not a pleasant experience being trapped in those cellars and we didn't know whether we'd ever make it out. We thought we might meet our deaths in those cellars. Believe me, the 82nd Airborne really looked good to us when they came in.

The heroes of Trois Ponts were Lt. Walters of 1st platoon

and Sgt. Miller. But none of us enjoyed our little battle at Trois Ponts.

Capt. Gamble: When the bridge across the Amblève was blown in his face by Lt. Walters and Sgt. Miller and the 1st squad of 1st platoon, Peiper and his Panzer Division turned north in his attempt to cross near Werbomont. Here again a handful of men under the command this time of Lt. Edelstein demolished the bridge before the onslaught of the Panzer armor.

I might add here that in addition to wiring the bridge across the Amblève River, Lt. Edelstein decided to lay a mine field on an intersecting road leading to the bridge site. Just as three of his men came out on a steep bank leading down to the road they were to mine they saw five German tanks coming up to the bridge. The tanks, of course, spotted them and opened fire with machine guns. Certainly the temptation for these men must have been to run, but they did not. They slipped down the bank, laid their mines, climbed back up the bank, all the time under fire, then leapfrogged down the road and found cover.

Their squad corporal had been left to blow the bridge, which he successfully accomplished. He and the man left with him caught the trucks and returned to Werbomont with them. The other men finally rendezvoused together on the Werbomont road, but their unit had gone. It seems cruel, but on such missions a time limit is given and, of course, one cannot jeopardize the lives of many for a few who might have met their demise in an attempt to accomplish their mission.

Fortunately these men came through in good style and hitched a ride in a jeep back to Werbomont.

During this time, we had been relieved at Werbomont by the 82nd Airborne and this handful of men were brought back to that point expecting to rejoin their Company. However, we had moved farther west and it was several days before they found the Company again.

Here I would like to say with all honesty and humility that I thought we were doing very little as far as the total war effort was concerned and it was at this time that I began really to wonder whether I had failed as an officer and leader. We were retreating, in my opinion, in a disorderly manner, and a great sense of responsibility suddenly burst upon me for these men about whom I knew very little at this time and actually knew very little of what they had done.

I must say it is a very lonely feeling to realize and feel the weight of such tremendous responsibility for certain objectives, as well as the lives of the men and suddenly begin to question your own decisions. This was the predicament in which I found myself these next hours.

At this moment I could not see, nor understand, the significance of what was happening. It was only after the German Panzer tide was stemmed that we could look back on these events and realize what our men accomplished and what a tremendous contribution was made by them during these two or three days. To have been in command of such men was both my honor and privilege. The tradition of the Corps of Engineers had certainly been enriched by their ingenuity and valor.

Sgt. Billington: After an apprehensive night back in Werbomont, we had orders the next morning to go down the road toward Trois Ponts and wire a fixed timber bridge over the Amblève River which C Company had built only a short six weeks earlier.

Parts of two squads of 2nd platoon, my 3rd and Cornes' 2nd, with Sgt. Pigg and the Lieut. took two trucks and set off. One of the trucks had bad valves and couldn't get up any steam. We got under way, however, went to the corner and turned down the Trois Ponts road. Refugees coming our way on bikes and on foot were all there was to be seen.

We went to the bottom of the hill, coming into a peaceful valley with this small stream on the far side. I believe it was the Amblève River which flowed on down and you had to cross again at Trois Ponts. Well, there was our bridge. We turned the trucks around, just in case, headed toward home and put the good one behind to push the bad one.

We got the bridge set up for demolition and then came a discussion as to where to hook up the detonator. Pigg said, "Hell, Billington, put the damned thing out where you can see!"

Well, the argument about whether you could see the bridge or not didn't add up to me. If Kraut tanks showed, you could sure hear 'em. I figured I was going to have to blow the bridge and I couldn't see standing out in the open waiting to turn that damned jigger with maybe Kraut tanks firing at me. So I finally decided to run the wire back to an old Kraut sentry box about 125 ft. back from the bridge. We got it all ready to go.

It turned out I was wrong about having to blow the bridge myself. The Lieut. remembered the two roads that intersected on the near side of the bridge. We couldn't let them go unprotected. One came in from the east, and the other was a byroad to Stavelot. I drew the upstream road and Bossert and Rondenelle[1] took the downstream, or Stavelot road.

We left Shorty Nickell[2] and Fred Chapin[3] at the bridge while we went to fix the roadblocks. I took Thorne[4] and Miller[5] with me.

We loaded up with mines and, walking, took a short cut over the hill to come out on the intersecting road. About a half or

[1] Pfc. John Rondenelle, 2nd squad, 2nd platoon.
[2] Pfc. Shorty Nickell, 2nd platoon.
[3] Cpl. Fred T. Chapin, assistant squad leader, 3rd squad, 2nd platoon.
[4] Pvt. Thorne, 3rd squad, 2nd platoon.
[5] Cpl. A. Miller.

three-quarters of a mile from the intersection we went up a farm road to a house, on around the barn, up a field road to the top of the hill. We were just starting down this steep bank when I looked up and lo! and behold! there were two or three Tigers coming toward the bridge! They started shooting! The Security man on the point never did show back to the party!

We heard the bridge go with a bang and then the sounds of motors racing. We slid the rest of the way down the bank, pulled a mine chain across a curve in the road and then clawed our way back up the steep bank and started down the farm road. We were in a hurry for the transportation was to wait for us but not for more than twenty minutes.

Just as we got to the point where we could see the trucks, the damn tanks began shooting at us with machine guns. We three hit the ditch and they couldn't get down low enough to get us because of the hill and the edge of the road. The tracers would hit the crown of the farm road and bounce off the hill. I remember thinking, "They can't get us here. We're safe."

We played leapfrog on down the road, running a short distance then hitting the ditch, which incidentally was full of the iciest water I ever felt. We were going good until we came to a pile of wood in the ditch. It looked as big as a city block to get around. I didn't see how we could make it, but by crawling on our bellies make it we did, and we finally found shelter behind the barn. We stood there and shook and hoped to hell they wouldn't begin throwing 88s at us. They didn't.

Thorne wanted to make the trucks, so he edged around the end of the barn and suddenly took off across the field. The Krauts saw him and began following him with tracers. But Thorne was weaving. He was bent over double, his coat hanging open and he looked like a wounded chicken. The bullets lent wings to his heels and he made the road safely.

Miller wanted to go one way and I wanted to go another so

we split. I went back up the hill to a farm pond and using the bank for cover worked my way around and into some woods, crossed through the woods to the road three-quarters of a mile from the bridge. The trucks were long gone and I thought my goose was sure cooked.

But about that time along came Thorne and Bossert and Miller and another straggler. We headed down the road. Then a jeep came along and we flagged it down for a ride. Much to our surprise it was Slim Jim Gavin.[6] He had been up looking over the territory. He took us back to Peggy's tavern at the crossroads near Werbomont. General Gavin told us if our outfit had pulled out to attach ourselves to the first outfit we could find or else we'd wind up in a collection point and might never get back to the 291st again.

We found all the gang had pulled out — everybody gone but us. Werbomont was working alive with the 82nd. There was nobody to tell us what to do. We went to the schoolhouse, which had been the CP and tried to grab a little sleep. During the night an Anti-aircraft outfit moved into the schoolhouse with us and the following morning said they were going to the rear, to First Army Headquarters. So the five of us decided we might as well attach ourselves to them.

Well, they had a screwy Lieutenant who was recon happy. Nothing would do but he had to reconnoiter the whole front. We spent the next four or five days riding up and down the front in the recon car. At first I was damned scared, but I began to feel he was a nut who wanted to be a Patton, Jr. and didn't have anyone with his Company he could order to go along so he leaned on some brave lads he was able to recruit. They had one Company that was cut off from the rest of the outfit and with someone to go along and hold hands he could be

[6] Major General James Gavin, Commander of 82nd Airborne Division.

an important adventurer. When I figured it out I began to enjoy the role of footloose and fancy free myself.

We got to Houffalize, La Roque, down as far as Metz in France, in sight of Bastogne, which was closed off, and to Neufchâteau. Next day after we were in Neufchâteau the Krauts shelled hell out of it. We came off unscratched with *nearly* a night's sleep for four or five nights.

Finally the Lt. decided to head back up to Huy and to First Army Headquarters at Chaudfontaine. On the way we saw some of the outfit on roadblocks. I thought, "This ain't for me. I'm too scared and lazy to tend roadblocks." But old Bossert was along and he had more loyalty to the 291st and didn't want to get reported lost. So . . .

Back with the outfit finally we were on roadblocks until New Year's. This was at Modave, where Battalion had moved for regrouping, near Dinant or Huy, I've forgotten which. We had some old pancakes somebody threw together for Christmas dinner. What a treat! Ate sitting in front of a big open fire in some rich guy's chateau. Only humor was a colored driver who stopped for the password. Everybody was paratrooper happy, scared of everybody else, afraid to trust any stranger even in an American uniform. This boy said, "Now, boys, you all know ain't no colored boys in Hitler's army. I bound to be a genuwine American."

When I got back to the Company, Fred Chapin had already made his way back. He told this story. When the Krauts came up in the tanks they started to shoot. He stayed behind to turn the key. Up went the bridge with a big bang. Shorty Nickell was already making tracks for the trucks. Chapin wasn't going to get left if he could help it. He was behind but the scare put wings on his feet. All at once his cartridge belt slid down below his knees, tripped him and he fell flat on his face and the Krauts went gunning right over his head. Up he got, grabbed the tail of the last truck and away they went.

Rondenelle had stayed behind on the other road to pull his daisy chain of mines across. A Kraut halftrack came along. Rondy yanked his necklace over and up went the halftrack. But he barely got away, for they really opened up on him. He took eight or nine days to make it back to the Company but finally did.

The guys out on point for Security went into Trois Ponts and joined up with Jean Miller's 1st platoon bunch there. *They* sure had guts, or were too scared to have good sense, or something. Jean turned that key with Panthers and infantry both gunning straight for him!

Hooks Kovacs remembers the same action as follows: Lt. Edelstein, Sgt. Pigg, Jeff Elliott, and about 12 men from a couple of squads loaded up in the truck I was driving. Lt. Edelstein and Jeff were in the jeep. I followed the jeep. We pulled out from the CP at Werbomont where Lt. Edelstein had got his orders. We drove about an hour, maybe more or less. We started down this winding road. All we could see were civilians headed to the rear, carrying all they owned on their backs, on foot and bicycles. They were telling us how far away the Bosch were — about three miles.

We came to the bottom of the valley where a bridge crossed a small stream. I think it was the Amblève River. When we reached about 100 feet from the approach to the bridge, the jeep stopped and I pulled up behind it. We all unloaded and Lt. Edelstein explained what our mission was. All he told me to do was turn my truck around, park it and leave the motor running. He told the other boys to disperse themselves along the road and wire the bridge for demolition. He told me that just as soon as the bridge was blown I was to walk to the truck and

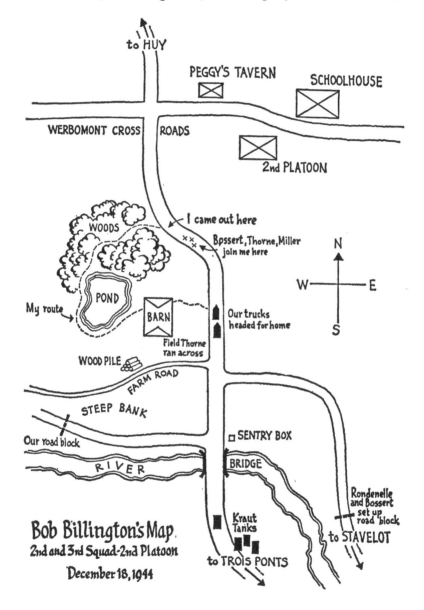

to HUY

PEGGY'S TAVERN

SCHOOLHOUSE

WERBOMONT CROSS ROADS

2nd PLATOON

I came out here

Bossert, Thorne, Miller join me here

WOODS

N

W — E

S

POND

My route →

BARN

Our trucks headed for home

Field Thorne ran across

WOOD PILE

FARM ROAD

STEEP BANK

Our road block

□ SENTRY BOX

RIVER

BRIDGE

Rondenelle and Bossert set up road block

to STAVELOT

Bob Billington's Map.
2nd and 3rd Squad-2nd Platoon
December 18, 1944

Kraut Tanks

to TROIS PONTS

get in and start out slow, to give the men a chance to run and catch the truck.

I followed through with my orders and was lying in a ditch along the road. I was watching for German infantrymen in the woods, which I thought would arrive before the tanks. As I was lying in the ditch an artillery shell hit on the road near the approach to the bridge on our side. I knew then the Germans had us zeroed in.

I still kept watching the woods for Infantrymen, but I happened to glance up and across the bridge I saw a German tank. He stopped at the turn of the road heading for the bridge. His turret was turning and I heard a lot of gun fire. Then I heard this big explosion, saw pink and blue smoke, pieces of timber flying in all directions, and I knew it was the bridge blown. I headed for the truck (and not jay walking). I got in and was starting out slow, according to orders, when Sgt. Pigg jumped in and I could hear men scrambling into the rear. I gradually picked up speed and began changing gears. Then we started upgrade on this winding road. Every so often we were in view of the enemy and they would fire at us with their machine guns. One of the ironies of the situation was that the truck had a couple of burnt out valves and wouldn't make but 12 mph.

When we reached the top of the hill I think there were only about five men, and Sgt. Pigg and me. We had a radio with us and tried to contact Lt. Edelstein or the CP. We couldn't get anyone. We met a tank destroyer outfit and they questioned us about information concerning the enemy down at the bridge. I don't remember who it was, but one of the men in the rear of the truck read the officer off for not being down at the bridge where the enemy was instead of sitting on their cans up where it was safe.

We drove a short distance to the main highway. Here we found the 82nd Airborne unloading all over the place from

Sgt. Henry E. Giles, 15042375. Company A, 291st Engineer Combat Battalion. Picture taken May 5, 1944, at Gloucester, England. Ribbons showing: Good Conduct, Pre-Pearl Harbor, European Theater.

Standing, Cpl. A. C. Schommer, Sgt. R. C. Billington, Kneeling, Sgt. E. W. (Bill) Keenan, S/Sgt. Paul J. Hinkel.

France: Company A officers & 1/Sgt. Standing: 1/Sgt. William H. Smith. Kneeling, left to right: 1/Lt. Archibald Taylor, 3rd platoon commander; 1/Lt. Albert Walters, 1st platoon commander; Captain James H. Gamble, Company commander: 1/Lt. Frank R. Hayes, administrative officer, H/S platoon; 1/Lt. Alvin E. Edelstein, 2nd platoon commander.

Lt. Col. David E. Pergrin, Battalion Commander

Stavelot, Belgium. Disabled Tiger Royal tank on outskirts of town.

Near Lanzerath, Belgium, February of 1945. Mine clearing for 82nd Airborne Division. Kneeling: Sgt. Frank C. Dolcha, 3rd platoon.

Malmédy, Belgium. All that was left of the town after three consecutive days of bombing, December 23, 24 and 25, by 322nd Bombardment Group of Ninth Air Command, American Air Force! In the foreground is what was left of B Company's Command Car.

Near Schmidt, Germany. Building the double-single Bailey bridge across the Roer River for 78th Infantry. Captain Gamble considered this the most difficult Bailey bridge the men of Company A built during the entire war because of its angle and terrain. This bridge was also built under heavy artillery fire.

The 291st M2 floating treadway bridge across the Rhine River. Town of Erpel in the background. Note convoy crossing. The treadway companies on the sign delivered the heavy equipment. They did no work on the bridge. Men are unidentified.

Long shot of 291st bridge across the Rhine with the Ludendorff railroad bridge in background. "Flak Hill" is on the far side of the river.

Ruins of Ludendorff railroad bridge at Remagen, Germany, after it collapsed. Sgt. Giles witnessed the collapse of the bridge at his machine-gun post.

Linz, Germany. Left, Pfc. Paul LaCoste; right, Sgt. Giles.

Germeter, Germany. Company A airstrip laid for 99th Infantry recon-naissance planes during the reduction of the Ruhr pocket. Note plane taking off at end of strip.

Company A men laying an airstrip near Heimbach, Germany, for the recon-naissance planes of the 78th Infantry. Standing: "Speedy" Dymond. Two men on left unidentified. Two men on right: Pfc. Louis Hernandez and Pvt. Nowakowski.

Near Kitzingen, Germany, late in April of 1945. A German jet shot down by American fighter planes. Still in support of 99th Infantry, the 291st was strafed on this German highway as they moved with the 99th toward the Danube River, into Bavaria.

A group of American Engineer soldiers doffed their steel helmets for a moment to try on straw hats in Carentan, France. L. to R. Rog, Mc-Cutcheon, Pink, Street, Implazo, Morello, Gregory, Marucci, Sgt. Giles. *Courtesy of Wide World Photos*

trucks and trailers. Boy, were they mad! They had thought they were due a leave in the States!

We continued to try to reach our CP by radio or Lt. Edelstein. We felt like a bunch of lost sheep. I was so mad, tired and scared that I told Sgt. Pigg to throw the radio away and let's head for Paris, stay there for a few days and then come back. Instead we kept working our way back, questioning different ones we met, until we located a Light Pontoon Equipment Engineer outfit from our Group. We told them what had happened. They were on alert. So we had a bite to eat and they told us to get some sleep. We got about a couple of hours sleep when some Lt. woke us up and took us out on a roadblock. We set charges in trees and put my truck behind a building because it had a .50 cal. machine gun mounted on it.

We stayed there a couple of days, then Lt. Edelstein found us. He didn't know where the CP had gone either. But at least we had a leader with us again and could recover some sense of order. Everything was chaos for a while, but finally the whole outfit got together again and eventually the entire Battalion was regrouped. But things were right frantic for a while.

Cpl. King: I don't recall where we went when we left Werbomont, but I do remember the helpless fear that returned as we slowly realized the great strength of the German breakthrough. There were days of great confusion — wondering where parts of the outfit were and even if they were still living. There were bitter cold nights of guard duty with everyone so jumpy it was a wonder we didn't slaughter each other.

Mrs. Vincent A. Fresina: I don't remember exactly where it was that Vince and a Lieutenant got separated from the Company, but believe it was near Stavelot. They were pinned down on a hillside for days. Finally Vince suggested they roll in the dark and crawl, which they did and they were able to catch up with some members of the Company at Malmédy. There Vince did his part in the defense of Malmédy. It was his Company, Company A, that blew two vital bridges across the Amblève River — at Trois Points and at Habiemont.

Cpl. Schommer: Although we were out of radio communications with Battalion Headquarters for a few days, they were still in contact with Group Headquarters and they continued to command the line companies. Radio communications were restored and it was at this time the value of radio communications was really appreciated. Throughout the confusion of the breakthrough, once the first surprise and disruption was over, the Battalion operated quite efficiently.

With personnel split up into small groups, small walkie-talkie radios were used by inexperienced operators and the code sets were very short-handed. For weeks operators worked 24 hour shifts. We ate and slept at the keys. Many nights, men who could not read Morse code would take over while a tired operator slept. He would listen for the call letters and if they came, he would wake the operator. I remember watching German tanks moving through a field only a few blocks away from the window of our CP one day.

[When the bridge near Werbomont was blown in his face, Commander Peiper had no alternative except to go still farther north seeking another crossing over the Amblève. Here, near Stoumont, he was finally entrapped in the mountainous terrain and, out of fuel, out of food, out of ammunition, his supply line cut, he had to abandon his vehicles and he and his men had to walk out, making their way back to the German lines as best they could.

In his book *Dark December*, Robert Merriam had this to say about the heroic action of the 291st Engineers and 51st Engineers at Trois Ponts, and a handful of 291st Engineers near Werbomont: "Here was a case where the fate of divisions and armies rested for a few brief moments on the shoulders of a handful of men; first, at the town of Trois Ponts, and then, only hours later, with another, smaller, handful of men, at the bridge just east of Werbomont. Had either of these groups failed in their job (and the temptation to run away must have been very great) the probability that Peiper would have got to the Meuse River the next morning would have been very high. And even though his was a lone panzer Kampfgruppe, such was the confusion of the time, the uncertainties and doubts raised by the German war of nerves, the lack of information at the higher headquarters, that it is most probable that Hodges, Bradley or Montgomery might have been thrown into a frenzy, which would have led to the forced withdrawal of all American troops behind the Meuse River. And the Germans, standing off with 2 SS Panzer Corps, waiting for just such a break, would have quickly followed through and exploited to the full any hole Peiper would have been able to make. But these two handfuls of American soldiers, despite the grave uncertainties as to the whereabouts of either friendly or enemy forces, chose to ride out the German attack. As a result Kampfgruppe Peiper was sacked in the canyons of the Amblève River, and the second major defeat had been dealt the Germans."

At dawn on December 21, in heavy fog, Sepp Dietrich's entire 6th Panzer Army mounted a furious offensive against the entire northern shoulder of the front, from Elsenborn Ridge farthest east to Malmédy, farthest west. He was making an all-out effort to smash through any soft spot he could find, enraged at having been held up since the 16th. The most had been expected of him and he had done the least, except for Commander Peiper's column.

Otto Skorzeny's troops of Operation Greif, now conventional tankers and infantrymen, hit Malmédy hard from two directions and for some time the outcome was in doubt. The attack was so vicious that, in fact, the west flank of the defense was turned for some time. It was during this terrible, smashing attack that Pfc. Wiley A. Holbrook was killed at his position.]

Capt. Gamble: On December 26th the Battalion was relieved at Malmédy. At Modave, near Huy, shortly thereafter the 291st was reunited, and it was there that we finally learned the entire story concerning all of the activities of the Battalion during the past several days.

May I digress momentarily to state at this time I first learned that my very close friend, Capt. John Conlin, CO of Company B, had been critically wounded during the bombings of Malmédy and had been evacuated to England. He was succeeded by Lt. and later Capt. Rhea, who ably filled Conlin's shoes with splendid leadership and engineering ability.

Cpl. Schommer: We next moved to Modave, a new location only a short distance away. I remember eating K-rations on Christmas Day. We also had a movie shown for our Company but there were only four men in camp. One man at a time could watch while the others worked or stood guard. The movie was Bing Crosby in *Going My Way*.

The radio was set up outside in a field where the operator could guard against paratroopers while on duty. It was very foggy for weeks and paratroopers were dropping all over the place. The Mess Sgt. reported seeing some on his daily trips to feed the boys. None visited our camp, however.

It was during this period that I operated radio for Capt. Gamble in the Command Car which John Coupe drove. The Capt. would visit the various units when possible, but would take the radio along. I remember one particular trip when the Capt. was in a foxhole with some officers and Coupe was walking around. I received a call and with the earphones on I couldn't hear the racket outside. But when I took the earphones off &

went to deliver the message to the Capt. I thought all hell had broken loose.

If you have ever heard screaming meemies, you know what I mean. Coupe had been trying frantically to warn me, but I couldn't hear him, either. A snow-covered field turned almost black with exploding shells. But there was a protecting hill where the car was parked, over which the shells lobbed in. There was no damage done, but if we hadn't been under that hill I wouldn't be here to remember it today.

Capt. Gamble: After reorganization at Modave, the 291st was assigned to the XVIII Airborne Corps, General Ridgeway commanding, with the specific mission of supporting the 30th Infantry Division. We moved north again through the same area over which we had retreated, or at least I might say Company A had retreated, building bridges, always under fire, at Trois Ponts, Malmédy, Poteau, as the 30th Division drove toward St. Vith.

T/4 Elliott: When the worst of it was over and we were pushing the Krauts back and headed down that way again, I took Sgt. Hinkel and a Light Col. from 78th Division back into Trois Ponts in a jeep one day. There were no tracks in the fresh snow. We went as far as we dared and walked the rest of the way. We went on the back road from Spa.

We met some Belgian underground guys. The Col. wanted to know how many Krauts there were in Trois Ponts.

Right where H/S motor pool was, three women had lived next door. We found them dead, murdered by the Krauts. The one that was pregnant had been disemboweled.

We came back out and then the Company went in the next morning to put a bridge in for the 78th and the 82nd Airborne.

Cpl. Schommer: When we were called on to build the bridge at Trois Ponts a small German unit was still entrenched across the river. When we arrived, our own tanks lined the road for many blocks. An infantry outfit was also there, but they could not advance.

From the bridge site we could see the Germans in their fox-holes waiting with machine guns facing the bridge site. This job looked rough!

Before starting the job, however, we were shown what had happened in a cellar of one of the houses. Apparently the Germans had gathered all of the people left in the town into the cellar of one of the houses and there they proceeded to punish them for befriending the Americans. Two small children actually had their heads smashed in. Men were dismembered and shot. One pregnant woman had been cut open and left to die. This scene was viewed by hundreds of GIs. This was as horrible a sight as that of the massacre of the men at Five Corners.

We started that bridge expecting those machine guns to start firing at any moment. I left the radio to help because all hands were needed. Surprising as it may seem, no shots were fired. Perhaps the German strategy was to allow the infantry to cross and catch them in a crossfire.

What the Germans didn't know, however, was that the tanks were to do the job. When the bridge was finished, the infantry withdrew and the tanks attacked. The tanks drove right over the enemy positions and literally buried them. Prisoners were then rounded up and brought to the bridge. Here they were stripped of all American clothing [if these men were wearing American uniforms they were troops of Operation Greif], and marched, some practically naked, most without shoes, to that particular cellar and forced to view the awful scene in it. From there, they were marched through the town into a wooded section, from whence shortly came the sounds of much shooting.

I had always read that Americans treated prisoners justly, but I wonder which prison camp these particular prisoners occupied. I have always been glad the 291st had no part in the executions.

There were many feats of bravery performed by the boys of the 291st which escaped notice. Likewise, credit was sometimes given to the wrong persons. During the period of almost utter confusion, when one unit did not know where the next unit was, it seemed as though we would build bridges one day and blow them the next. Mine fields would be laid by one outfit and picked up by another the same night.

On one occasion I was with two other boys clearing a road during the night. An officer from another outfit stopped us and asked, "What the hell do you think you're doing?" We told him we were clearing the road. He said, "Are you working for the Germans? My engineers just finished laying those mines and you are a mile deep into the German lines!"

He asked the name of our outfit and told us not to move until he returned. He never did return, however. One of our jeeps came and picked us up and returned us to our camp. We never heard any more of the incident but it was typical of the confusion that existed when no one seemed exactly sure which side occupied which town.

Cpl. King: I remember when we began to move forward again my dismay at seeing the litter of all those American tanks that had been that "impregnable" line of defense. Things didn't turn out right for them at all.

The real story of that battle was in the heroism of some of the other fellows. I hope some of them will be able to tell their story. I do recall they set off demolition charges, blew up bridges under fire, manned roadblocks constantly, and as terrified as we all were, did their jobs and did them well. Why the entire outfit wasn't decimated I'll never know. They were under enough fire and ran enough chances to have been.

Capt. Gamble: When St. Vith was taken we were assigned to support the 82nd Airborne Division in its attack against the Siegfried Line. With driving snowstorms and three and four foot drifts of snow we had our problems during those days.

Sgt. Abe Caplan, 1st platoon: The Battalion was assigned to support of 30th Infantry Division and we assisted in building the bridge at Trois Ponts which 1st squad of 1st platoon had blown.

One Thursday evening in January, my squad was called out to go into the woods in search of Germans in American uniforms who had parachuted into that area. We searched all one day and night, but none were found.

Occasionally we would get into Spa, where we could bathe or see a movie. This was a welcome respite since most of us billeted in the house outside were on constant call to go on any mission which might be assigned to us.

Some thirty men of 1st platoon lived in this house and we slept wherever we could find a place for our bed rolls. The lady of the house played the mandolin. She was also a member of the local church choir. She often entertained us with her playing and singing and this we enjoyed thoroughly.

Slowly the Allied forces took the offensive and we were on the move again. Many road clearing assignments for 82nd Airborne. We built the double triple Bailey across the Our for them, under heavy artillery fire, in sleet, snow and below zero weather.

This is a summary of the Battle of the Bulge as I saw it.

Cpl. Schommer: After we retook St. Vith, Battalion Headquarters was stationed there and we began to take stock of our equipment. We had several radios and mine detectors that were damaged and I made arrangements to take them in for replacements. John King drove the mail jeep that night and we arrived at Battalion in St. Vith just after dark. We picked up the mail and the new equipment, were just about ready to leave when an artillery barrage started coming in.

We decided to make ourselves scarce but quick. As we started, a truck that was parked just off the road backed out of a driveway just as a shell exploded directly in front of it. The flash of the explosion and the sound of the crash as he hit us was all I remembered for quite a while. When I came to, I was on a cot in the field hospital.

I was told later what happened. Apparently the truck tried to get out fast after the shell landed and backed into our moving jeep. I was sitting over the right wheel and was knocked out of the jeep into a ditch. In the excitement I wasn't missed until after the jeep was well on its way back to camp. The boys returned then and found me still in the ditch. A flashlight in my overcoat pocket was driven into my hip and I couldn't move my legs.

That night I was put on an ambulance train and taken to a hosptial in Paris. I was sure glad to get out of that area because those shells kept coming in all night. It's tough enough to sweat out a barrage in a foxhole, but from a cot in a hospital tent it was pure hell. I'll never forget the sight of some of the poor guys who were put on that train that night. Some had arms shot off, some were without legs, some blinded, nearly all were crying with pain or fright.

On arrival in Paris, we were processed for Purple Hearts. What a tough time I had trying to convince them I wasn't wounded in action, but in an accident. Since all of my brothers were in action at that time, I didn't want my folks to worry about me. As it turned out, I only succeeded in talking myself out of five points toward discharge!

When I got out of the hospital three weeks later and finally worked my way back through the replacement depot system to the outfit, the Battle of the Bulge was over and we were on the move way over in Germany.

The Battle of the Bulge—291st
Lt. Col. David E. Pergrin

THE "Battle of the Bulge" started for the 291st on December
16th, when "Jerry" dropped long-range 310-mm. fire on Malmédy, where Captain John Conlin's Company B was headquar-
tered. John telephoned the rather unusual circumstances to me
at Bn. Hq. in Haute Bodeux. I advised John that Captain Gamble was on the move to Amblève, south of Malmédy, and I had
plans to visit A Company and would stop on my way through to
check out the damage. T/5 Curtis Ledet drove the Command
Car and on arrival Captain Conlin had all road damage repaired; however, several buildings had been damaged in John's
favorite village.

We had our usual fine visit with Captain Gamble and his ef-
ficient and enthusiastic Company A and headed back to Bn.
Hq. after dark through the 106th Infantry Division's thinly but
effectively dispersed lines. The outpost guards were extremely
jittery and challenging for password identification. However,
we arrived back at Bn. Hq. about 1 A.M. on December 17, without incident.

Captain Colin phoned at 9 A.M., December 17, that Lieutenant Frank Rhea had noticed unusual activity near Butgenbach
while on road patrol. Conlin's words were, "Colonel, this may

be our opportunity to get a crack at the Krauts." John was a hard-hitting Irishman and nothing suited him better than to be advised "to prepare a defense and we would be there to join the party."

Colonel W. H. Anderson called from Group Headquarters shortly thereafter and advised, "The Bosches are loose east of Malmédy. Take the necessary action to defend."

Major Edward R. Lampp, Captain Lloyd B. Sheetz and I headed to Malmédy after advising Gamble at Amblève and Captain Moyer of C Company at La Gleize of the German breakthrough. Gamble was contacted by radio from Malmédy and advised to fall back on the Stavelot–Trois Ponts–Werbomont line. Gamble had little time to indicate that he was on his way and that Jerry was in A Company's backyard!

At 11 A.M. Lampp, Sheetz, Conlin and I reviewed our defense of the Malmédy-Stavelot area and the forces at our disposal. It was decided to defend the roadnet and all tank approaches to the villages of Malmédy and Stavelot.

East of Malmédy, on the route to Butgenbach, all trees were prepared for demolition with 1/4 lb. blocks of TNT. Where the road went through a cut, mines were strung across the road and a squad of Company B defended it with a machine gun and bazooka. The location of this roadblock was only 1/2 mile west of "Five Corners" where the Malmédy Massacre occurred. South of Malmédy on a winding secondary road, through sharply ascending terrain, a similar roadblock was established.

North of Malmédy on a back road toward Spa (Headquarters of 1st U.S. Army) a mine and "abbatis" defense was prepared.

The major defensive position was the west end of Malmédy, where Route N-16 swings under a railroad viaduct over a bridge span and thence up the hill toward Stavelot and Spa. Both the railroad viaduct and the bridge span were prepared for demolition, and Lieutenant Rhea spread a thin infantry line along the railroad embankment using B Company Engineers.

Finally, the northern route out of Malmédy to Eupen needed a roadblock and it was obvious we were running thin of troops and defensive equipment.

Captain "Larry" Moyer was given orders to come into Malmédy with two platoons of C Company and set up a roadblock with the squad in Stavelot at the south approach to that village.

11:30 A.M. found the defenses organized on the roadnet perimeter and Major Lampp left for Bn. Hq. at Haute Bodeux to coordinate the line of defense with A Company when it arrived from Amblève. Communications with 1111th Group and Bn. Hq. were still maintained and Colonel Anderson was advised of the 291st situation.

12 noon, a Company of 7th Armored Division entered Malmédy with orders to proceed to St. Vith. I personally advised the major in the lead vehicle that one of our patrols had reported a German tank column of considerable strength within three miles of Malmédy. I requested that he build up our line of defenses, using his tanks. He advised that his orders were to move to St. Vith, and requested route directions to avoid a head-on meeting with the German Tank Column. The route suggested was back to Stavelot and then south to Vielsalm. This portion of the Combat Command of the 7th Armored Division then departed west out of Malmédy and with it came the departure of other units from Malmédy, except the 629th Engineer Light Equipment Company, 962nd Maintenance Company, and the Military Government.

Shortly after the departure of the CCR 7th Armored, Battery B, 285th Field Artillery Observation Battalion, arrived and was advised of the position of the enemy. The officer in the lead jeep chose to move on his original route to St. Vith and thought there would be ample time to clear at Five Corners (Baugnez) prior to any conflict with the German Tank Column.

12:45 P.M. our roadblock south of Malmédy reported an American jeep loaded with Germans in American uniforms had hit the mines at the roadblock. The four Germans were killed and the tires from the jeep were in a tree thirty feet in the air. (Operation Greif — Skorzeny men).

1:15 P.M. the roadblock east of Malmédy reported tank and machinegun fire at Five Corners. I anticipated that this would be Battery B, 285th FAO, making contact with the tank column. I got Sergeant Bill Crickenberger with his jeep and submachine gun and headed east on N-32 to reconnoiter the situation and determine if we could assist with the meager force at our disposal. Bill and I moved by jeep to the high ground overlooking Five Corners and then approached the wooded area to the south on foot. Upon reaching the woods, three American soldiers came limping out screaming incoherently. One of the three was a lieutenant, who had been wounded in the heel. (If my memory serves me at this late date, this man was 2/Lt. Virgil Lary). The firing had ceased at this time (2:30 P.M.), so we took the three men back to the Bn. Aid Station and were able to develop the facts concerning the massacre.

It would have been futile to use the 291st forces and meager weapons in attack against Peiper's Tiger tanks. During the next several hours, seventeen more of 140 men of Battery B were treated for wounds at the Aid Station and this, along with other casualties of our own, indicated the need for the Bn. Medics. Captain Kamen was requested to come in from Haute Bodeux with the men and medical supplies. At the same time, we ordered more mines and demolitions from Bn. Supply.

The period between 3 P.M. and 7 P.M. showed much activity

at the perimeter roadblocks. B Company knocked off a jeep of Skorzeny's masquerading troops, a probing tank, and two German scouts on motorcycles.

Peiper's tank column had swung south of Malmédy and knifed toward Stavelot about two miles to the west of Malmédy. The lead tank was knocked out by the Company C roadblock south of Stavelot and Peiper regrouped for a dawn attack into Stavelot. At this point elements of Kampfgruppe Peiper had probed the Malmédy-Stavelot defenses but had not been able to penetrate. If he had pushed on through, there would have been little to stop his progress.

Lieutenant Self and the Bn. Dental Officer, Captain Paul Kamen, pushed through Stavelot into Malmédy when the road was under fire from Peiper's artillery and small arms.

The patrol from Company B on the north road to Spa intercepted elements of the 99th Infantry Battalion at 9:30 P.M. The patrol was advised to bring these men in from the back road, since our defenses at the west end of Malmédy were under tank and artillery fire from the flats along the Amblève River in the direction of Stavelot. Lieutenant Colonel H. D. Hansen was in command of this battalion and at 10 P.M. we were able to confer at the Command Post at the east end of Malmédy and set up a more formidable defense.

Throughout the night of December 17–18, our roadblocks reported heavy enemy activity, particularly west and south of Malmédy. Lieutenant Donald Davis, along with Lieutenant Rhea of B Company had strengthened this area. Contact was lost with Major Lampp and Company A, as well as Group Headquarters. Sleep was out of the question, although we were beginning to realize that our line of defense had a better than 50-50 chance of holding. Lieutenant Robert Wilson from First Army's AA Defense brought in three of their 90-mm.

guns to aid in stopping tanks. "Jerry" was shelling the village from all sides and we expected a dawn attack somewhere around the perimeter.

The attack at dawn was at Stavelot, however, where our single squad had been reinforced during the night by a company of Lieutenant Colonel Hansen's Infantry and a tank destroyer platoon.

Our communications had been maintained very ably by Sergeant John Scanlon to roadblocks and with other elements of the Battalion. Without the fine efforts of John we would not have been able to order in demolitions and guns which were required.

The attack of Peiper's column was effective at Stavelot and when Major Sollis retreated into Malmédy we had lost one roadblock of our defense.

During the morning of December 18, Company C captured another jeepload of Skorzeny's troops and B Company captured two paratroopers (von der Heydte's Folly).

Major Sollis' report of the Stavelot fight indicated that the villagers had assisted the Yanks in the tank fights by exposing the position of German tanks.

About 7 P.M. on the 18th of December, contact was made with the 30th Division's 120th Infantry Regiment. At this time, elements of the entire battalion were so integrated in the defenses with minefields and demolitions that the Regimental Commander requested from General L. S. Hobbs to attach the 291st to his regiment.

At the same time the First Army Engineers were requesting that the Battalion be pulled from the line to Spa in order to regroup. At 10 P.M. I received orders to move my Headquarters to Spa and work out a 24-hour withdrawal of the 291st from the line. Captains Moyer, Sheetz, and Conlin, along with the small Bn. Staff, hurriedly slipped into Spa and bedded down in what was formerly First Army Hq. billets. Hopefully, this was our first night's sleep since December 16.

At 4 A.M. of the 19th, the 30th Division had succeeded in having the Battalion attached to the 120th Infantry Regiment. "Back to Malmédy" was the order and by 5 A.M. I had loaded into my command car and was on my way into a period of the most unbelievable eight days of my life.

At precisely the time Corporal Ledet had wheeled our command car around the curve on N-32 west of Malmédy into the valley of the Amblève River, just short of the bridge span, "Jerry," consisting of strong infantry commanded by Otto Skorzeny, set off flares for a predawn attack against the west end of Malmédy. The command car was struck by small arms in the crossfire and it was a relief to reach the outpost at the railroad viaduct, where Pfc. Wiley A. Holbrook identified Ledet and me.

During this attack, the enemy penetrated deeply into the north, reaching the Amblève River and the railroad embankment at the west end of Malmédy. Their mission was to capture the Wooden Bridge over the Amblève and overrun the artillery positions in the high ground above Malmédy.

The attack was thwarted by the 30th Infantry Division, but again the 291st played a vital part with roadblocks and mines. The actions of Lieutenants Frank W. Rhea and Ralph W. McCarty, along with T/5 John H. Noland and Vincent J. Consiglio of Company B, plus Corporal Isaac O. McDonald of Company A, resulted in blowing the Wooden Bridge and the railroad viaduct in the face of the enemy attack. Pfc. Wiley A. Holbrook and Pvt. William C. Mitchell were killed as the enemy infantry attempted to overrun these positions.

The enemy lost three tanks to mines, bazookas and demolitions during the attack. The Regimental and Battalion Commanders of the 30th Division crossed over the high ground along with myself to review the damage done by this attack. We ran a segment of observed artillery fire to reach the railroad embankment and Wooden Bridge, which the boys had blown just as an enemy tank came over the edge of the abutment. Vincent Consiglio was able to fill me in on the action, as well as Lieutenant McCarty. Immediately this area was strengthened with troops, and again it was predominantly 291st Engineers. The railroad embankment was lined with Company A, B, C men under Lieutenants Rhea and Davis.

The remainder of December 19 was spent in preparing minefields beyond the 120th Infantry lines, generally in the face of artillery fire from the German buildup.

December 20 was a repeat of strong attacks around the perimeter defense; however, the attack at the west end of Malmédy was the one that made the deepest penetration of the original line. If there had been no defenses of the vital Malmédy roadnet, Jochem Peiper's probes of tank units could have raced through and had an excellent opportunity to drive to the Meuse by way of Spa and Liége as a spearhead for Sepp Dietrich's delayed columns.

The defenses in Malmédy continued to be exploited through foggy overcast skies until the afternoon of December 22, when we received our first bombing from the air. We were unable to determine the identity of the planes. The village square received the brunt of this bombing and a Company kitchen of the 120th Infantry was buried beneath the debris of a three-story building. This bombing, along with artillery fire, had caused fires to break out in the center of town. Captain Conlin and Captain Moyer were ordered to withdraw troops from the line and organize firefighting brigades to protect the line of defense from being overrun from the rear by fire.

[On the afternoon of December 22, the first clear, sunny day, six B–26s of the 322nd Bombardment Group of Ninth Air Command had as their target the town of Zulpich, Germany, a railhead which was serving the German offensive. The flight leader was having trouble finding his target. Finally, sighting a town in the hills, he decided he was over Lammersum, six miles northeast of Zulpich. He thought that was close enough so he released his bombs. The accompanying planes did likewise. The town was Malmédy, thirty-nine miles from Lammersum.]

Reports were coming in from the Infantry, as well as from civilians, of casualties resulting from the fires and bombing. We worked continuously extricating the dead and wounded through the night of December 22, but had gained control of the situation by noon of the 23rd, except for digging out the 120th Infantry Division's kitchen personnel.

Moyer, Conlin and I were directing our men with this tedious task and were able to clear the last debris from an opening into the basement of the building where some twenty soldiers had been buried alive. Moyer and I were just in the act of going through the opening, and Conlin was on the street to check for further falling debris, when our own Air Force (and this time they could be identified) gave the town a full-fledged bombing. Moyer and I, along with other troops of the 291st, were trapped in the basement under falling debris. We were able to dig our way out after an hour or so and we found Conlin badly wounded on the street. This was a great blow to all of us, since Conlin's inspired leadership and loyalty had carried us through a rough period.

Our only recourse to ease the thoughts of this loss was to push harder to open up the roadnet through Malmédy, which had been completely destroyed. The 291st was again fighting fires, extricating wounded, and bulldozing avenues for supply traffic to flow to the soldiers on the perimeter defense. This type of action continued through the 24th when we were bombed again, but finally, on the evening of December 25, order had been restored in Malmédy.

John Conlin's favorite village no longer looked like a picturesque Ardennes community, but more like a burned-out pile of cinders and rubble shoved back by bulldozers. Many civilians and soldiers had been killed, wounded, or entrapped in cellars. However, partly through his efforts, the gallant men of the 291st were able to drink a toast of champagne on Christmas Day. The drinks had been left behind by a unit which had departed from the scene on December 17. However, this unit was a Corps Medical Bn. which could have done little to aid in the cause of defense. We were grateful to them for not only leaving their liquor supply but also some Christmas packages which made a fine addition to our Christmas celebration of short rations.

Lieutenant Rhea succeeded Conlin as B Company's leader and we all got our parting shot from Hitler's Bulge crowd on December 26. Rhea, Captain Moyer and myself decided to make a ground coverage of our still integrated "Infantry Engineers." We experienced little difficulty around the perimeter from enemy fire until we crossed an open field after leaving the blown railroad overpass at the west end of the village. The open field had to be crossed in order to get to Lieutenant Davis' dug-in troops along the railroad embankment.

Skorzeny's artillery observers picked us up as we reached the center of the open field and immediately directed 88-mm. fire among us. We came through this barrage without any serious casualties and returned to the Battalion CP to find a message from Major General L. S. Hobbs, Commander of the 30th Infantry Division. The message indicated that the 291st was to be removed from the defensive positions of the 120th Infantry and sent to Modave to regroup and be re-equipped for the attack against the Bulge. General Hobbs requested that I report to him after completing the withdrawal of our 291st forces.

The meeting with General Hobbs found an exceedingly bedraggled Lieutenant Colonel hearing of his troops and officers being highly extolled for actions both individually and as a unit. The most satisfying words, however, were, "I should like to have the 291st as part of my Division, but Colonel, you, your officers and men need a well-earned rest."

Citations and Awards for Bulge action
Silver Star — 2/Lt. Ralph W. McCarty
Silver Star — T/5 John H. Noland
Bronze Star — Major Edward R. Lampp
Bronze Star — Captain James H. Gamble
Bronze Star — Captain William L. McKinsey
Bronze Star — Captain Lawrence R. Moyer
Bronze Star — Captain John T. Conlin
Bronze Star — 1/Lt. Frank W. Rhea
Bronze Star — 2/Lt. John K. Brenna
Bronze Star — Sgt. Jean B. Miller
Bronze Star — Cpl. Isaac O. McDonald
Bronze Star — T/5 Vincent J. Consiglio
Bronze Star — T/5 Herbert F. Helgerson
Bronze Star — Pfc. John F. Iles
Bronze Star — Pfc. Camillo a Bosco
Bronze Star — Captain Lloyd B. Sheetz

[I quote in full the Award of the Silver Star Medal Citation to Lieutenant Colonel David E. Pergrin:

Lieutenant Colonel David E. Pergrin, 0388317, 291st Engineer Combat Battalion, United States Army, is awarded the Silver Star for gallantry in action against an enemy of the United States on 24 December 1944, in Belgium. When the town of Malmédy was bombed, causing many fires and panic among the civilian population, Colonel Pergrin assumed the responsibility for fire control, clearing streets of debris, and recovery of entrapped civilian and military personnel. While in the execution of his duties, Colonel Pergrin was wounded by an exploding bomb. Instead of seeking the comparative safety of an aid station, Colonel Pergrin elected to disregard his wounds and with complete disregard for his personal safety, gallantly continued to expose himself in the performance of his duties, despite the fact that airplanes were still overhead. When the streets were at last cleared of debris and it was seen that the fires would be under control, he departed for the aid station for medical treatment. After receiving succor, he immediately returned to the town and worked tirelessly without sleep for twenty-four hours. The unselfish devotion to duty displayed by Colonel Pergrin reflects high credit on himself and the Armed Forces. Entered military service from Pennsylvania.

Signed: L. S. Hobbs
Major General — U.S. Army
Commanding 30th Infantry Division

For its action on the Amblève Line, the Malmédy–Stavelot–Trois Ponts–Werbomont area, the 291st received the Distinguished Unit Citation and the fourragère, the French Croix de Guerre Unit Citation.]

Liége—Hospital—Replacement Depot

Liége
Monday, Jan. 1, 1945

HOSPITAL again. Have been checked in but the doctor hasn't seen me yet. And durned if my ears haven't begun hurting. Started last night. Both are draining worse. This will fix me up good when the doctors look at them, but maybe it's best for me to get this over with once and for all. Two and a half months is a long time for an infection to hang on. This second go-round I'll try to be more patient. It seems pretty certain that they get better when I'm warm & dry, get worse when I'm exposed to the weather, wet feet & clothing & cold.

The hospital here is part of a civilian hospital. Army seems to have taken over one wing. There are four of us in this "ward." Myself, a fellow by the name of Gardner who is recovering from pneumonia, one Stearns, who has trench foot, and Webster, who has a kidney infection. Gardner is a tanker, was with 2nd Armored. Stearns is a dogface, a Pvt. from 99th Infantry. Webster is a Sgt. — a paratrooper with 82nd Airborne. None of us is wounded. Just a bunch of old crocks.

Webster is pretty cocky, as most paratroopers are. They are the apple of the brass's eye & the darlings of the press & most of them think that singlehandedly they are winning the war.

But I think he's a good joe. I'm a good listener & he's a big talker, so he's been holding forth. Right now he's bitching about the Bastogne deal because the 101st was sent there & the 82nd isn't getting as good a press as the 101st. He says the 82nd is fighting just as hard, having it just as rough, but the press has made a big deal out of Bastogne, especially since Gen McAuliffe said Nuts to the Kraut surrender ultimatum. I had to laugh, but I know how he feels. We think the 291st is the best Engineer outfit on the continent. I told him I thought the 82nd had covered itself with plenty of glory.

Webster made the jump in Normandy the night before D-day. He said that was the roughest deal he'd ever had. Said he got down all right but landed waist deep in the middle of a swamp. Had to cut all his equipment away to get out. Said he waded around in that damned swamp for hours & thought he never was going to find dry land. They had these little tin crickets to signal with and he said when he finally got out of that swamp he started popping his cricket. He'd lost his gun, ammo, his pack, everything he had — but he hung onto his cricket. Said he just went wandering around popping that damned cricket.

Then the Krauts heard him & opened up on him with a machine gun. He got so scared then he quit trying to find his group & hid in a hedgerow until daylight. Then right down the road he saw his Lieut. & two or three of the other boys. He joined them & they got themselves sorted out & squared around, located themselves from a road sign & finally made their way to their assembly area, about six miles away.

This was behind Utah Beach & by that time the invasion was on & the boys were wading ashore. But he said he was lucky at that. Some of the boys came down right in the middle of Ste. Mère Eglise & there were a bunch of Krauts there & the town was burning & the Krauts picked them off as fast as they drifted in.

Brother, he can have the 82nd Airborne & its headlines! I'll stick to the good old 291st. We may not make headlines but we don't have to jump either. Except from artillery fire & such.

And right now, from buzz bombs again. The Krauts were sending them over when I was here before, but nothing like they are now. They have been going over all morning, one right after the other. The boys say all you can do when you hear an engine konk out is roll out of bed & get under, fast. Everybody freezes when we hear one. Just freeze & sweat it out, then when it's gone over relax a little till the next one comes along. But the way they're throwing them in, you don't get much relief. Webster said, "You might just as well get used to it. They don't *ever* quit, day or night."

Well, I've got news for him. You don't ever get used to them. You don't ever get over being afraid. The first time you're scared to death in war & live through it you think, well, it won't be so bad next time. But it is. Every time you're scared is just like the first time & there's no such thing as getting used to it. It's always the same, *every* time, and just as bad.

Well — Happy New Year!

Tuesday, Jan. 2, 1945

I must be jinxed good. The doctor, a Capt. named Spring, examined my ears this morning. He said I wasn't supposed to be dismissed from the hospital in Paris, that the ear specialist there had recommended I be *reclassified* and put on *non-combat* duty! He said, "And right now I would have to agree with him. Your ears are in bad shape & if you neglect them now you might be deaf for life."

It hit me like a ton of bricks. Good Lord! To have to leave the outfit & be reclassified. I said, "Sir, I'd rather not be reclassified. I'd rather take my chances & stay with my own outfit."

He didn't say anything. Just walked over to the window & looked out for a little while. About that time a buzz bomb came over & we all froze until it had passed on. Then he said, "Well, we'll see what a little treatment does. We won't rush the cadence."

I said, "Do you have to follow the Paris doctor's suggestion, sir?"

He said, "No. I can make the decision." He grinned, then, & said, "How the hell did you get yourself hustled out of that Paris hospital so fast? You'd have been in a rear echelon outfit long before now if you hadn't got away."

I told him I didn't have anything to do with it. Some new doctor came around one morning & signed me out. Capt. Spring sort of snorted & said the guy got too big for his pants. Said he was probably some little veterinarian throwing his weight around. He said we'd see & after checking the other boys he left.

Gardner is still too sick to pay much attention to anything, but Stearns & Webster were listening while the Capt. talked to me. When he had gone Stearns said, "If you was a dogface, you'd jump at the chance to be reclassified. Boy, I wish I had your luck. If you'd been up in the lines when them Krauts commenced coming through, you wouldn't never want no more combat. It was hell, just hell, that's all."

I didn't say anything, for I know it must have been. And I know the infantry have it the roughest of anybody. But Stearns kept on grumbling until Webster got fed up & told him to shut up. Said, "Don't think you're the only one who's had it rough. All of us have, one time or another. Giles is right to want to stick with his own outfit. So do I. If this thing I've got doesn't turn out to be a kidney stone & I don't have to be operated on, I'll be heading back to my outfit & glad to."

Stearns said, "I'd trade for your kidney infection, too. All I got is a lousy case of trench foot & first thing you know they'll have me back up in the damned line in a foxhole again."

I was beginning to steam a little with him acting as if he was the only one ever had to live in a foxhole. I know we don't have to go out & face cold steel, but by God we haven't had an easy war. So I told him a few things. He said, "Yeah, but you get to live in houses, back from the front. You can sleep good."

That really browned me off. "Twice," I told him, "twice since we landed in France have I slept in a house. It's been dogtents the rest of the time." I also, since I'd got started, told him I'd heard the 99th had a damned good rest area they could go back to every few days. We haven't had that first rest since the day we landed. A few days between jobs before we moved on, yes, but never once sent back into a real rest area.

He shut up, then. Flounced over in bed & turned his back on us. Webster looked at me & shrugged & motioned outside. We are both walking cases & can come & go. Went down to the dayroom. Webster said, "I'm glad you told him off. He's done nothing but bitch since he got here."

I asked how long he'd been here. Webster said, "Three days & if I have to listen to much more of his crap I'm gonna try to get him transferred out of our ward. He'll drive you nuts."

We both wrote letters, then came back up to the room. And I have now read J's letter for Sept. 15th. It's a real temptation to cut loose & read them all, but I won't. This new development may mean months before I have any more mail. I pray this treatment works. I mean I'm *really* praying. I don't think I could take having to finish out the war away from the outfit. Oh, you can do anything you have to do. I didn't think I could go two months without mail, but I did. But I sure as hell don't want to be reclassified & mean to do all I can not to be.

Wednesday, Jan. 3, 1945

The Capt. is really working on my ears. He cleans them every morning, puts drops in them & he is also giving me three or four different kinds of pills to take. He won't say yet how they're doing, whether they're improving, but I can tell myself they're some better. The drainage is slowing up already. They hurt a little when the medicine wears off, but not much.

Buzz bombs! One just now konked out & hit some place awfully close. Shook all the windows. All of us but Gardner rolled under the beds when the thing konked out. After the explosion & we'd crawled out we sort of laughed at how silly we looked lying all scrooched up under the beds. But, man, that one was close.

I remember reading in S & S once that Gen. Eisenhower said he was glad when he could get to France. The buzz bombs in England were making a nervous wreck of him. Me, too. We counted this morning & 47 went over in three hours. Only this last one konked out in the area, but one is too many.

Webster's pus count is better & he's not having so much pain. So he is more hopeful, too. Stearns still bitching. About the food here now. It's damned good food & he ought to be grateful for it. He *must* have been on K-rations or a line company's slop long enough for this to taste wonderful. He's just a born bitcher.

He laughs at us for freezing when the doodlebugs go over. Says if we'd taken Kraut artillery they wouldn't sound so bad to us. We both have taken Kraut artillery & plenty of it. But I've decided to ignore him. I notice he rolled out of that bed as fast as we did when that one quit a while ago. I'm glad his feet are getting better. Maybe they'll sign him out before long. He gets tedious. But he scratches at his feet all the time. Webster says he's trying to infect them so he can stay in the hospital. Maybe so. I wouldn't put it past him.

The next letter from Janice was Oct. 2nd. And finally I know where Nash was sent — Italy. He's with the 15th Air Corps. J. says every time the newspapers mention a strike by the 15th, with six, eight or ten Liberators missing, Libby gets panicky. Said she finally sat her down & told her Nash did not fly every mission the 15th flew & since she has no way of know‑ ing when he flies, why not quit looking at the headlines. But poor kid. She knows damn well & good he has to fly 50 before he can go home. But that was two months ago. By now he's worked off a lot of them.

Been catching up on my reading a little. The Red Cross has some fairly new magazines — *Time, Newsweek, Sat. Eve. Post, Esquire,* etc. Webster reads a lot, too. He also likes crosswords, but we haven't been able to find any yet.

Thursday, Jan. 4, 1945

Still sweating out the Capt's decision. He won't say yet. But there isn't a bit of drainage today & there's been no pain. I was proud to tell him that. He just grinned. He's a good joe. Big, heavy guy, about 40 I'd say, with a nose that's squashed all over his face. It sure has been broken at some time. He also walks with quite a limp. I asked Webster if he knew why. He said, "Hell, he got hit in Italy. Nearly lost his leg. They say he's still got a silver plate in his hip." One of the nurses told Webster. He was evacuated to England & Webster says the nurse told him the Capt. could have gone home for good, got out for keeps, but he wouldn't. Soon as he could use his leg he asked for another assignment & was sent to France. The nurses are really crazy about him. I don't mean in a sexy way, but as a doctor. He goes over & helps with the civilians, too, they say. Always has time to help & they say he's the best they ever saw with children. Tells them funny stories & takes them candy, etc. He's a swell fellow.

Webster & I have been talking about the offensive. S & S told of it today. Finally, *we* are on the offensive. Kicked off yesterday. This soon they don't give the positions of any of the outfits, so we don't know. But, just kidding, Webster said, "Now if you & I were there, Giles, *you* would be clearing my road & building *my* bridge for me."

I decided I knew him well enough by now that this was a good time to have some fun with him. As if I'd just thought of it, I said, "Webster, I believe it was my outfit you boys relieved at Werbomont."

He said, "I didn't know we relieved anybody. Who was 291st attached to?"

I said, "Nobody. Just Company A, 291st Engineers."

"Company!"

"Well," I said, "almost the Company. There were parts of 2nd and 3rd platoons there." I said, "Of course, most of 1st platoon had their hands full down at Trois Ponts. But their 2nd squad was helping out down at St. Vith." I went on, "And of course, 1st squad of my platoon were in Malmédy with the Battalion. All our guns & gunners were in Malmédy & all our bazookas & ammo."

"Oh, hell," he said, "I thought you meant it."

"I do," I said.

"Now, listen, Giles, don't try to tell me that two or three platoons held Werbomont till we got there."

"That's what they did, though."

"What with, for God's sake?"

"Guts. And blowing a few bridges — and laying mine traps."

He studied a minute or two. "Well," he said, finally, "somebody did blow the bridge there . . ."

I said, "Oh, don't feel bad about it Webster. In the 291st we consider one squad equal to a platoon in any other branch of the service. One of our platoons is equal to a Company, & any of our Companies is equal to a full Battalion with any other outfit."

He goggled a minute, then threw a pillow at me. But he wanted to know the whole story & as best as I could, from what I heard from the boys, I told him. And it lacks a lot of being the whole story. He just shook his head. "My God! A little squad here & a little squad there, laying mines, having the guts to stick & turn a key & blow a bridge with Kraut tanks & infantry firing on 'em. I dunno . . . I dunno. I believe I'd be running yet."

I thought he had been roasted enough, so turned it off. "You didn't run in Normandy, did you?"

"Well . . . no."

We went back to our magazines for a while, but finally Webster put his down. He said, "You know, Giles, I guess you had a lot of the same indoctrination we had — you know, about *esprit de corps,* & all that crap. But that damned outfit of yours . . ."

I laughed. Said, "Hell, we invented it. We had to. We're a bastard outfit. We don't have a patch except the big "A." We're all we've got. Just the 291st."

"Well, by God," he said, "in my book, you're all you need!"

But by that time I was beginning to feel like a durned preacher so I switched the talk back to the offensive.

The weather is miserable for it. There's a blowing snowstorm today. And it must be pure living hell to be out in it. And the boys probably are — probably working on bridges right now, for they had to blow all of them to stop the Krauts.

Stearns won't even look at a S & S. Says he doesn't want to read about the war or hear about it or think about it. And he wishes we'd shut up about it. He's the biggest grouch I ever was around & he has absolutely no sense of humor. Nothing ever strikes him as funny. The buzz bombs are worse than ever

& one hit right out in the courtyard this morning, tore a hell of a hole in it & one of our window panes cracked. Lt. Gregg, our floor nurse, was in the room at the time & she ducked, just like the rest of us, under a bed.

Happened she dived under my bed with me. When we crawled out, she sort of shook herself down & hitched up her slacks & said, "Well, I've lived in hopes of going to bed with a man, but not *under* one." Webster & I went into convulsions & she laughed as hard as we did. She's an old maid, homely as they come, with buck teeth, freckles all over her face, rough red hair, & I don't suppose a man ever made a pass at her. The way she said it & the way she looked was the funniest thing I ever saw. Stearns didn't even crack a smile. She looked over at him & said, "What's eating *you* today?"

He said his feet hurt. She said, "Sure they do. But you'll do no more clawing on 'em. I've got 'em tied up with a running bowline, my friend, & I'd just like to see you get that undone."

He began cussing & she told him to shut up or she'd dose him with castor oil. Just the same she got some aspirin for the pain.

I asked her where she ever heard of a running bowline. We are taught knots & hitches, etc. for building pontoon bridges. She said her kid brother was in the Navy & when he was in boot camp he was always writing home about such things. When he came home for a visit one time she made him teach her a few.

Read J's letter for Oct. 4th. She has got a real thing about that fireplace. Well, she can have one. If I'm able to buy the Old Place from Dad, that house already has one. I grew up there & used to dress every morning on the hearth. Last time I was home I walked over there & looked at the house. Didn't think that one day I'd want it for my own. But it's what I want the most now. Dad was storing hay in the house but it was still in pretty good shape. Wouldn't take much to fix it up.

Webster isn't married but he has a limey girl he's pretty crazy about. Thinks they may marry. We have done what all G.I.s do — showed our pictures, talked about our girls. He writes to his girl every day, too. He's wanting some mail bad. Envies me my stack of letters, but says he couldn't ration them the way I'm doing. I told him he could if he had gone without as long as I did once & might have to again.

Friday, Jan. 5, 1945

Ears still doing O.K. if that means anything. Capt. still saying nothing.

Stearns was moved this morning. Lieut. Gregg did it. I think she knew he was steaming us. We asked her where he went. She said in a room with a bunch of others with trench foot. Said they could all bitch together. I must say it's a real relief to have him gone. Webster is a swell fellow & Gardner is O.K. But he's a quiet boy anytime & he is still having enough fever to make him feel bad.

Lt. Gregg gave me the money to have my hair cut this morning. I'd just had a shower & put on clean pajamas when she came in. It's been over two months since my hair was cut — nearly three, in fact. I was combing it & Lieut. Gregg said, teasing, "Why don't you braid it & tie it with ribbons?"

I laughed & said, "If my pay ever catches up with me I'll have it cut."

She said, "How long since you got paid?"

Told her I got $3 in November. Hadn't had a real pay since Oct. She didn't say anything. Left the room & in a minute she came back with the price of a haircut. Said the Red Cross had an emergency fund for such things. But Webster & I think she went no further than her own purse. Webster was kidding me. Said I had her snowed. I haven't. She's just as good to all the boys.

She may bawl hell out of 'em, if they're like Stearns, but she doesn't ever neglect them.

She found us something more to read today, too. Three pocketbooks. Webster has started on the murder mystery & I've begun *Cannery Row*. The other is a collection of short stories. Also she found us a N.Y. *Times* crossword & man, is it ever a stinker! Don't think the two of us together can crack it. You forget the crossword vocabulary unless you work at them regularly.

Read J's letter for Oct. 6th. She said it was a wonderful, wonderful day. Then she told how hard it was raining & blowing. But she had eight letters. When she's happy her letters almost shine with it.

Sunday, Jan. 7, 1945

Capt. Spring still doesn't say anything. My ears are doing fine, though. No pain. No drainage. So, I'm hoping. But every time he comes in I start sweating. Feel a little bit as if I were walking on eggs, but maybe none of them will crack under me.

They have church here in the hospital chapel on Sundays. Webster wanted to go, so I went with him. This hospital is run by the Catholics & I guess they had mass earlier, but the Protestant chaplain uses the chapel, too. First time I've been to church since England. No, I went to mass that time in Luxembourg with LaCoste. Anyway, it made me think of how we all went every chance we had just before we shipped out at Southampton. Webster said they did, too. Before they made the drop in Normandy. Said everybody went.

Gardner is feeling a little better today, talking a little & by george, he's from Buechel, Kentucky, which is practically a suburb of Louisville. Told him J. lived in Louisville & he asked where. When I told him he said, "I know exactly where Hepburn Avenue is — just off Bardstown Road."

I told him she caught the bus to work every morning at Bardstown Road & Highland.

He said, "That's the Broadway bus. I used to ride it to work myself. My dad used to drive me to the end of the bus line & I'd be the first one on. By the time we got to Bardstown & Highland, though, it would be filled up."

I told him she had said she had to stand most of the time. It's a very curious coincidence — that here, right in the room with me, is a boy who has maybe even seen Janice. Seen her get on the same bus. It's given me a queer feeling — good, but strange — of what a really small world it is.

We talk a lot about the offensive. It's going mighty damned slow. Those Krauts aren't giving up an inch without fighting for it. They aren't turning & running this time. We get the S & S here the same day it is published for it's published in Liége. The front is 25 miles long in a kind of half circle. 82nd Airborne seems to be pretty much in the middle, attacking back down through Trois Ponts & Werbomont. There's no way I can know where the 291st is, but I would guess along in the same area. And the weather couldn't be worse. Cold, blowing, sleeting & snowing. I don't think I ever saw more snow than there's been in Belgium this winter. It's a bitch, taking all this back from the Krauts. When you think we had it, and had it for such a long time, then have to slog back over it, it makes you sick.[1]

Webster & I still plugging away on the *Times* crossword. Get about a dozen words a day.

Read J's letter for Oct. 7th. She says Nash is not too impressed with what he's seen of Italy. Says there may be other

---

[1] During the month-long offensive drive to rid Belgium of German troops, the 291st was under the XVIII Airborne Corps, General Matthew Ridgeway commanding. At various times it was supporting 78th Infantry, 30th Infantry, 82nd Airborne, all of whom, and for purposes of the offensive only, came under General Ridgeway's command at the time.

parts of it in better shape but where he is the land is poor and the people are poor & ignorant.[2]

I don't think many of us are impressed with what we've seen overseas. There's just no place as good as the U.S.A. War is a poor time for appreciating a foreign country, I know. Most of the time you don't even see it. Either you're too scared or too tired. But I know one thing. I've had all of it I want. When I get home I don't ever want to see Europe again & I doubt if I'll ever want to leave Kentucky again. And the way these buzz bombs keep zooming around over us all the time I'm beginning to wonder if I'll ever get back to Kentucky.

Another one konked out in the area this morning. Right across the street. A bunch of civilians were killed & many more injured. The civilian wing of the hospital was pretty busy for a while.

And you can tell we're taking casualties in the battles. Our wing is so full it's overflowing & even the halls are full. We have a new man in with us in the last hour. Been operated on for a bad leg wound. He was out when they brought him in. Still is, for that matter. But Lt. Gregg asked us to keep an eye on him. Said when the anesthetic began to wear off he might get restless & if he did, call her. A while ago, I thought he was dead. He's so still & white. Told Webster & we checked. He was breathing but so lightly we had to stand over to make sure. We wondered if we ought to find Lt. Gregg. Decided not to. She's having the legs run off her & as long as he's breathing he must surely be O.K.

Later: He died. He never did get restless & he never did come out of the anesthetic. But all at once he began to struggle for breath. Webster went running for Lt. Gregg while I stayed with him. I didn't have the least idea what to do for him, but thought maybe if I'd hold his head up, it would help. Thank

2 Lt. Nash Hancock was near Taranto, in the bootheel of Italy.

God, Lt. Gregg got here & the doctor. It's an awful thing to watch a man die. Like the coward I am I wanted to run away. But they needed us, so I held the plasma bottle while Lt. Gregg worked with him & the doctor was injecting something else. I never saw two people work harder or faster. But he was too far gone. When it was over, Lt. Gregg turned around & I could see she was crying. I couldn't believe he was gone. Stupid like, I said, "Is that all?" She turned on me like I had caused it & yelled, "Goddammit it to hell, yes, that's all! That's all for one more poor sonofabitch!"

When they rolled him out, it left an awfully empty place.

Monday, Jan. 8, 1945

Today has been a real sweat, a real sweat. Capt. came in this morning & studied my chart. Every day when he does that I hold my breath. He put the chart down finally & said, "Well, Giles, how are the ears today?"

I told him they were fine.

He said, "I have to decide about you today, one way or the other." I figured it, for there was something different in the way he asked me. So my pulse started racing. I thought, here it comes. He didn't say anything more for a while. Began pacing the floor. He's a floor pacer when he's thinking. Back & forth, back & forth, & I just sat there & sweated.

Finally he stopped & looked at me right straight & said, "You *ought* to be reclassified. Your ears are in good enough shape right now, but this condition is chronic. It's going to bother you every time you're exposed to bad weather. You have no business in a combat outfit."

I asked if I could say something then. He told me to go ahead. So I told him my side of it. The picture as I saw it. I had it all worked out, just what to say when this came up. I told him that reclassifying me wouldn't guarantee I'd be in out of the weather. I might draw just as rough an assignment as far as housing was concerned in the rear. I also might draw rougher work. I told him I had been Weapon Sgt. with my outfit for two years — they were all my friends. They would do anything to help me. A new outfit wouldn't. I said I thought I had a better chance of taking good care of myself with my own outfit than any other way. I also said since replacements were so short I thought, if I was physically able at all, I ought to be where I could do the most good. I could do it with my own outfit, but I might just be a useless Sgt. some place else.

Well, he quit pacing around to listen to me & he really did listen. He didn't take his eyes off me while I was talking & I could tell he was hearing every word I said & I could tell he knew I meant it & there was truth in it. I had it all worked out, but so much was riding on it I was sort of rushing the cadence along toward the last & a little out of breath.

When I got through, he began pacing again. It seemed to me an hour before he made up his mind. I looked over at Webster, who was pretending to be reading an S & S & he winked at me. I took it to mean he thought I'd done all right. Suddenly the Capt. turned around & laughed & said, "All right, you win. I'm going to let you go back to your outfit. But," he said, "by God if you lose your hearing & ever put in for a service-connected disability, don't ask me to certify you, for I won't."

Damned if I didn't get tears in my eyes. Couldn't help it. He saw them & gave my shoulder a punch & said, "Hell, kid, we need your bed. We'll get you started out of here tomorrow."

I asked if I had to go back through the repple depple system. He said I would. Said there wasn't anything he could do about that. But I don't mind it as much as I did the last time. I know what Capt. Gamble said. And Capt. Spring needn't worry. If I go deaf he can be damned sure I'll never put in for a service-connected pension.[3]

When he left, Webster & Gardner both said they wanted to shake hands with me. Said I'd make a good lawyer. Webster said, "Damned if I didn't almost cry myself."

I hope he makes it next. He's a grand fellow & they're pretty sure now he doesn't have a kidney stone.

Gardner has a long way to go yet. He's still running a slow fever & Webster thinks he has T.B. Well, that would be a hell of a way to do it, but if he does have T.B. it will sure send him back to the States & out of the war.

Lieut. Gregg came in to have a look at another new fellow we got this morning & I told her I made it. She grinned all over her face & said, "I suppose you know what a damned fool you are. Had a good chance for a nice cushy job at the rear & fouled it up. Got to go back to your blasted engineers & freeze your damned ass off. But I love you!" And durned if she didn't give me a big hug and kiss. I love her, too — in the nicest way there is. She's one swell fellow, too.

Replacement Depot
Thursday, Jan. 11, 1945

Back in the same old replacement depot but in the other wing this time. Last time I was in the east wing on the second floor — this time in the west wing on 3rd floor.

Sort of hated to tell Webster & Gardner goodbye. We wished each other well, said good luck & all that. Then Webster grinned & said, "See you on the Rhine, boy. Maybe you can build me a bridge across that one." I told him not if I could help it. They could build their own across that one.

---

[3] To this day Henry Giles has trouble with his ears, but he is not deaf. To this day, also, he has never put in for a service-connected disability.

Couldn't find Lt. Gregg to tell her goodbye. But there was a note pinned to my B. bag. "You owe me a beer in Berlin. Good luck, you idiot!"

Capt. Spring gave me a little advice. Told me to try to keep my ears protected. Wrap a scarf or something around my head. And he gave me a big box of aspirins. Grinned when he did & said, "This is so if they begin hurting you won't have to report to the Medics." Those people were wonderful to me & I won't forget it. A guy is lucky to be sent to that hospital. They make you feel like you're important & somebody.

The place here is just the same. Same old dayroom I spent so many miserable hours in — even many of the same guys. White is still here, but Hessler is gone. Asked White if he had a roommate. Said he did but there was room for me if I wanted to come in with them. I asked the 1/Sgt. about it & he said, "Hell, I thought we were rid of you. I don't give a damn where you stay. Just make yourself at home, buddy." Nothing about the way they treat you has changed here, either.

White took me up to dump my stuff & I met his roommate — his name is Craig & of all things he was a nightclub singer back in the States. Said he didn't mind if I moved in with them. He is a good looking fellow. Guess in show business they have to be. I asked him why he wasn't in Special Services. He laughed. Said, "You ever know the army to put a guy where he belongs?"

I asked White about him later & he grinned. "He's a cook. And his own cooking give him the G.I.s so bad he had to go to the hospital." Well, that adds up. Then White said, "Boy, I sure am glad to see you back. Maybe my girl will get some decent letters now. That Craig can't think of a damned thing to say." White is the fellow from eastern Kentucky I wrote letters for before — so here I go again.

The buzz bombs are still with us, worse if anything. I'd

like to be with the outfit that finds their launching site. It would be a pleasure to wire it for detonation. The thing about these things is, they keep you all tensed up for so long waiting to see if they're going to quit. You never know & each one you hear may be the one that blows you to hell and gone.

Wrote First Sarge the first thing, but with this offensive the boys are pretty busy, I know. May take a little longer to send for me than we thought. But they'll know where I am, anyway.

Saturday, Jan. 13, 1945

Feel bad from lack of sleep. Buzz bombs worse than ever. Didn't sleep more than two hours last night & not much sleep for three nights. The damned Krauts have gone crazy. Seems as if being stopped in their big push they've just cut loose to do all the damage they can wherever they can. Two of the bombs have landed in the area this morning — one down the street & the other right in the courtyard. That one shook the building & blew out some window panes, one of ours among them. We've hung a blanket over it. All we can do is what we did in the hospital — roll under the bed when one konks out. I sure wish their supply of those things would run out.

Craig has a pleasant voice, but not what I'd call a great one. Sometimes he sings for us. But he's a moody cuss & often won't. Says he's just not in the mood. He spends a lot of time in the sack. That's O.K. as long as he does his part keeping the joint policed up, but he's lazy & dirty. Always opening a can of hash or unwrapping a candy bar & throwing the litter under his bunk. He skips his turn going after coal, too. It's down in the basement, which means four flights to haul it up. I asked White if he'd always been this way & he said more or less. White is very neat, clean & organized, but it's not right for him to do Craig's work, too.

Today it was Craig's turn to go after the coal & the fire

was dying down & he just lay there in the sack. White picked up the bucket, but I told him to put it down. Went over & shook Craig, told him it was his turn to take care of the fire. He sort of yawned himself awake & got up & went after the coal. Didn't argue about it at all. White laughed & said, "Guess he has to have a Sgt. make him work."

Craig makes fun of White behind his back. Mocks the way he talks. Says he's the most ignorant man he ever saw. Depends what you mean by ignorance. White can take care of himself & he's a damned good infantryman. He made expert[4] with no trouble & he told me one time he had eight notches on his gun stock. That is eight Krauts that rifle has accounted for. The best Craig could do was end up cooking.

When I was here before I asked White about making expert. He just laughed about it. Said, "Hell, Sgt. Giles, them big targets the army uses was duck soup to us old country boys. I was raised up & guess you was, too, with a squirrel's eye for a target."

Well, not quite. I'm not that good & never was. I can usually hit the head but not always dead center. Dad can, but he's always been a better shot than I. Last time I was home on furlough we went squirrel hunting together. He brought down six to my four & all his were clean. I had one gut shot in mine. Dad laughed & said, "Son, the army's ruining your shooting eye."

White owns his own place back home, too. Has a nice little farm there. Doesn't have to take a thing off anybody. Craig makes so much of his nightclub singing but I'd bet my last dollar it was in joints & dumps. Nearly all city guys think a country boy is an ignorant hillbilly. But some of the most ignorant cusses I've run into in the army have been guys from Brooklyn & the Bronx & some of the other eastern big cities. What White does to the English language is pure compared to what

4 Expert marksman.

some of them do. Craig himself says "Joisey." Says he used to sing in a club over in Joisey. Ah, what the hell. It takes all kinds.

Have laughed over J's last letter — Oct. 13th. Between Libby & the war I'll say one thing, she sure never has time to be bored. Seems Libby is about to be dishonorably discharged from the *army!* She heard something about civilian air patrol. She thought it had something to do with plane spotting or some other civilian air guard. Signed up for it, then found it was really civilians flying patrol. So, she just dropped it. Didn't even know it had anything to do with the army. Now, it's taking all kinds of credentials & witnesses to prove she never was sworn in, never belonged and can't be "dishonorably discharged" from something she never belonged to!

Wednesday, Jan. 17, 1945

Snow & more snow & more snow. It's done very little but snow all this winter. The offensive seems to be picking up, though, in spite of it. S & S reports the 1st & 3rd armies have joined up at Houffalize pinching off a pocket of 15,000 Krauts. And the Russians have opened an offensive on their front — driving toward the Vistula. That should take some of the heat off the western front. Our armies are driving toward St. Vith, now. I watch for news about XVIII Airborne Corps. Because of the sector I believe the outfit is with them.

Just had a hell of a surprise. One of the Sgts. came through the dayroom where I'm writing calling my name. When I answered he told me I was on KP tomorrow. Well, the day an NCO has to do KP hasn't come yet, so I knew he was kidding. He had two letters for me from Janice, written last November & addressed to this depot. Maybe some of the others will begin to show up, now.

Later: Just at that point there was a hell of an explosion &

the whole building shivered & shook. Some of the windows began shattering & falling & everybody flattened to the floor. Terrified. I thought the roof would start falling any minute & some plaster did crack & fall. It was a sickening feeling.

When it was over & we got up, White said, "Listen, if my outfit don't come git me pretty soon I'm going AWOL back to it. There ain't nothing up front any worse than these damn buzz bombs." I believe it.

One of the Sgts. came in after a while & said the front end of the east wing had taken a direct hit. He said nobody in the building was killed, but one man was pretty bad hurt. Worst, though, some civilians were passing & a little girl was killed. Some of the fellows went out to see her, but I didn't want to. They said half her head was blown off. Her father & mother were injured, but she was the one who was killed. Maybe they had to go some place, maybe they didn't have anyone to leave her with, but it's a terrible thing for little kids, who don't know what it's all about & have had nothing to do with the war, to have to get killed because of it. Well, some things you just have to put out of your mind. There's nothing you can do about it.

When White & I went upstairs Craig was still rolled in a ball under his bed. The floor was covered with loose plaster & one big chunk was in the middle of my bed. Makes you wonder how long the law of averages is going to work in your favor.

Nothing to do but sweat.

Saturday, Jan. 20, 1945

Saturday. That was the night, back in Texas, everybody used to come charging into the barracks headed for showers. "Lend me a tie, somebody."

"Anybody got any shoe polish?"

"I need another buck. Somebody loan me a buck."

"Hell, I've not got a clean shirt. Who's got a shirt my size?"

Hubba, hubba, hubba. Everybody off to town & a fine time. Just another night, now.

Holbrook was the one who never had a clean shirt. He's still much on my mind & it depresses me to think he's gone. The first of 2nd platoon to get it. They said they thought that morning all the Krauts in Belgium had hit them in Malmédy, it was so rough. And for a while they thought their goose was cooked. They got it the roughest on the west side of town where Holbrook was positioned.

When we were in Marle, where the French kids came around the area all the time, someone took a picture of several of us with some of the kids. When it came, I sent it to Janice. Holbrook was in the picture, a little boy squatting between his knees. I hope she has kept the picture.[5] Nobody could know then that Holbrook had only three more months to live. It was a good war, then, & we thought it would all be over by Christmas. He didn't get to live till Christmas.

I remember the afternoon he & Black Mac & I went out scrounging for eggs — rounded up a couple dozen. Holbrook was a big guy & needed a lot of food. But he wouldn't take but his part. I would guess that he or Mac either could have eaten the whole lot & not felt too full.

I've got to quit thinking about him, too. It doesn't bring him back & doesn't do me any good.

Pulled guard last night & it was colder than frozen hell. Snow is at least two feet deep & you walk in a kind of trench through it. Two on & four off, but that two hours can seem like all night. The wind was blowing a gale, too, last night. Goes right through your overcoat & all your clothes. Makes it bitter. Hands cold through my gloves.

[5] The picture was kept. It has even sadder memories, for a later casualty was also in the group.

Wednesday, Jan. 24, 1945

Craig's outfit came for him today. He'd just as soon they hadn't. He's been warm here & although he's scared to death of the buzz bombs he's had plenty of sack time. Was complaining while he was getting his stuff together that he was taking cold & didn't have any handkerchiefs. Gave him two of mine.

I've been wishing like hell the outfit would send for me, but I know they're having it rough. Just to be sure they don't forget, though, I wrote First Sarge again today.

First Sarge. Only time I ever feel like I get anything on him is on payday. Regular army gets paid first. He has a rubber face & he always looked so pained. "Sgt. McCarl!" — "Sgt. Love!" — "Sgt. Giles!" Then he comes next. He always does it the same way, with that disgusted look on his face, but there's nothing he can do about it. Regulations. Old army men come first on payday.

Today's S & S says 1st Army gained *three* miles yesterday. Last summer they sometimes moved fifty miles! But the news is better all the way around. Krauts are beginning to retreat in big batches now, Air Corps strafing whole columns stuck on the roads. Boys are flying in this clear weather & really getting in some good knocks. The Russians are only 165 miles from Berlin. Adolf had better begin to worry, but good.

Only had three of the 27 letters left, so today read them all. She was definitely going down home for Thanksgiving. Thanksgiving! My God, when was that?

Monday, Jan. 29, 1945

White & I were sitting in the dayroom today talking about the 30th Inf. advance (that's his outfit) when damned if his Company Clerk didn't walk in. I sure was glad for the fellow. He has been right here in this depot since last October. Almost four months his platoon has done without him when he could have been with them all the time. Sure is a hell of a system.

S & S is full of good news tonight. The headlines are: Bulge is gone. 3rd Army has retaken most of Luxembourg. St. Vith has been retaken & the Krauts are running hard to get back into Germany. The British & 9th armies up north are back to the Roer River. Six weeks & a lot of good men lost & we're back where we were on December 16th.

Also big story about arctic-tested clothing going to joes at front. Article says Arctic shoe pacs, socks, mittens, mufflers & ponchos will be issued. It's about time. Especially with the shoes. The ones we wear now leak like a sieve. And they say wet feet is what causes trench foot. We had wet feet even back in October in the mud. If they could have gotten this winter clothing up to us then, when it was beginning to be needed, maybe there wouldn't have been so much trench foot. I read some time ago where there were over 12,000 cases in 1st Army alone. I predict, however, we'll get this winter clothing about next summer.

Played Bingo tonight. Red Cross got it up. Gave pies & cakes for prizes. Didn't win anything but it was a way of passing some time.

near St. Vith

Wednesday, Jan. 31, 1945

Back with the outfit again. The Capt. sent Joe Willis for me.[6] Never was as glad to see anybody & think this time I have it made.

I can sure understand a little better why they couldn't come sooner. They have been in support of 30th Inf. most of the time & they have moved pretty far forward since I saw them

6 T/4 Joe Willis, H/S platoon.

last — back down through Trois Ponts, Malmédy, Spa, back to Hockai & Poteau, etc. Even Amblève where they almost got it when the Krauts first broke through. They've been building fixed & Baileys right back over the same creeks & rivers they bridged earlier, then had to blow them. And they've had a hell of a hard January.

Snow, ice, sleet, rain, wind, cold! Out in it all the time. My God! They all look ten years older & ten years dirtier & ten years tireder. But this is the best damned outfit in the whole ETO. They all came around today to shake hands & say, "Glad to see you back." "Good to see you again." "Hope your ears are O.K. now." Black Mac, LaCoste, Billington, Pigg, Cornes, Bossert, Chapin, Schommer — everybody. And, by george, Jeff Elliott is back with the platoon — driving 2nd squad's truck.

You could never forget a bunch of fellows like these in Company A. I have been in a good many outfits in my time & known a lot of fellows, but none have I liked more than the boys here — officers & men alike. Capt. Gamble even stopped to shake hands & say he was glad I was back. Coming back was just like coming home. I'm back where I belong & where, if it hadn't been for that damned replacement depot system, I could have been a long time ago.

Riding down here yesterday gave me some idea of what it's been like. The whole countryside is frozen, drifts two & three feet deep, but burned out tanks, halftracks, jeeps, every kind of vehicle are everywhere & most of the villages are nothing but rubble. We came through Malmédy & there's nothing there — nothing but walls & chimney stacks & ruin. That's what our own air force did. Willis showed me where Holbrook was killed. Then when we came through Baugnez he showed me where the massacre took place. Said they helped Graves Registration find the bodies which had been snowed under & frozen.

One thing — this offensive has been expensive to us, but I hope it has been the ruin of the Krauts. S & S says they lost 50,000 killed & wounded & 40,000 prisoners. Our losses were 40,000 killed & wounded, 18,000 missing. These figures released by the War Department but not final.[7]

The Bn. is holed up here waiting for the next assignment. It won't be long for they've been here several days.

We didn't have very good facilities for laundry & bathing at the replacement depot & I was so cruddy I did a little laundry today. A suit of long johns, my socks & the fatigue jacket I've been wearing, more or less living in, for three months. Also boiled my white handkerchiefs with something that turned them green in spots. My socks, I suppose. Everybody is trying to get cleaned up a little. Much washing of bodies & clothing going on.

We're in houses here, or rather in cellars. Hq squad is in a hole in the ground under a bombed-out house — dirt floor, low ceiling — you can't stand up straight, but at least it's underground & with the Krauts still throwing 88s around it feels good.

Had a big laugh at one of the fellows today. I was telling a bunch of them about the buzz bombs in Liége. They've had a few but nothing like we got in Liége. Anyway, this fellow said, "Don't tell me nothing about them buzz bombs. I was on pass in Liége one time back in November. If you think you had it bad in the hospital & repple depple, man, you oughta have one of them things konk out on you in a whorehouse!" He went on in greater detail till he had us all rolling. He's a droll guy, anyway. The situation was too easy to imagine.

---

[7] Final and official casualties were: American losses, 76,890 men; 8607 killed; 47,139 wounded; 21,144 missing. German High Command estimates were: 81,834 casualties; 12,652 killed; 38,600 wounded; 30,582 missing.

Lanzerath, Belgium
Saturday, Feb. 3, 1945

Began moving the 1st in support of the 82nd Airborne — if you can call it support when the snow drifts are so deep our boys with the bulldozers had to go ahead & clear a road for them & the minesweepers had to go ahead of the bulldozers.

It's wonderful how much confidence it gives any outfit to have the minesweepers going ahead of them. I believe these paratroopers would feel a lot less nervous making a jump than they do convoying down a road that hasn't been cleared. And there were plenty of antitank mines on the shoulders of this road. The detectors would find them, then the boys would have to dig them out of the snow. Actually the anti-personnel mines, used mostly in mine fields, kill more men than these Regals. They explode in the air after you've stepped on the tripper and the charge is full of scraps of metal. You've usually had it or else you've got half a face left, no eyes or no nose left. But none of them are pleasant.

Job here is to build a Bailey across the Our River for the 82nd. Have been thinking of Webster & wondering if he made it back to his group yet.

We're back under artillery fire again. Began to run into some incoming mail on the way up & just a few 88s drifting in sort of lazy like, hit or miss, as if the Krauts were just lobbing them over to keep in practice. But even *one* coming in makes you begin to squirm & wiggle.

It was cold riding up here yesterday. We finally got into the edge of this little burg & stopped in front of three or four farmhouses. Somebody said, "O.K. this is it."

We piled out & stood around till Pigg came over & said, "2nd platoon this way."

We went up the road a little way & then up a sort of driveway. 2nd and 3rd squads took the house across the driveway

& 1st & Hq took this one. The upper floor is wrecked but the lower floor is still all right. Five of us from Hq squad took a look at the cellar & decided that would be our home for the night. Some of the boys don't like cellars. And it's true if a house took a direct hit you could be buried. But a grave vault wouldn't give me claustrophobia when 88s are coming in.

We dumped our stuff down & looked around. The floor was dirt & muddy from seepage & thaw, so the first thing we did was go up on the second floor to find something to lay over the mud. We ripped some boards off the walls & found some big wide shelves in a closet & lugged them down. Told the other boys where to find them & we got to work & built ourselves a pretty dry floor. Pigg yelled down for somebody to come get his stuff. Said he had to go find 1/Sgt. & see if the kitchen was going to get set up. Hooks went up for it.[8]

Then we blacked out the windows with blankets, lit candles & were at home. Cold down here, though. Pigg came back pretty soon & yelled the kitchen wouldn't get set up. There is a stove in the kitchen of this house, so we got a fire to going & heated up our rations a little & ate. Sat around & talked a while, played a little poker, then I came on back down here to write.

Later: The damndest thing just happened. I have been constipated for three or four days but suddenly felt I might be successful if I went to the latrine. It was out back of the other house. It was quiet outside, nothing coming in, so all I dreaded was getting out in the cold again. Went through the kitchen where a poker game was still going on, but didn't say anything to anybody.

I went around & found the trench. Had just started letting my pants down when — zoom — here came one screaming in!

[8] T/4 Louis Kovacs, driver of Hq. platoon truck, on which Henry Giles' machine gun was mounted.

And it was going to be close. I flattened in the slush & as scared as I was that icy stuff sent a shock all over me. But I dug in my chin & hung on till the explosion was over. Could hear the shrapnel plunking all over the place.

There was a stone wall about six feet away & I thought if I could make that wall I'd be safer behind it. While it was quiet I got up & started to run. Forgot my pants were unbuttoned. Took three steps & they slid down around my ankles & acted just like the trip on a muskrat trap. I went down rolling like a ball. About that time another 88 came zooming in. I just lay there where I was & tried to squirm in as deep as I could.

I never did make it to that wall. Two more came in on the tail of the first two & I thought, my God, I've had it. There's no way out of this. Then there was an interval & I wondered if I could make it to the house before any more came over, but about that time I was the most unconstipated man you ever saw & 88s or no 88s had to cut loose. It would have been funny if I hadn't been so damned terrified.

Well, that was all of it. No more shells. Everything got quiet. I didn't bother to button up. Just hauled my pants up & made a bee line for the house. When I came inside, Pigg grabbed me & shook me — what for, I don't know. I was already shaking like a leaf. He just shook me & said, "Are you all right? Are you all right?"

I couldn't yet talk but I could nod I *was* all right. Then Black Mac came over & shook me. He looked mad as hell. He said, "Were you out in that stuff? My God, haven't you got any sense at all."

By that time I had some breath back. What I said doubled them all up, & it just came off the end of my tongue without thinking. I said, "Well, they don't furnish chamber pots in these dumps we stay in."

I was as wet as a river rat, of course, so I stripped down to my long johns & hung my clothes up to dry. Then came on down to finish writing. I was in the middle of a letter to Janice when I had to go. I looked at what I'd written & tried to make sense out of it. I'd been saying, "Tell Libby when I get back we'll . . ." I couldn't for the life of me think what it was I had been going to tell Libby we'd do. Just struck it out & started over.

Sometimes it strikes me as one of the oddest things in war that the people at home can't possibly have any idea what's going on sometimes when we write. And maybe best they don't, either.

Sunday, Feb. 4, 1945

This morning the bridge was sighted in, Company B began hauling up the sections & we started assembling & pushing. *It is going to be a bitch.* The river is 189 feet wide here & the chasm is 100 feet deep. The weather is lousy — snowing & blowing. And we have plenty of artillery fire. That's my idea of real T. S.[9] It's round the clock, boys, & don't spare the horses. Capt. Gamble the big boss.

Tired. No mail last night, but it came up tonight. Six letters from J. & one from home. The one from home has left me feeling depressed. It had the news that Dallas has been killed in the Pacific.[10] It's strange to think I'll never see him again. He has sort of been in the picture of good things when I get back to the ridge. We were in the same grade at school, the same age, we hunted & fished together, we had a muskrat line we used to run on freezing cold mornings. We even enlisted on the same day. Meant to stick together & both of us wanted Engineers. Dallas balked, though, when he learned we'd be sent to California. He didn't want to get that far from home.

9 G.I. term, untranslatable in polite English.
10 Dallas Badger, Knifley, Kentucky.

I liked the sound of California so we decided to go our separate ways. He drew Infantry, poor kid. Last time I saw him was just before he shipped out to the Pacific. He looked me up & we had a binge together in Paso Robles. I keep thinking how he didn't want to go to California because it was too far from home. He had to go a hell of a lot farther — & be killed there.

The weather couldn't be worse. Still a lot of old snow & ice & drifts & it keeps on blowing & snowing. And cold. My God! My idea of heaven is never to be cold again in all my life.

Tuesday, Feb. 6, 1945

Well, we did it, but it wasn't easy. This was mostly a Company A bridge, with some help from B. Capt. Gamble was in charge. It took all hands *but* the cooks & round the clock to get this one across on time. I worked on it the last day & night. It was a real killer — a double triple.[11]

Wonder who decided hell was fire & brimstone? It's not. It's hard-packed, slippery old snow, slush in the ruts, fog & drizzle & sleet, more snow, steel sections like ice through your gloves & hands so numb & frozen they don't have any feeling so that the bolts slip through your fingers & some damned section chief is cussing you out for dropping them. Shoes & overshoes that leak so that your feet, wet to begin with, get wetter, then they freeze till they have no feeling & you stumble carrying your part of a panel. It's 88s whizzing in now & then while you're hung out over a 100 ft. drop. That'll sure make you flinch & duck. Hell is *cold,* not fire.

I wish somebody, some day, would tell what a lot of damned hard work it is to build a Bailey under even the best conditions. I know they are a marvelous invention. And I know they help

---

[11] A double triple Bailey bridge was two panels thick and three panels high with a single-span treadway floor.

the war effort. But I'd like to boil Sir Henry Bailey in oil, myself, for ever inventing them.

You have to have enough sections to build two bridges to get one across. You have to build back on the bank to balance the weight you push forward. Assemble the panels, & every panel weighs a ton or two it seems. When you get a section assembled you either roll it back for weight or roll it forward for thrust. The balance changes constantly. You begin on the near bank & shove your sections across hanging them in midair, hinged onto the section that was hooked on before. And if you slip, there's a 100 foot drop waiting for you.

One end of this bridge is in Belgium, the other end in Germany. Well, the 82nd is crossing with dry feet. I thought about Webster again, but he'd be lost in a Division so there was no use looking for him. But I sure hope he made it back in time.

Pigg said the Lieut. told him there was an S & S reporter around for a while yesterday & that this is one 291st bridge that will get written up. That will be quite an experience for us. I don't think we've ever had that first line in S & S before. Engineers just work. They don't get credit.

Mail call. Seven letters from J. In one she said she was two-thirds through with her book. This is the first word I've had about how she was doing with it. She said it was the hardest work she ever did & she felt like a fool even trying to write a book, but having gone this far she meant to finish it. I don't know how she makes herself keep on with it, at night after a full day in the office. But that girl doesn't know the meaning of the word quit.

I'm forever losing my candles, so I've rigged up an electric candle. Took two flashlight batteries, about a foot of tape, six inches of copper wire, a bulb & rigged them up & it makes a pretty decent light — about like three candles. Hope this information doesn't get into enemy hands. Lieut. Hayes calls it "Giles' secret weapon."

Which reminds me of a joke going the rounds now. The Germans have tried V1 & V2, now they mean to try a new V weapon — V-quit. Only they haven't. We can't tell if they're even short on ammo.

Germany — 1945

From Walheim to Remagen

Walheim
Friday, Feb. 9, 1945

TODAY, moved here, into Germany. In support of the 78th Infantry. Don't know where they're headed, but it'll be hot, for this is all a hot front now. Still getting some 88s. Had two or three pretty days after we finished the bridge & before we were reassigned, but it's turned bad again. The warm days just made the melt & slush worse underfoot.

We're in houses here, but it's just a bivouac. Move on tomorrow. This is desolate country. We are in the middle of the Huertgen Forest. For a long time today we came through the battlefield — nothing but stumps of pine trees, limbs all blown off, upper halves splintered. You could sure tell there had been one hell of a battle. It was weird & spooky & gave you the creeps. I don't see how men ever fought in this mess. No wonder the 4th Inf. took 7,000 casualties.

Then we came out of the battlefield into a part of the forest that looked natural, but very gloomy. Big pines, wet & drippy & mud very foul underfoot. This village is right in the middle of it. Much fear of mines & booby traps.

We are also in the Siegfried Line. I was surprised when I saw the dragon's teeth. I have heard & read a lot about the

Siegfried Line. Back in England the people used to sing about hanging their washing on the Siegfried Line. I don't know what I really expected. Some kind of underground bunker system that would be practically impenetrable as near as I could tell. But these dragon's teeth are just columns of concrete & they really are in a line — as straight as if they'd been drawn up by string. But the Krauts had to leave roads between them for themselves. We came down through one of the roads to this dirty little town.

There is nobody in this village. Everyone has skedaddled. We have it all to ourselves.

This is the part of the war I have dreaded the most — being in Germany. I even dreaded crossing the border and knowing I was in Germany. But I don't remember now any special feeling when we did cross. I have always thought the Krauts would fight like devils for every inch of German soil — and in a way, they are. I dreaded this Siegfried Line. I still dread the Rhine. It stands to reason they have their backs to the wall & that lunatic Hitler will fight till the last German is dead before he gives up.

Have been talking to Schommer & Hooks tonight. They think, as I do, we have a lot of sweat ahead of us yet. We were wishing we had a bottle. Might be some in these cellars in the village but only the houses we are in have been cleared by the billeting boys. Nobody wants to risk looking. A bunch of wine bottles would be a good place for a booby trap.

Didn't think the mail would get up tonight but it did. Six letters for me, all of them recent, which I like. Nash is squadron leader now. Should think he would make Capt. pretty soon. He had more flying time than his Col. when he went overseas, but that doesn't seem to count. J. told a good story he wrote to Libby. Seems the air force boys, like all G.I.s, are always on the hunt for something to drink. There is a port city near their airfield with a lot of British ships. Nash & his crew made a deal with some of the British Navy boys. The British see to it that their boys have plenty to drink. Anyway, the merchant marine boys wanted very much to have some rides in a Liberator. Nash & his crew took them up in trade for a case of Scotch. They went aboard the ship to enjoy it. Very much of a good time was had by all. Next thing Nash knew he woke up on a British ship and for all he knew it was headed for sea. Said he came damned near joining the British merchant marine!

[The Battle of Huertgen Forest had been fought in November of 1944, in an effort to reach and put out of commission the two big dams, Schwammenuauel and Urfttalsperre, on the upper Roer River. Before the Battle of the Bulge, an all-out offensive across the Roer and toward the Rhine was being planned. These dams posed a threat to the Roer crossings. It was necessary for them to be in Allied hands or destroyed, to insure the lower river crossings of Ninth Army and the British offensive. At one time 28th Infantry actually reached the town of Schmidt, just above the dams, but were so battle weary they could not hold the town. All efforts to blow the dams from the air had proved futile, also.

Now, the entire Allied front, from the British on the far north, through the Ninth Army supporting them, the First Army in the middle, the Third in the Saar, and the Seventh in the Vosges, were poised for their biggest offensive of the war. It was scheduled for February 7. The British and Canadians did get off, in a very bloody and costly battle, but on February 7 (how very good German Intelligence was) the Germans blew up the two dams on the Roer and the floodwaters, added to the melts and thaws which had already swollen the river, made it necessary for the American armies to wait until the river had receded.

The 78th Infantry, to which 291st Engineers were now attached, had as their objective the town of Schmidt and advance elements, ahead of the 291st, were already engaged in bitter fighting.]

Siegfried Line
Saturday, Feb. 10, 1945

I think it is rather historic & worth mentioning that tonight some of us from Hq squad are bivouacked in the middle of Adolf's famous Siegfried Line & in one of his damned pillboxes.

We had come into the billeting area, which is another crummy village, & some of the boys saw this pillbox up in the neck of a little hollow. Several of us wanted to see it.

All you could see at first was the top, like a scorched round egg, & the rest was hidden by weeds & underbrush. I suppose the 78th worked it over with flamethrowers which gave it the scorched look. When we got closer we could see the slit around the top where the guns poked out. That gave you the creeps. They are made of concrete. Pigg said, "Hell, let's be historic. Let's make the damned thing our home for the night."

Frankly, I was nervous. I said, "Aren't we supposed to stay in houses? This damned thing may not be clear."

Pigg said, "We'll clear it."

We went inside. I don't mind admitting I felt pretty queasy about it. I read in S & S not long ago about a guy who picked up a book in an empty house, opened it, and had his head blown off. But actually, if you know how to look, a booby trap isn't too hard to find. There's always got to be a wire. If you check door hinges, before you open a door — if you check a stove door & the lids — if you look behind pictures — if you look all around the windows — if you look under chair seats. There's no way a booby trap can really be hidden. It's carelessness that explodes them.

We checked very carefully & the place turned out to be O.K.

I imagine the Krauts had to leave in such a hurry they didn't have time to do anything but save their skins.

I was surprised how small a pillbox really is. I always thought of them as huge things with connecting tunnels. But this one is just a little room, with an addition. It has a sour smell, like sweat & urine & old dirty clothing. It is well known among us that the common Kraut soldier lives like a pig. He doesn't bathe, he doesn't keep his clothing clean. They nearly all have lice & don't seem to mind it. But the bunker was dry & once we knew it was clear, I was willing to stay in it. Not for history — although I realize it is historic — but for safety. They are still throwing 88s all over us. It feels wonderfully safe to be underground.

There are two rooms in this pillbox. The biggest room has a table, some chairs & six bunks, three to each side of two walls. The bunks still had some Kraut blankets on them & some musty old straw under them. The floor is cold, made of cement. We talked about using the bunks. We are all afraid of the lice.

We dumped our stuff & went into the next room. It was more like a dungeon than a room. No windows. Just a cell. It was their kitchen, I suppose, for there is a stove for cooking & some beat up old pots & pans. We checked the stove & the pots & pans for booby traps. They were clear. By that time it was getting dark. I went out & got some wood, collected a can of gas, & got a fire to going. In the meantime, some of the boys had scoured the pots & pans. We heated up our rations & ate & then talked some more about whether to use the bunks or not. Finally, I thought to hell with it. I'm not going to sleep on that cold cement floor. So I got a can of delousing powder & began pouring it on the Kraut blankets & straw & some of the other boys caught on & began doing the same. Then we just heaved the whole mess out in the woods.

Deloused the bunks, then, & for good measure, ourselves!

The other squads are in houses, but some of them came over for a poker game. With a fire going & candles lit, the smell doesn't seem too bad, though some of the other fellows turned up their noses a little when they first came in. Billington, J. B. Miller, Schommer, Pigg & I were in the game. Black Mac & some others were kibitzing.

King had told us the mail was on the way up. When it came, Pinkie,[1] who wasn't in the game said he'd go for all of us in the game. Turned out I was the only one who had any. I didn't get out of the game, just went on playing, but started reading my letters between times. Someone would yell when I was high, or it was my turn to open or bet & I passed the deal. By the time I'd finished reading my five letters I had won every pot & tucked away just about enough to buy a whiskey sour back home. Black Mac said, "You ought to have letters every time you play poker."

Billington said, "The hell he will. That's the last time he reads his mail in a game *I'm* in with him."

When the game broke up I wasn't sleepy yet. Had my letter to write besides & wanted to read the S & S that came up. Came back into the kitchen so the others could go to bed.

Janice doesn't know I'm back with the outfit yet. Still worrying about my ears & the replacement depot.

There's one thing in S & S that has really burned me up. Some stupid congressman has introduced a bill to draft women into the armed services. When that happens there'll be a mutiny in the ETO, I can tell the congressmen. Very few servicemen want their wives or girls in the women's services. It may not be fair & I know there are many fine women in the WACs & WAVEs, but a few rotten apples have made the whole barrel smell. Whatever good they do, they are exposed to the smut and the pawing & the foul talk about them behind their backs.

1 Cpl. John D. Pink, 2nd platoon.

They're in a man's world, at war, & have to take it. And service-men, who know better than anybody how raw it is, are the last who want their own women mixed up in it. I don't believe this bill will go through.[2]

Heimbach, Roer River

Sunday, Feb. 12, 1945

Moved in here last night in snow & mud & slush so deep even the jeeps got mired down. In dogtents, too. 78th are still trying to take Schmidt, not too far away. They are having a hell of a rough time of it, we hear.

Job here is a couple of airstrips for the 78th's recon planes. Lord knows how many mines have been sowed in the fields se-lected for the sites. The boys are cleaning them out today. Dead cows all over the place that have tripped off some of the mines. Fresina[3] & Flaherty tell me they have found both types of Tellers and some Regals.[4]

Speedy said the strips were going to sink to China as fast as they were laid. Pigg said, "That ain't our worry. Just get 'em laid."

Most of the boys are calling Speedy "Sarge" now. He's no goldbrick but he's slow & he'll stand around & stand around, figuring maybe this is the best way to do a job, or that is the best way — and in the meantime the detail has got most of the work done. Since Sgts. usually stand around & boss, the boys have begun calling him Sarge.

If you ever had time to look around & if you weren't always so wet & cold & miserable, this country might look rather pretty.

2 It didn't.

3 Pfc. Vincent A. Fresina, 1st platoon. Pfc. Fresina & Cpl. John Flaherty did much of the mine detection and clearing for Company A.

4 Teller mines were round, about 18 inches in diameter. Some were about six inches thick, others not so thick. The larger held a load of nine pounds of TNT. Regal mines were long and bar shaped.

There are mountains here, some still snow-covered & the town is down in a valley. But, by george, nothing looks good to you when you're half sick & hungry & cold & sleeping in dogtents. That goes for 3/4 of the outfit. Some have the G.I.s — some have chilblains & frostbitten toes & fingers — some have sore throats & colds. Some have trench foot. There's hardly a whole, well man in the outfit.

My right ear is draining again, but not hurting yet. Can't think why it keeps on draining — what the infection can be. But my knees are giving me more trouble than anything right now. Every morning they're stiff & sore. Takes me about an hour to work the stiffness out of them. Sometimes they ache pretty bad at night. If we could just get inside for a while, my ears & knees both would be helped. But, that's war for you. As long as you can stand up & put one foot in front of the other, you keep going.

Waiting on mail call. The guy who got the anonymous letter about his wife stopped by a little while ago. Said they had patched things up & while it was still shaky things were better than they were. He isn't in 2nd platoon any more so I don't see much of him. But I'm glad he has something started toward a little peace of mind.

Then Love came by to bring me a bottle of grain alcohol & fruit juice he'd mixed up. We chewed the fat a while. Finally wound up agreeing it had been a long, long road from California to the Roer — too damned long. More than we asked for, more than we wanted & a hell of a lot rougher. He met a girl in Joplin when we were at Crowder. Been writing to her all this time. Now seems to think they may marry. He's putting in for one of these rotation furloughs. S & S says a lot more will be granted now. Tried to talk me into putting in for one, too. But I don't want one. When I go home, I want to go for good. I think it would be a hell of a lot worse to go home, then have to come back, than it will be to sweat it out. But I hope he gets his. He's a good old boy & I like him a lot.

Cornes began calling me "Uncle Henry" the other day & the whole outfit has picked it up. Until they get tired of it, that's all I'll hear. We always run one thing into the ground before we sicken of it & drop it. Or something new comes along. One corny joke or routine will keep going for three or four weeks.

Mail call. Seven letters & one from home. Nash has his second cluster for his Air Medal. 30 missions! Brother!

The letter from home made me sad. Edward was killed on Christmas Day in Belgium.[5] He was in the company of a lot of other good guys that got it that day, but they didn't happen to be related to me.

Mama's letters are always sad these days. She can't help it, I know, but they sure don't do much for my morale. When Cora Mae writes she chatters all over the place — tells all the local gossip, what's going on around home, & I nearly always get a good laugh or two & feel better. Wish she'd write oftener.[6]

Thursday, Feb. 15, 1945

Came in tired tonight. Had a work detail loading some timbers. First thing Pinkie said was, "Hey! We got a movie tonight! Good deal, huh?"

A movie. Who'd have thought Special Services would catch up with us in *this* burg. Much excitement because it's been a while since the outfit saw a movie. Sombody said it was Rita Hayworth, somebody else said no, it was Betty Grable. Nobody really cared. Anything, anybody, it was something different to do for one night.

---

5 Edward Bottoms, Knifley, Kentucky, a cousin of Henry Giles.
6 Cora Mae Giles, Henry's youngest sister, at this time sixteen.

Later: They had the movie in a stone barn, hay all over the floor for us to sit in. It was *Start Cheering*. Lots of good music, lots of pretty girls dancing, lots of good jokes. But the best thing, it wasn't about the war or the army. One thing we can't stand is these phony war pictures where some handsome movie actor leads his troops onto a beach & on to victory & comes out without a hair on his head out of place.

When we came out the fellows were all talking about how good it was to see places that weren't all bombed out & people who looked happy, etc. It doesn't really seem possible there's such a place left in the world.

I was having that dazed feeling I always have for a little while after a movie. I've always had that feeling. I grew up so far back in the sticks I never saw a movie until I was about sixteen. Then somebody started a little show on Saturday nights in Knifley. A bunch of us used to walk over, six miles there, see the movie, then walk the six miles back. It would take me most of the way home to get back inside myself again.

I thought perhaps I was the only person who ever felt dazed that way after a couple of hours in a show, but when I told Janice she said she always felt the same way for a while. Said she would come out blinking, & it would take her a few seconds to realize where she was, get her directions sorted out & think which way to head for Broadway & the bus. Get back to reality.

Back to reality! For us, tonight, it was mud & slush to our knees, slipping, sliding, cussing our way back to our palatial residences — puptents.

Saw a funny thing happen today. Two of the boys were carrying a heavy piece of timber. The one in front slipped in the mud & dropped his end, which made the one in back ram into the timber & hurt himself. He cussed the guy up one side & down the other & he is one of our best & most imaginative cussers. I have heard him say that a good cusser doesn't have to repeat himself until he runs out of breath. The guy in front really got it. It was drizzling, a cold, sleety rain. He just stood there, all hunched in the rain & took it. Never said a word. A picture of misery if I ever saw one.

When the fellow had run out of breath, they both stood there a minute. Then the cusser took out his pack of cigarettes, flipped one up & held it out to the front guy, then took one himself. They both smoked & when they'd finished, they picked up the timber & went on. All over & forgotten.

Schmidt
Sunday, Feb. 18, 1945

Finished the air strips at Heimbach & moved here right on the tail of the 78th. They finally took the place. Nothing left of it but rubble, more mud, snow & slush. Job here, for Company A, a Bailey to help get the 78th across the Roer. Rest of the Battalion at Heimbach & Blens. Another Bailey at Blens, but not our baby, thank God.

Pigg decided he was sick of dogtents, so he got hold of a pyramidal & we have spent most of the day fixing it up. We laid sandbags & logs around the base to make it tight & put a truck tarp down for a floor. It's not the Ritz but it's better than puptents. Even have a stove we looted from a bombed-out house. Pigg said, "Damn, my name may be Pigg, but I'm sick & tired of living like one." Any improvement, just a tarp for a floor, a little more head room in a pyramidal, makes you feel 100% better.

Was trying to write J. a little while ago & after I'd told her about our tent my mind was an absolute blank. Couldn't think of a damned thing to say. Finally I said, "What in the hell can I tell her?"

Schommer said, "Tell her you love her."

"I've already told her that."

"Well, hell, tell her again. You can't tell a woman you love her too often." So, I just reported the conversation & signed off. Shortest letter I ever wrote her.

Some of the boys were visiting — Billington, Cornes, Black Mac, John Coupe, etc. Coupe didn't know much about J. except that he'd heard of her. He said, "Who is this Janice that Giles is always writing to?" Billington said, "Well, I'll tell you what I know about her. She writes Giles every day & twice on Sunday & she works at a preacher factory." I had to laugh. But I wonder how Louisville Presbyterian Seminary would like that description.

According to S & S the Russian offensive is looking mighty good. Sure ought to take some of the heat off this front. They are only 80 miles from Berlin. Reminds me of something Nash said in closing a letter to Libby: "God bless you & the Russian drive." Amen, to that.

Some of the boys are beginning to get their Christmas packages. The Battle of the Bulge fouled everybody up. Hooks got a fruitcake from his folks, which we all have enjoyed, & Pinkie got a box of homemade candy. I think the Krauts must have got mine. None have showed up & I know Janice sent five, the folks sent one, J's mother & sister each sent one. Doubt I'll ever see any of them.

Monday, Feb. 19th

Too tired tonight. Worked on the bridge today. It's a bitch. Slipped in the slick once & had trouble regaining my footing. Mac grabbed & I do believe I might have gone into the drink if he hadn't. Gave me heart failure. As cold as the water is & as fast as the current is, I don't much think I'd have made it out.

[Bob Billington says: Schmidt was one of the worst deals we drew. Snow, mud to our eyebrows, awful weather, in dogtents & one of the meanest bridges we ever built.

There was four to six inches of wet snow to begin with. Schmidt was nothing but a few houses knocked to rubble. My, oh my! We slept O.K. but what a mess!

What made the bridge such a job was that the road made a right angle turn at the foot of a steep hill & there wasn't any room for leverage. We had to launch it thusly, and balance it across an old pier left from a narrow stone bridge that had been there. That bridge nearly killed us.]

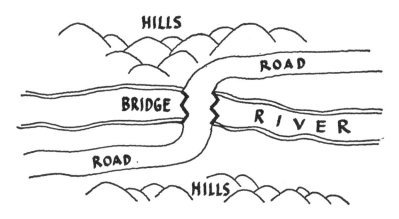

Friday, Feb. 23, 1945

Well, the outfit can take another bow. We just built the goddamndest Bailey anybody ever built across any blasted river. A triple single. The only thing that made it possible was there was an old stone pier we could use for balance. We just had to risk it & throw it over. Damned nasty river, too. Not very wide, but awfully swift.

We also had just enough shelling to make it uncomfortable. By God, if this outfit doesn't draw some of the meanest

jobs of any Engineer outfit on the continent I just want to see
some that are rougher.

But the 78th began crossing today. Now, we have the Siegfried Line behind us, the Roer behind us, next comes the Rhine.
It makes me have goosebumps to think of that one.

After the 78th began crossing today a bunch of us went downstream on the river & threw in a few hand grenades. Result
— fish for chow tonight. The river has some nice trout in it
& it would be great to have a rod & the peace to fish it, but for
food & quick at that, a hand grenade does fine. Managed to get
mine cooked but they stuck to the mess kit & crumbled pretty
badly. Didn't matter. They tasted fine anyway.

Drew my back pay today & got all of it for October, November,
December & January. It made a nice little batch of money.
Asked Lt. Hayes to send $60 of it by cable to Janice for her
birthday. Hope it reaches her, but it's only a month off.

We also drew rations today. Seven packs of cigarettes, six
candy bars, a bar of Lux soap & a can of Prince Albert pipe tobacco. Not bad. Also got the only block of writing paper.
Lieut. Hayes laughed when I asked for it. It's a standing joke in
the outfit how much I write. If any man in this outfit remembers me when the war is over, what he'll remember most is me
forever writing! I mostly write here at night, when there's
more time than usual. But I scribble to J. at every chance —
on rest breaks during convoy, noon breaks, sometimes before
chow in the morning just to be sure *something* gets written to
her every day.

Tuesday, Feb. 27, 1945

We're in some little Kraut village. No idea what the name
of it is. Rolled in here last night, our first stand east of the
Roer. The 78th finally got themselves across the river. We're

in houses. No bridges immediately ahead of us, just some road jobs.

Some of the boys got a shower rigged up for us in an old barn here. Even had a stove put in to take some of the chill off. The shower is an old gasoline drum with holes punched in the bottom, but they have it rigged with a valve to turn the water on & off & it was good & hot.

Never felt so good as to get clean again — lathered and lathered and lathered. Then I had a complete change of *all* clean clothes, except pants, to put on. I've been saving them for this occasion. When I had finished & shaved, I felt like a million dollars. Just being clean, with clean clothes, makes you feel like a different person. LaCoste said he knew he washed five pounds of dirt off — said he felt that much lighter. It could almost be true, believe me, the way we've been living.

Some of us have been issued combat boots — I'm afraid mostly officers & NCOs. They're wonderful — and what a relief not to have to lace those leggins. LaCoste, who didn't get any, said, "Who cares? I just as soon lace leggins as buckle buckles. We get an inspection right quick some day, Sgt. Giles, & you'll be unbuckled!"

What a guy. He doesn't like Germany because they don't understand his French!

We got our personal copies of the Presidential Unit Citation for the Malmédy action today. Lieut. Hayes said I could send mine to Janice. This entitles us to wear the Blue Ribbon, the only one that may be worn on the right side of the blouse. I don't feel I have much right to it, but Pigg said, "What the hell? Didn't you freeze your damned ass off at roadblocks?" Well, it was a unit citation & I'm 291st & I did what I was asked to do — all I could do. Sort of depresses me, though, to think of Holbrook & the others who earned the right more than anyone to wear it & never will.

The 291st Engineer Combat Battalion, United States Army, is cited for outstanding performance of duty in action against the enemy from 17 through 26 December 1944, in Belgium. On 17 December 1944, at the beginning of the German Ardennes break-through, the *291st Engineer Combat Battalion* was assigned the mission of establishing and manning roadblocks south and east of Malmédy, and with the defense of the town itself. The battalion set up essential roadblocks and prepared hasty defenses. Shortly thereafter, numerically superior enemy infantry and armored columns moving in the direction of Malmédy were engaged. Though greatly outnumbered and constantly subjected to heavy enemy artillery, mortar and small arms fire, the officers and men of the *291st Engineer Combat Battalion* stubbornly resisted all enemy attempts to drive through their positions. Repeated attacks were made by enemy armor and infantry on roadblocks and defensive positions and, in each instance, were thrown back with heavy losses by the resolute and determined resistance. This resistance marked the stopping place of the enemy advance on axis Bullingen-Waimes-Malmédy-Stavelot-La Gleize-Stoumont-Chevron-Werbomont, later learned to be the route designated for the First Panzer Corps. The determination, devotion to duty and unyielding fighting spirit displayed by the personnel of *291st Engineer Combat Battalion* in delaying and containing a powerful enemy force along a route of vital importance to the Allied effort is worthy of high praise.

North of Zulpich
Thursday, March 1, 1945

The Kraut names are so befuddling to me I can't get them right, except some of the larger places. But we seem to be heading generally in a northeast direction. Somebody said Cologne & the Rhine. I don't know.

When you move so often a new town doesn't mean anything & you don't much care what it is. All you want to know is, are you going to be in houses, & how good a deal it is. We barrel along & somebody says the bivouac area is just ahead & somebody else says, "Where are we?"

Somebody else says, "Hell, who cares? Just so we get houses."

Second platoon are in this big house. It's been bombed but most of the furniture has been taken out, too. Just a few beat up old stands & tables & chairs & such left here. I was in charge of getting it cleaned up & ready, when here came two old German women. They hurried in & began moving the stuff out. Didn't quite know what to do & was thinking I'd better tell them to "Raus," when Pigg came in. He said, "Hell, let 'em move it out. Save the boys the trouble of throwing it out."

They came back with brooms, then, & got all the plaster & glass & stuff swept out. I must say they saved us quite a work detail. But it was our first experience with civilians & it felt rather strange.

Lately, some of the people are still in the towns we come through but they sure get their white sheets & tablecloths hung out in a hurry. At first we were pretty nervous of them, for we'd been told all the civilians would be sniping at us. If they have, we haven't seen or heard of it.[7] They just get the hell that white rag out their windows to show they're through & please be nice & leave them alone.

We have a fire going in the cookstove in the kitchen & I have staked out one corner for my bedroll. I'd like to sleep warm tonight & need to, because of my ears & knees. If we can find some eggs & potatoes we mean to eat well tonight.

---

[7] Hitler had ordered all civilians to resist to the last man, woman and child. The 291st did not run into any civilian resistance. In his book, *A Soldier's Story*, General Bradley says Third Army ran into stiff civilian resistance at Aschaffenburg, near Frankfurt. So far as he knew it was the only place Hitler's order was obeyed.

Later: We found them & plenty of them. And just politely, or maybe impolitely, took what we wanted. We found all we needed in sheds & storehouses & henhouses. Then Jeff found a couple of dozen bottles of wine in a cellar. That was the best loot of all. I was so grateful to him I told him I'd cook his supper for him. And he was right grateful for that. Everybody's been peeling potatoes, frying them, scrambling eggs, etc. Biggest cooking spree you ever saw. And all washed down with that good wine.

Somebody handed me the S & S for Feb. 22nd & while waiting for mail call I've been reading it. The news is good everywhere now. Third Army has taken Saarburg, everybody is across the Roer up here & through the Siegfried Line & things are looking up. I'm letting myself hope again, just a little the war may be over this summer. I thought by Christmas last fall, I remember — so my hopes are always a little thin. We have a routine. When somebody says maybe it will be over by summer, everybody sings out, "What summer?"

There is also a little mention of the 291st bridge at Lanzerath in this issue of S & S & since nobody else has "butts" on it, I'll mail it to Janice.

WITH THE XVIII AIRBORNE CORPS. Under heavy artillery fire, the 291st Engr. Combat Bn. recently completed a double triple Bailey Bridge stretching 180 feet, with one end in Belgium and the other in Germany. The bridge has a drop of 100 ft.

Two companies of the battalion, commanded by Captain James H. Gamble of Chilhowie, Va., and 1/Lt. Warren R. Rombough of Terre Haute, Ind., worked day and night to complete the job.

Section chiefs on the job were Sgt. Frank C. Dolcha[8] and Sgt. Sheldon T. Smith, New York; S/Sgt. Albert D. Melton, Ken-

---

[8] 3rd platoon, Company A.

tucky; S/Sgt. Malvin E. Champion, Texas,[9] and S/Sgt. William R. Miller, Louisiana.

Mail call. Three letters & one from home. Mama says William[10] has been badly wounded & is being evacuated to the U. S. If this war lasts long enough there may not be enough Giles' left to carry on the name.

The *Courier-Journal* also came tonight. Had a big laugh over a picture of some stateside soldiers being presented their Good Conduct medals. Back in the old army you really earned them. It took you three long years without a blot on your service record. Now, everybody gets one at the end of the first year. I used to be proud of mine but they're not worth a nickel any more. Too damned cheap. Billington & I have been working on the crossword, but too much noise going on.

Everybody talking about what it's going to be like to cross the Rhine. That's where we're headed. "Rough," they say, "plenty rough. They'll make it hot for us on the Rhine. It's their last stand."

"Don't even talk about it. It'll be the worst one yet."

Black Mac started singing "One More River to Cross," but didn't get beyond the first line when someone threw a shoe at him.

Somebody said, "How big is the damned thing."

"I dunno. Big as the Mississippi, I guess."

"Oh, my God!"

Speedy said, "I sure wish it *would* be the last one we have to do."

Somebody else. "It'll be the last one for some of us."

"Shuddup! You wanta jinx us?"

Jeff said, "Maybe we won't have to build one across the Rhine."

9 3rd platoon leader, Company A.
10 William Giles, Knifley, Kentucky, another cousin of Henry Giles.

"Whaddya think they're gonna do? Leave one standing for us?"

"No, but S & S says the Navy is supposed to help with the Rhine crossings — assault boats & barges & stuff."

Billington. "Oh, we'll have to build one. If there's just *one* bridge built across the Rhine the 291st will build it."

Somebody threw a shoe at him & there was a scuffle & then the cards were broken out & the usual poker game began.

We finally broke it up & began going to bed. One of the boys was sitting there scratching & pondering. After a while he lay down, gave a big sigh & said, "I have prayed so long & so hard I've run out of anything to say. I'm not going to say my prayers tonight."

Another day ended, and surely another day nearer home.

Saturday, March 3, 1945

Sometimes I think we're chasing our tails here. We keep zigzagging around, mostly making one-night stands. Filling potholes in the roads. We've turned south, now, and I think we're near Euskirchen.

But the weather is a little better. The days are getting longer & during the day it's almost warm, especially if the sun is shining.

In houses here, and that's always a good deal. But I think the boys are the bluest tonight I've ever seen them. A bunch of them are in another room now singing — and they are singing the loneliest songs they know. It's because of what was in S & S today. I got a copy first & saw the news first. It said most of the troops now in the ETO would be sent straight to the Pacific. I read the headline out loud. "You're lying!" Two guys jerked the paper away from me.

You talk about feeling sunk. And mad. "What the hell goes on in the U.S. anyway?"

"4Fs by the millions!"

"Plenty of stateside soldiers for the Pacific!"

"Why pick on us? Isn't one goddamned war enough?"

"They can't do that to us."

"Who says they can't? They will. It'll be just like 'em."

It went on and on until I got sick of hearing them argue & came in here. I'm tired. Awfully tired. Sometimes I'm so beat when we come in & get our stuff dumped I just feel like hitting the sack right straight. Don't want ever to move again. Too much effort. But I know if I give in to it I just might *not* make it. Best to scramble around, get chow, then if we're lucky enough to find a little booze, let down a little & know you've got one more day made.

Mac says he's tired like that, too. Says, "Hell, I don't ever get rested."

And Billington says, "God, I was born tired & this war is just making an old man out of me."

Pigg & Cornes & Jeff have come in where I am now. They're still talking & bitching. Jeff liberated some chickens today, about half a dozen, & we broiled them. Guess you could call it that — anyway we browned them. Enough for several of us to have a couple of good pieces. Also he found some more wine. That boy is a damned good "liberator." I don't know but what we'd starve to death if he didn't race that truck of his all over a place soon as we get into an area. He usually comes up with something. He usually sees that I get some of what he finds, for I'll cook it for him.

Jeff just asked Cornes, "Would you rather stay here & be in the army of occupation than go the CBI?"

Cornes said, "Hell, yes, wouldn't you? I'd even enlist for a three-year hitch to get out of going there."

I said, "I've got over five years in this army already & I don't want to stay here *or* go to the CBI. I just want to go home."

Mail call. And I just got hit over the head with a ton of letters! 45 from Janice, 12 from home & a V-mail from J's sister. I didn't even know where to begin. Have they ever been batted around. Forwarded and reforwarded and re-reforwarded. They were tied all in a batch & the boys groaned when they saw them. Those who got no mail cried the blues — no justice, they said. I reminded them I went over two months without these letters.

Sorted through the batch & read the first dozen, but decided to wait till tomorrow to finish. There are 30 for December, two for Oct. 14 for Nov. & one each for Jan. & Feb.

Sgt of the Guard tonight.

Brück (I think)
near Arweiler
Monday, March 5, 1945

Quartered here in an old schoolhouse the Krauts used for a barracks. A lot of policing up to do before we could use it. They must have got out in a hurry, for they left a lot of junk.

One thing I found was a pretty good Mauser. The firing mechanism has been fouled up but I'm hoping I can fix it. This is turning into a lootin', tootin' war these days. I don't know of anybody taking stuff from houses where people are living, but the boys help themselves from the bombed-out houses or the ones the Krauts have skipped out of. We aren't supposed to. According to regulations we can take & keep any kind of German army equipment we find, field glasses, pistols, rifles, etc. But nobody pays any attention & nobody cares. After what they did to France & Belgium, most of us feel they have it coming to them.

We look first for wine or liquor, then for eggs & potatoes, chickens, anything to eat. Then, for whatever junk anybody wants. Not too much luck. Some of the fellows have come up with a few things — field glasses, books, clocks, etc. I have been looking for a German Mauser. Don't want any souvenirs. But I would like to have a Mauser .22 for squirrel hunting when I get home. Fellow near Mortain had one he'd captured & I fired it a few times. It's the lightest, most accurate .22 I ever saw.

Some of us who play musical instruments are keeping our eyes open for them. Jeff, who is the best liberator of us all, has promised he'll find me a guitar or mandolin, come hell or high water. He'll do it, if there's a whole one left in Germany.

Was asking Lieut. Hayes about the regulations for shipping this Mauser home if I can fix it. He said it was O.K. No regulations against it. Also told me C Company is at Euskirchen — bridge job — Bn. at Rheinbach. We're filling what Bob Billington calls "tank traps" in roads around here.

Days are longer & today I heard a bird singing. Weather mixed between foul one day & good the next, but I *do* believe spring is on the way. How glad I'll be. I hope to hell I *never* have to be as cold again in my life as I have been most of this winter.

Have finished reading all my letters. I think I must surely have enough Airmail stamps now to last me the duration. J. sent 50 in several different letters. But some of the boys are usually without any, so depends how long the war lasts how long the stamps will last.

Tuesday, March 6, 1945

Durned if I didn't nearly burn us out this morning! There's a Kraut heating stove in the building. It didn't have any stovepipe, but we fixed that. Only it was loose, so we packed a sandbag under it, then wadded a truck tarp in the cracks for blackout. Well, as usual, the old country boy woke first this morning. Mornings are still very chilly so I built up a roaring good fire.

All at once I noticed the tarp around the stovepipe was on fire. I yanked it out & tried to stamp the fire out & couldn't, so I dragged it out in the snow & put it out with slush & mud. Then I remembered the sandbag was smoldering. Raced in & got my helmet & filled it with snow & slush & poured it on the sandbag. Took several trips to get it all out. By that time the place was full of smoke & guys were fogging up coughing, sneezing, yelling what the hell was going on! Pigg yelled, "Goddammit, ain't it enough for us to take Kraut fire without you adding to it?"

LaCoste said, "What you got against 2nd platoon, Sgt. Giles?"

I said, "After all the fires I've built trying to keep you guys warm, this is the thanks I get!"

Schommer said, "I don't think he was trying to burn us out. I think he was just trying to smoke us out."

After I'd finished chasing my tail three times around the barn all the damage done was to my cap — the wool one we wear under our helmets. It had been damp & I put it on top the stove to dry. Meant to watch it, naturally. But in all the excitement I forgot it. Man, it's the most pan-fried cap you ever saw! Everybody has been advising me what to do with it. Unprintable, naturally. Love took one look & said, "We'll tack it to the wall & print 'Sgt. Giles was here!.' " Me and Kilroy!

Have found I can't fix the firing mechanism on the Mauser. The Krauts probably have the same instructions we have. When we abandon a piece of equipment we're supposed to destroy it beyond usefulness to the enemy. But I'll keep looking. Maybe I'll be lucky & find one.

Jeff found a pretty good mandolin today & brought it to me. I'd almost forgotten how to tune one, but Black Mac helped & together we got it tuned up. Tonight we had a good song fest, with enough booze to oil throats pretty well. Mac wouldn't take the mandolin. I'm almost sure he could handle it better than I, but he's too modest. Anyway, a bunch of us sat around & sang for a couple of hours tonight, me picking that fool, cracked mandolin. Mostly my hillbilly stuff. We went to town on "Little Maggie," "Mountain Dew," "Crawdad Hole," "Red River Valley," etc. We have some good harmonizers in the bunch, too. But Cornes tickles me. When he gets real mellow he always wants to sing the same song — "If my cow comes wandering home, milk her, etc." It's a real lulu.

Some of the officers came over & most of the fellows from the other platoons heard us & came around. We have always sung a little, but an instrument makes a world of difference. We have decided to look for a clarinet or bass fiddle for Loftis, more mandolins & guitars, so we can have ourselves a real band.

I'm going to bed tonight feeling better than I have in a long time. Just getting my hands on an instrument again made me feel ten years younger.

Wednesday, March 7, 1945

Heard today the 291st is being given some kind of French decoration for the action at Malmédy. No details yet. But it would entitle us to wear a lot of gold braid around the left shoulder. Damned if we're not going home decked out like real heroes with all the fruit salad we're collecting. We have two more Battle Stars now, too. One for Northern France & one for the Ardennes. I only hope I won't have to stay over here so long it will take two blouses to hold the decorations.[11]

We've eaten pretty well tonight. I found some eggs in a henhouse down the road, about a dozen. Pinkie found some potatoes

11 This was the fourragère — the French Croix de Guerre unit citation. The boys never got to wear the gold braid, for the official citation was not finally made until 1946. But the 291st record lists the award.

& onions & Jeff brought in three or four chickens & some wine. I don't particularly like to cook, but I'm hungry most of the time & do like to eat, so I get the job of cooking pretty often. What I did tonight was stew the chickens, then put in the potatoes & onions. Boiled the eggs & chopped them in. With Jeff's wine, it went down fine.

Somebody found an old phonograph with a bunch of German records & brought them in. We played them for a while, but I can't say we enjoyed them. Tired of them pretty soon & Jeff said, "Giles, get your mandolin."

Don't know why I happened to think of "Rising Sun" but I did. I don't know where the songs come from when I have a guitar or mandolin in my hands. The chords set them off, I guess. Anyway, I began to pick it. Mac's good old face lit up & he began singing it. Somebody picked up the tenor & I took the bass. We went to town on it. Jeff was so crazy about it he made us sing it half a dozen times so he could learn the words.[12]

There is a house in New Orleans
They call the Rising Sun;
It's been the ruin of many a poor boy,
And me, O Lord, for one.

Go fill the wine glass to the brim,
Let the drinks go merrily 'round;
We'll drink to the life of a ramblin' poor boy,
Who goes from town to town.

I'm going back to New Orleans,
For my road is almost run;
I'll spend the rest of my wrecked life,
Beneath the Rising Sun.

[12] This is a song straight out of Bourbon Street, New Orleans, very old and nearly all guitarists, old-time jazz buffs, etc., know it. I thought the words might be interesting if included.

Don't suppose Jeff ever heard it before, but it's a standard down south. Mac thought of "Careless Love," then, and we went on to "Salty Dog," "Birmingham Jail," "When the Saints Go Marching In," etc. By that time half the Company was gathered around. I *wish* we could find something for Loftis to play — either a clarinet or bass fiddle. I know he's itching to get his hands on something. That boy is a real genius. He's from Oklahoma & used to play with bands that played all over Oklahoma & Texas. Maybe we'll find him something pretty soon. Everybody's looking.

Mail call. Three letters from Janice. In one she said she was trying to learn to play Beethoven's "Moonlight Sonata," really well. I read that part out loud. I often read parts of her letters aloud to the fellows, just as they read interesting things from their letters. But that threw Billington into convulsions. He said, "What I want to hear is Giles' hillbilly mandolin & his girl's Beethoven piano! Man, what a concert that would be!" He razzed me good about it. Said I'd either have to learn Beethoven or she'd have to learn hillbilly before it would work. I betcha we make out all right, though.[13]

We've really seen some happy people today — some French prisoners of war the 78th have released. Grinning all over their faces, making the V sign. They're on their way home, now. Some of them are awfully thin. We have heard the Krauts have been working them in the underground places where some of the V weapons are made. Cologne, I think — and since it's fallen they're free. What we heard is that the Krauts took them underground, never let them come up, fed them as little as possible, & when they got too weak to work took them out & shot them. There were always plenty more where they came from. And some people think these Nazis are

13 Henry was correct. I have become an enthusiastic country music fan, and he has learned to appreciate Beethoven.

human beings! I thought of the LeClairs back in Marle. Hoped their son might be in this batch who were starting home today.

Thursday, March 8, 1945

Was just beginning to write when First Sarge came in & said they'd had the news at CP that a bridge has been found across the Rhine. Some place called Remagen & not too far from us. 9th Armored found it & there's a bridgehead already across. That's great news. Great news. And First Army is *first* across the Rhine. Guess we'll cross on that bridge with the 78th. We like that idea, anyway. It would be pure luck not to have to build one, but it would sure suit the hell out of us.

We've been pretty excited about it. Nobody expected to find a bridge intact. Everybody figured the Krauts would blow every one of them as fast as they got across. But 9th Armored must have been so hot on their tails they didn't have time. Whatever the reason, this is sure good for our spirits. My God, I have dreaded that Rhine like nothing else. S & S has called it Fortress Rhine. But think — here we are across it!

Tried to celebrate in the proper way & did right well. Had to piece out the wine with some grain alcohol & the mixture caused a few heaves, but nothing to get excited about. Also caused me to try something I rarely do — yodel.

Jeff came in this afternoon with another mandolin. This is a fine instrument in perfect condition & I mean to hang onto it. Black Mac took the other one, although, like me, his real instrument is the guitar. We got tuned up together tonight & with most of the platoon hanging around & joining in did some real singing.

Feeling mighty damned good I got started on some western songs with yodeling choruses. Jeff laughed till he was rolling on the floor. Said when I reached for a high note both eyes crossed & it took both eyebrows to bring it down. Well, me with a bass voice trying to hit high C would be something to see, I'm sure. Must have looked like a fool. But I don't mind playing the fool as long as we can have some fun with it.

When the singing ended, everybody rolled into the sack, feeling pretty hopeful. Maybe this damned mess is actually going to end one of these days.

Remagen

[MUCH has been written about the bridge at Remagen but in my opinion the most definitive book concerning the entire action, American and German, is *The Bridge at Remagen*, by Lieutenant Colonel Ken Hechler, USAR. Col. Hechler was in the army historical section at the time, was present much of the time during the action, and had an opportunity later to interview both American and German commanders and troops. I lean very heavily on him for the following interpretation.

On March 7, 2/Lt. Karl Timmermann, the brand-new (one day) commander of Company A, 27th Armored Infantry Battalion, 9th Armored Division, was given the point position as the Battalion pressed to the Rhine. On that day the Company was in the small town of Stadt Mechenheim, only a short ten miles from Remagen, a town on the west bank of the Rhine.

The advance reached the heights above the town at about noon. It was known to American commanders that a railroad bridge was located at Remagen but not only did no one expect to find any bridge intact, Remagen was not a good place to cross the Rhine. The terrain on the east bank was rough and hilly and promised too much difficulty in occupying and breaking out of. Crossings north and south in much flatter country were therefore planned. Between these crossings the overall advance strategy was simply to force all German troops out of the Rhineland west of the river.

From the heights overlooking the town two men of Company A spied the bridge still standing. They called Lieutenant Timmermann, who notified his Battalion commander and Task Force commander. The first reaction was to knock the bridge out with artillery fire. Permission was denied because of the presence of "friendly" troops. Up the chain of command to Corps Commander, then Army, then Group, finally to SHAEF went the news of the bridge. The decision was then handed down to take it if possible, establish a bridgehead with reinforcements promised immediately. Though Remagen was not in the planning, a bridge was a bridge and General Eisenhower decided immediately to exploit the discovery.

Lieutenant Timmermann was ordered to advance and take Remagen, which he did. Company A then advanced to the bridge approach, reinforced with other elements of the Battalion. Here he was also given the mission of crossing and taking the bridge.

Just as Company A was preparing to move onto the bridge, a great explosion occurred, clouds of dust and smoke billowed up and hid the span, and it was believed the Germans had blown it up. When the dust had settled, however, the bridge was still standing.

Joined, now, by 9th Armored Engineers 1/Lt. Hugh B. Mott, Sergeant Eugene Dorland, and Sergeant John A. Reynolds, Company A set out on their dangerous crossing. The engineers methodically found and destroyed the bridge wiring, found the charges of explosives and dumped them, as Company A continued the crossing. There was some fire fighting but eventually the Company was across, and reinforcements began to join them. Within twenty-four hours 8000 troops had crossed, with tanks and artillery.

There has been much speculation concerning the reason the bridge was not blown in time. It seems to have been pretty much a comedy of errors — much confusion about command, who was responsible, who could give orders to whom.

The Ludendorff Bridge was a double track railroad bridge which spanned the Rhine between the twin towns of Remagen on the west bank and Erpel on the east bank. One track had been planked over by the Germans for vehicular traffic. On the east side of the river the tracks disappeared into a long tunnel under the 600-foot hill, the Erpeler Ley. This hill was later given the name of Flak Hill by the Americans. The bridge had been much weakened from the heavy bombings by Allied planes during the fall and winter of 1944–45. In fact it had been reported knocked out more than once. But the Germans always managed to repair it and keep their trains running across it. Since February its primary use had been for hospital trains bringing German wounded back, and for the retreat of German troops from the Roer.

In nominal command at Remagen was Captain Willi Bragte, but the only troops to whom he could give a direct order were 36 riflemen. A company of bridge engineers was stationed there and their commander, Captain Karl Friesenhahn was charged with maintenance of the bridge and with its destruction if it became necessary. But he could not give the order to demolish it. Some Volkssturm (People's Army) troops were in Remagen also, but they did not come under Captain Bragte's command, nor did the multiple gun anti-aircraft batteries atop the Erpeler Ley. Any order from one unit to another had to go through a chain of command.

The German High Command had given some thought to the defenses in the Remagen area, but believing the Americans would avoid the bad terrain around Remagen, they had concentrated most of their defenses at Bonn and Coblenz. Through a series of changes in Corps Commands, Captain Bragte often did not know to whom he was responsible. The final change occurred at 1 A.M. on March 7, when General Otto Hirzfeld, commander of LXVII Corps, embattled all the previous day north of Bonn, was messaged that the Remagen area was now under his command. He was 40 miles north of Bonn, knew nothing of the Remagen situation, and was already up to his neck in trouble.

Unable to go himself, he sent his adjutant, Major Hans Scheller to Remagen. Major Scheller was told that if he found it necessary he was to demolish the bridge. After great difficulty, Major Scheller arrived at the bridge around noon on March 7. Company A, 27th Armored Infantry Battalion, were at the same time on the heights overlooking the bridge.

Captain Bragte had positioned his 36 riflemen above Remagen on high ground. Worried about them, he asked permission to withdraw them and move them to Erpel on the east bank. Major Scheller felt the defense ought to be made in Remagen on the west bank so he refused permission. To reinforce them, he made an effort to commandeer some of the troops streaming in retreat across the bridge. It was like trying to catch the wind in nets. Nobody would stop, everybody was getting away while the getting was good.

Major Scheller, seeing the futility of this procedure, soon gave the command to remove the Command Post to the east bank under the Erpeler Ley — to the tunnel. Captain Bragte tried to telephone his riflemen to withdraw, but they had already been overrun.

The bridge had long been wired for demolition and during this time Captain Friesenhahn was busy testing his circuits, making certain they were in working order. His only responsibility and his only concern was that the bridge should blow when the order came. Captain Bragte was worried about the overall defense of Remagen and Erpel. Major Scheller, familiar with the problem at Corps Headquarters knew there were many retreating German troops who needed to use the bridge before it was blown. He was worried about them.

The picture for delay was thus set.

By this time 9th Armored Artillery was firing across the river and the sound of tanks and machine guns and small arms fire could be heard in Remagen as Lt. Timmermann's troops made their advance. Captain Friesenhahn asked permission to arm the charges and proceed with the demolition. An artillery captain was pleading, at the same time, with Major Scheller to wait. His artillery battalion was trying desperately to reach the bridge. They would be cut off and captured if it was blown prematurely. Major Sheller decided to wait a little longer.

The west approach to the bridge had long been wired for preliminary demolition as a delaying action. Captain Friesenhahn was ordered to station himself there and to set off the preliminary demolition when he deemed it necessary. With four engineers, he waited until the American troops were in sight. Then he gave the order to set off the charge. A crater 30 feet wide was blown across the bridge approach. The bridge engineers raced back across to the tunnel. It was about ten minutes to three when Captain Friesenhahn reached the tunnel and again asked permission to blow the main charge.

About this time, phosphorus shells fired by the American tanks began to take effect and a heavy smoke screen was formed on the Erpel side of the bridge. Then heavy artillery fire began. Finally, Major Scheller gave the order to set off the main charge.

But both Captains Bragte and Friesenhahn felt there had been so much confusion in command they must have a written order to clarify responsibility. It is therefore a matter of record that Major Scheller gave the order at 3:20 P.M.

By this time the tunnel was crowded with civilians, Volkssturmers, German soldiers caught in the retreat, foreign workers and prisoners. Captain Friesenhahn took his place just inside the tunnel to turn the key. Nothing happened. He wound the key again and again and still nothing happened. He realized then that the American shelling had caused a defect in the firing mechanism.

Emergency demolition charges had been placed in the center span, but they had to be set off by primer fuse. Captain Friesenhahn asked for volunteers to race to the center of the bridge and light the fuse. Only one man volunteered, a Sergeant Faust. He made his way out onto the bridge and lit the primer. He then raced back to the tunnel. The charge went off, the center of the span seemed to rise into the air and for a moment both Americans and Germans thought the demolition was complete. But the span settled back down on its foundations and the bridge still stood. Captain Friesenhahn had been forced to make do with what was sent him for the emergency charges. He had asked for 600 kilograms of army explosive. What he got was 300 kilograms of an inferior industrial explosive and it was not enough.

Shortly thereafter the Americans were across the bridge and eventually the entire German contingent in the tunnel surrendered with the exception of Major Scheller who, unable to report the failure to blow the bridge to General Hirzfeld by telephone, had commandeered a bicycle and set off to inform him personally.

By the time the 291st Engineers reached Remagen on March 9–10, the Germans had rallied and, horrified by this new disaster, they were massing two Panzer Divisions in the hills beyond Erpel. The Luftwaffe was called on to make an all-out effort to destroy the Ludendorff Bridge and any pontoon bridges American engineers might attempt to build.

Captain James H. Gamble of Company A, says: We moved to the Rhine quite rapidly, where work sites for the M2 treadway bridge were dispersed along the west bank of the Rhine river. Col. Pergrin organized the Battalion in such a manner that Company A and Company B were to inflate floats and assemble the bays. Company C would align the bridge, string the supporting guy and bridle cables and build the near and far shore approaches.

This was a very difficult operation, the bridge site being only a short distance downriver from the Ludendorff railroad bridge. It was a prime target for enemy aircraft and 88 millimeter artillery. The constant shelling and bombing by aircraft resulted in some 32 casualties and much equipment was destroyed before the bridge was finally completed at 1700 hours on March 11th.

I might add at this point that this was our first acquaintance with a Jet aircraft which the Germans were flying at that time and according to information received later they had only some ten minutes flying time.

I must say that the bridging of the Rhine was a difficult and rather exasperating experience but we had the entire Battalion intact and there was certainly comfort in numbers. Here again we can commend the entire organization for its tremendous effort and success in the bridging of the Rhine, but in my own thinking nothing can compare to the individual decisions and the refusal to run under adverse circumstances such as were displayed by the men of the 291st during those first days of the Bulge.

As the Journal continues, these were the conditions under which American troops, among them the 291st Engineers, were working — constant shelling from the German artillery in the heights across the river, bombings and strafings from German planes, and eventually eleven rounds of V-2 rocket bombs.]

Remagen
Friday, March 9, 1945

We're here, but nobody else is yet. We got rolled out about midnight last night. Let's go, let's go, roll out boys, come on, let's go.

Much confusion & bitching. Everybody half asleep. My God, these night moves. Tired as hell, sleeping away, somebody rolls you over, come on, let's go, we're moving.

"Moving where? Why?"

"Let's go where?"

"What the hell's the matter? What's happened?"

First Sarge coming in, "We're going to Remagen — build a bridge. And it's don't spare the horses."

Groans & moans, me among them, with knees stiff, trying to roll up my pack, get all my stuff together, make sure I wasn't leaving anything. Everybody grumbling. "Why in the hell we got to build a bridge there? I thought they *had* their damned bridge."

"How many bridges they need, for Christ's sake?"

First Sarge hustling in again. *"Get on the ball!* Trucks are ready."

We got loaded up & on the road around 1:30. Very dark night & drizzling rain, some fog & a bad convoy all the way round. Much traffic & many long waits & delays. Everybody off the trucks every stop just to stretch & get a little circulation back into feet & legs. I walked down the line once, talked to Jeff. Asked him what the hell was going on. He said, "It's the goddamndest mess of traffic I ever saw. The whole damned First Army must be going to cross on that bridge. Never saw such a headache in my life. Can't get *no* place."

We finally did. Got in just before daylight. Went straight to the bridge. Then sat there & waited to see what next. Most of us half asleep & not giving a damn. Couldn't see anything anyway. Then Pigg came up & we started moving. "What now? Where we going?"

Pigg said, "Aw, the whole damned thing is snaffed up. Nobody here but us yet. First Sarge said we'd bed down."

About that time a shell roared in & landed up in the town, where we were headed. The bridge is about a mile upstream from the town. *That* woke us up! "What the hell? Thought this place was *taken!*"

"We been plenty more places supposed to be taken."

"Goddamn! Artillery fire again!"

Somebody laughed. "The old 291st. Always in the hottest spots. You can bet on it every time."

Much confusion trying to get around in the town. Much traffic & the streets narrow & winding. Tanks still smoking, buildings still burning, very much a feeling of being in the middle of a battle & not knowing whether we were coming or going.

Finally pulled up in front of a big building. Somebody said it was a church. Anyway, it had a good big basement. We set up in it, glad to be hiding out from the shells. We didn't take time to look it over much, or to clean it up. Just unrolled our beds & fell in.

Nobody called us this morning, so we slept till nearly noon. Then we got up & looked the place over & decided we had us a pretty good deal. There's a good stove in the basement & plenty of coal to burn in it.

Pigg went out to find First Sarge & see what the score was & the rest of us pitched in to make a home of the place. About that time here came a couple of women. They grabbed our brooms & began sweeping & cleaning. Both were young. They kept grinning at us & sort of rubbing around, trying to make time. They found the atmosphere a trifle cool. No takers. So they left of their own accord. They were just trying to feel us out & when they got the cold shoulder, they quit. One of them was a real looker — blonde, with pretty long hair & very full-bosomed. She made the best possible use of herself, too. But there were no takers. If any of the boys have taken on anything since we got into Germany, I've not seen or heard of it.

You wouldn't think these Kraut women could stomach an American. But they seem to be out for themselves with anybody. Crawling around, grinning & smirking, rubbing it in. By God, I'd hate to think of American women acting so foul under the same circumstances & I don't think they would. I think they would be too proud.

We got ourselves squared around & the place began to look decent. Pigg said Battalion had radioed they were having trouble getting here. They were farther away than we were & they've run into the same traffic troubles. Also been strafed by Kraut planes. So we've got some time off. Pigg said, "Make the most of it. We'll be working our tails off when they get here."

That's the beautiful truth.

McCarl had rolled the kitchen boys out earlier, so we had hot food. In chow line we saw & heard some more shells, but they were up near the bridge. Decided that was what the Krauts were throwing their stuff at — trying to knock out the bridge. A little sobering, to think of getting out on that river & hitching pontoons together.

About that time here came the damndest long flat bed truck you ever saw loaded with boats. Somebody yelled, "Here comes the Navy."

It was the truth. Bringing up assault boats. But that driver had his problems. The street was so narrow he couldn't get his truck around a corner. He must have been having that kind of trouble all night or else he didn't give a damn. Just gunned the thing and sheared the corner of a building off & kept going.

After chow, LaCoste & Black Mac & I decided to walk down to the river. We figured the Krauts wouldn't be shelling this far down. There has been a fine walkway or promenade or something built all along the river with cafés with open porches so people could sit & eat & look out over the river. They're all empty now, but a lot of tables & chairs are still there. We sat down & wished we could order a few beers. But that day has past for these people.

The Rhine. I don't know what I expected. Another Mississippi, I suppose. But it isn't nearly as wide as I thought it would be. About six or seven hundred yards, I'd say. I told the boys the Ohio was a lot wider & for my money a lot prettier. Mac kept watching the river & finally he said, "The damn thing flows the wrong way, Sarge. It flows north."

I couldn't help laughing. Said, "Mac, where have you been since we left France? All the rivers flow north in this part of Europe — the Roer flowed north, the Our, the Meuse, all of 'em."

"Not the Our," he said.

"Yes, the Our."

"Well, hell, I sure been turned around then."

LaCoste said, "Jesus Christ, what difference does it make? They flow straight up, we gotta bridge 'em."

Mac shook his head. "No, I don't think even the 291st could bridge a waterspout, LaCoste."

LaCoste saw a pretty girl & whistled at her. I said, *"Nein, nein, verboten."*

"Don't *nein* me no *neins*, Sgt. Giles," he said, "& don't *verboten* me no *verbotens*. Soon as I find one that understands *schlafen* & *ja*, I'll make time again." He wouldn't, but we've been riding him about losing his touch since we got into territory where his French doesn't count. He knows about ten words of German just like the rest of us.

From where we were we had a good view of the railroad bridge. It has three spans, on two piers. The middle span has arched framework. There are a couple of squatty stone towers at each end & on the other side the railroad tracks go into a tunnel under a big hill that comes right down to the river. And there's a hell of a lot of traffic going over in a steady stream.

A shell whistled in every once in a while & dropped in the river. And then some Kraut planes flew in, six of them, one right after the other. Came in low, flew across parallel to the bridge & dropped their eggs. No hits. Everything of ours opened up on them — much noise, much firing. No hits there, either.

Mac kept watching the river. The current is pretty fast. He shook his head finally & said, "It ain't gonna be easy. It sure ain't gonna be no piece of cake."

I said, "It's gonna be a sonofabitch & you know it. And somebody is gonna get hurt."

LaCoste groaned. "I say my beads every day & I go to mass every chance I get, but the goddamned 291st gotta be in the *wrong* place at the *right* time every time."

I said, "Maybe if you'd quit cussing it would help."

He looked astonished. "Who's cussing?"

"You were. Just then."

He shrugged. "That's not cussing. That's army talk."

We didn't go up to the railroad bridge. A little too hot up there & we figure we've got plenty of time. When we got back to the area some of the other boys said they'd been. Jeff, Cornes, a few others. They said 9th Armored had a big sign up over this end of the bridge that said, "Cross the Rhine with dry feet — compliments of 9th Armored Division."

Jeff said we're really putting the stuff across. The MPs have got their hands full with traffic. One of them told him the Krauts were beginning to throw in a lot heavier fire just last night & today. Billington said, "They waited to give the old 291st a real welcoming party."

The name of the town across the river is Erpel & the big hill is called Flak Hill.

As usual, Jeff had some loot. The most interesting was enough wine that those who wanted it could have half a bottle a piece. Which blurred the edges very nicely.

No mail yet, of course.

Remagen
Monday, March 12, 1945

And mark it down! At 5:00 P.M. yesterday, March 11, *the first vehicle crossed the Rhine River on the first American bridge built — the 291st floating treadway!*

That is history, in a way. For the record, the bridge took 32 hours & it is not only the first bridge to be built across the Rhine, it is the longest tactical bridge yet built on the continent. It is 1220 feet long. As Billington says, "We sure give 'em a hell of a target."

Battalion & the other companies got in about daylight the 10th. We got rolled out & the heat was on. Round the clock till the bridge was finished. Artillery fire & bombings the whole time. The bridge could have been built faster except for that. We lost two cranes & four aircompressors & several pontoons. Also had a good many men hurt & one killed.

Priester was ripped open by a piece of hot iron. I didn't see it, for I was upstream with my gun positioned, but the boys told me about it. Said he was just standing there when a shell landed too close. Piece of shrapnel just ripped him wide open. The boys said it was such a hell of a hole they could see his guts & liver. They said he stood[1] there a few seconds fumbling with his guts trying to hold them together, a kind of silly grin on his face as if he didn't believe it. Then he said, "Boys, I've

[1] There were 31 wounded and Pvt. Merion A. Priester, 2nd platoon, Company A, was killed.

had it," and fell over. They said he was dead by the time he hit the ground.[2]

Nice, quiet boy, very good kid. This is 2nd platoon's second killed in action. And they've both been good, decent kids. You want to forget that kind of thing as fast as you can & alcohol is the best little aid to forgetting you can find. I think the Col. saw to it we had plenty last night. The outfit had sure earned a spree.

I worked on the bridge part of the first day, helping inflate floats. Then Pigg came around & told me the Capt. wanted me to take my gun upstream & position it & try to help get some of the damned Kraut planes. Hooks & I put the truck about midway between the railroad bridge & our bridge & I didn't leave it till dark last night.

And, my God, how the Krauts were throwing it in. I guess the idea of us trying to put a bridge across infuriated them. 47 planes came over Saturday, the first day. I doubt if I hit one, but I sure was in there trying. Got that old 50 cal. mighty damned hot. Somebody got a few — about a third of them, I'd say. But everything that will fire is shooting at them. All the artillery we have lined up, ack-ack, machineguns, & guys even take potshots with M1s, carbines & pistols. It is wild & woolly, let me tell you.

They come in over the hills & have to fly pretty low. Mostly they are Stukas, which are easier to hit because they're slower. But there were some Folkewulfs & Messerschmitts, too. They come in & fly parallel to the bridges for more accurate bombing. Haven't hit much yet, though. Most of the bombs fall in the river. They're mainly trying to hit the railroad bridge, but

---

2 Bob Billington says: "We had laid out the approach for the bridge and the necessary bridle line and were trying to get the anchors in on a large tree when the shells began to come in like rain. That was when Priester got killed."

take a pass at both pontoons once in a while, too. 51st Engineers finished a pontoon upstream from the railroad bridge about three hours after we'd finished ours. Our boys worked like maniacs to get through first. We *weren't* going to let 51st beat us. Ours was a harder bridge, too. They built a heavy pontoon, but we built a floating treadway. And ours is longer.

The artillery fire is so good it *has* to be observed. It was artillery that did the damage while the boys were working. Those guns up in the hills across the river couldn't lay it in that accurately unless they had observers. Next question is, where? The talk is, right here in Remagen.

Company A helped assemble the bays & also worked on the bridle lines. B Company mostly inflated floats, but they also helped assemble the bays. C Company did most of the work of lining up the bridge with guys & bridle lines. But everybody did a little bit of everything.

We've had a good laugh over Black Mac. Pushing those bays out he decided he liked being a sailor. Then a shell hit too close in the water, the explosion & waterspout blasted the bay clear out of the river & Mac & the boys got dunked. Pigg said when Mac was pulled out he said, right peevishly, "Goddammit, I didn't enlist in the damned Navy!"

LaCoste, with a sober face, said, "Mac, what was you trying to do? Bridge me a waterspout?"

Many, many near misses like that. Everytime the boys pushed a bay out into the river & had to stay out there putting into practice their bowline knots & hitches & half hitches hanging them together, they were almost on suicide missions. How we got by with as few in the whole Battalion hurt as we did, & with only one killed, nobody knows.

There were wire service reporters & photographers & Stars &

Stripes reporters & photographers all over the place yesterday, taking pictures, interviewing the Col. & anybody else they could buttonhole. They have told us that next to finding the bridge, this first bridge across by the Americans will be the biggest story since the Bulge. Our bridge will be featured, they say. I wrote Janice & told her to watch the headlines as of this date. That's all I could say, but she'll know it's our bridge. When the story about it comes out in S & S I hope I can get a copy to send her.

We heard that Col. Anderson[3] was here himself to help Col. Pergrin lay out the bridge. I wouldn't know myself, but some of the boys said there *was* a full Col. here, standing around with Col. Pergrin watching most of the time. Both of them as cool as cucumbers. Paying no more attention to the shells & bombs than if they'd been in their own back yards. No ducking or flinching. Pigg saw him & Billington said Pigg wiggled his eyebrows around & said, "What the hell's a full Col. doing up here where he don't *have* to be? Don't he know he could get hisself killed?"

But this was such a big deal, it took some real engineers to handle it. The equipment had to come from a special bridge equipment outfit. We don't carry this kind of heavy stuff around with us.

S & S for March 10th said we had more than 8,000 troops across the railroad bridge within 24 hours. Well, a hell of a lot more have crossed since & many of them over our bridge. We've seen some of the 78th crossing & some of the 99th. First Army is really building this bridgehead up. Don't think we can be pushed back, now.

We got a big kick out of the 9th Armored sign first day we were here. Well, we have our own sign up now:

3 Col. W. H. Anderson, Commander, 1111th Engineer Combat Group.

The Longest Tactical Bridge Built
The First across the Rhine
Constructed by
291 Eng. C. Bn.

And our tails are high! *The 291st built the first bridge across the Rhine.* By george, we have a right to feel good. Our morale is high. You could tell it best this morning when B Company's bugler went to town on the chow call. He is the hottest bugler in the army. Since Texas, when he's feeling good he'll finish a call then break it into a beat — like "Boogie Woogie Bugle Boy," or "Hot Lips," or "When the Saints Go Marching In," or "St. Louis Blues." Anything fast, swinging, with a real beat. And he's so good it just raises the hair on your head. I always like it when B Company is near us, just to hear him. We call him the Boogie Woogie Bugle Boy & this morning that was what he sent out so clear & fast & loud if the Krauts didn't hear him on the other side of the river they had to be deaf. What he was telling 'em, loud & clear, was "Look out! The 291st is on its way!" My God, it put a lump in your throat, raised goosebumps on your arms & sent thrills down your spine.

We really tied one on last night, too. There was plenty for everybody & for several days more. We sure gargled it down, for it was mostly champagne. When everybody was rolling I saw one of the boys crawling on his hands & knees trying to find his bed. Hooks asked him what he was doing. So drunk his eyes were crossed, he squinted around & said, "My bed has got up & walked away."

Somebody else said, "Why don't you get up & walk away & find it?"

He looked down at his limber legs & said, "I can't. I'm paralyzed." He was. On wine and champagne.

Today, everybody had a well-earned day off. Jeff blew a

bank vault & came in loaded with Kraut paper money. Reichsmarks. Worthless, we figured. The bank had been bombed-
out but there was this vault intact. Jeff couldn't resist it. I took
a few of the banknotes to send home to Robert as souvenirs.[4]

[The money was perfectly good, as the boys later discovered.
Bob Billington says: "I remember all those Reichsmarks Jeff
found in the bank vault he blew. We all thought they were
worthless and only kept a few for souvenirs. When we got to
Munich we learned they were perfectly good exchange. No
wonder I'm not rich today. I lost a fortune right there in Remagen."

Speedy Dymond says: "During some leisure time in Remagen
we were looking around and I picked up a little German paper
money in the road. A bank nearby had been bombed-out and
it looked as if everything of worth was gone. There was a lot
more of the money lying around. I supposed it was worthless
so I only picked up a few notes for souvenirs. Later, when we
were in Munich I got a hair cut and showed a 20-mark note to
the barber. To my surprise he took it and gave me a handful of
change. It was then we all learned the money was perfectly
good. I often think of all that money we left behind. If I had
all I saw just being ground into the mud I probably wouldn't
have to be working today!"]

Remagen
Wednesday, March 14, 1945

Still on my gun trying to bring down a few Kraut planes.
In between times much gun cleaning to do. If anything, the
Krauts have intensified their efforts to knock out all the bridges.

Last night we heard our first V-2. I thought I had heard explosions. Didn't think anything could be louder or worse than

4 Robert Giles, Henry's younger brother.

an artillery barrage. But, man, the biggest & best artillery in the world can't begin to compare with a V-2.

Some of us had gone to bed & I had gone to sleep, when suddenly the end of the world came! I was jolted six inches off the floor. Glass & plaster flew in all directions, the building shook all over & I was deafened, felt like my guts had been sucked right back into my backbone. Everybody in a panic. *"What in the name of God was that?"*

"My God, what are they throwing at us now? What kind of secret weapon have they come up with now?"

We were scared to move, afraid to do a damned thing but huddle. But the building didn't come down around our ears & whatever it was — we couldn't figure it at the time — hadn't made a direct hit on us. We were all tensed up waiting for the next one. But that was all. Finally we got to jabbering about it. Somebody said, "They must have got the railroad bridge. Must have hit it with a blockbuster."

We all decided that was probably it — they loaded up with about a dozen blockbusters & made a night raid.

Finally Pigg said, "Well, hell, even if it's judgment day, I'm gonna get some sleep. If Gabriel blows his horn, wake me, willya?"

That brought a laugh and we all turned back in. That's a good platoon Sgt. for you. He may be so scared he's about to have a s —— t hemorrhage himself, but he's got to keep hold of himself. And that's where Pigg shines. There never is a time when he can't come up with something that makes the boys let down & laugh. I think it's natural with him, just his way. But it's a damned good way.

This morning we learned what it was. V-2. It landed up on the hill from us. Tore a hell of a hole up there. And some of the H/S boys got roughed up a little for it was nearer them. Nobody killed, though, thank God. Just a few more Purple

Hearts. But I hope to hell they don't have many more of those things.

Today's S & S had the story about our bridge in it. It was a good story & it did say we were first across, but we shared the headlines with 51st. Maybe that's fair, but it made me laugh at the way I felt for a little while. I remembered how mad Webster was about the 101st Airborne getting all the headlines at Bastogne. You can't help it, though, when you know your outfit has done the damndest good job an outfit can do & you don't get as much credit for it as you think you should. There were only two copies of the paper & some other fellows had "butts" on them, so I couldn't get one to send to Janice.

We've all had a big laugh about Jeff's latest loot. He brought in a canary today, cage & all! Somebody said, "Hell, Jeff, he wouldn't make one good bite boiled, baked, stewed or fried."

Jeff said, "This boy's not to eat. He's gonna be our mascot."

Hooks said, "Don't expect *me* to haul him around."

Jeff said, "*I'll* take care of the hauling."

Durned if the little fellow didn't start singing right about then & I guess we all fell for him. He just warbled his little old heart out, as if he knew he'd found himself a good home. He's awfully small. Wouldn't fill the palm of your hand. All yellow, with the silkiest feathers. And the least little legs. We got to batting names around to give him. Jeff was still looking at him & he said, "Damned if he hasn't got legs like a spider. No bigger."

So — Spider is his name.

I have the worst mashed thumb a man ever had. In loading up my gun today I fumbled & the cover caught my left thumb with a leverage shearing effect. Over half the nail is black & there are two big blood blisters on the other side. I cut a hole in the nail to relieve the pressure but it's throbbing pretty bad anyway. I was in a hell of a hurry for we had about six planes sighted & I wanted to get in on the action. Somebody got one while I was loading. Saw it go spinning down on top Flak Hill.

I'll bet Adolf is chewing up rugs by the dozens these days because his boys haven't been able to knock out these bridges & we're still pouring troops & equipment across. S & S says the whole German High Command is looking for the guys who didn't blow the bridge in time. Says they are to be courtmartialed & shot.

[From the highest command on down, many officers were investigated in connection with the German failure at Remagen. In a sorry tale of shifting blame and guilt even Field Marshal Model joined in an effort to find a few scapegoats to satisfy Hitler. All general officers were finally cleared, but six men were court-martialed.

1. Major Hans Scheller was convicted for failing to give the order to blow the bridge in time and for leaving his command. He was executed by a firing squad.

2. Lieutenant Karl Peters, the young commander of an antiaircraft battery, was convicted for failure to destroy all of his weapons. His battery was equipped with a top-secret weapon, a series of rocket launchers. His orders were to destroy them before allowing them to fall into enemy hands. He was trying to get the battery across from Erpel to Remagen when the situation deteriorated so hopelessly he gave the order to destroy the guns already on the west bank. He did not, however, remain to see it done. He returned to the east bank to try to save the rest of his battery. He was executed at the same time as Major Scheller.

3. Major August Kraft, commander of the engineer battalion, one company of whose troops were at Remagen, was convicted for not going personally to the bridge site on March 7th. He was handcuffed and shot to death in the back of his neck.

4. Major Herbert Strobel, commander of an engineer regi-

mental staff charged with protecting river crossings, was convicted of failing to lead a counterattack immediately when the Rhine was breached. He was shot to death in the same manner and at the same time as Major Kraft.

5. Captain Willi Bragte, in nominal defense of Remagen, was convicted in absentia for surrendering the troops in the tunnel. Since he had been captured the death sentence could never be carried out.

6. Captain Karl Friesenhahn, in command of the bridge engineers, was tried but acquitted. It was found that he had made every effort to have the bridge blown in time. Captain Friesenhahn was also captured so that his trial was held in absentia.]

Thursday, March 15, 1945

Krauts still pouring it in on all the bridges, but making very few hits. My thumb is sore as hell but it's quit throbbing. All during these days there's been very little that's been real to me but that gun, keeping it loaded & keeping it firing. Jack & Arlie say the same thing. I don't know, it's a kind of wild excitement. Everybody on a machine gun tries to be first to spot a plane. The minute you see one you haul back with a long burst, then every gun on the river gets into the act. In a way, it's as if there wasn't any other world but that truck & gun. There are long empty stretches with no planes — two or three hours, sometimes. Then I crawl in the cab & snatch a little sleep. I'm beginning to feel as if that damned truck cab was my only home. Then here they come again.

But, my God, something went zooming over the river today the like of which I've never seen before. I saw it out of the corner of my eye, knew it was a new kind of plane, tried to line it up, gave it a long burst, then stood there goggling till I got to laughing at the way it left my tracers behind. They were arcing off into nothing but empty space, it got away so fast. The talk everywhere tonight is that it was one of the new jet propelled planes. Fast! My Lord. Nothing could hit that thing. It zoomed in, dropped a load & was gone before you could get a good breath. By george, if they have many more of those things we're in trouble.[5]

We've been seeing a lot of our own air strength going over the last couple of days. Big formations of bombers. Latrine rumors have it they are softening up the Ruhr for the next big push.

We had a big laugh over an article in S & S tonight. It said Remagen had been evacuated by all American troops because it had been learned observers were directing the artillery fire onto the town. Said a German officer had been found with a communications radio and it was suspected several more were still hidden out. Evacuated! We haven't been. We're still sitting right here taking it. Wish to God somebody would evacuate us.

Wrote Janice tonight she could send me a fountain pen. She offered to send me another one when she learned mine was lost, but I hated to let her. I know they're expensive & hard to get. But I've borrowed from the other boys too much. Besides it isn't always convenient to wait till they get through.

As much as we've moved around, all of us have lost half our stuff, though. It takes a whole platoon to come up with paper, envelopes, stamps, pens, for anybody to get a letter written. Every night it's the same. "Anybody got any ink? My pen's dry."

"Somebody loan me a pen?"

"I'm out of stamps. Anybody got any?"

---

[5] Speedy Dymond says: "I had a close call at Remagen coming back from the bridge one day. I saw a plane coming but couldn't recognize it at first. When I did, I hit the dirt and the pilot let out a blast of fire which struck the road just a few feet ahead of me. One of the boys was in a truck, which was probably the plane's target. The truckdriver started to fire at the plane and so did I. We saw some smoke from the plane as it went over the ridge, so we may have hit it."

"Who's got some writing paper?"

And not only writing materials. Everything. "Hell, I'm out of cigarettes. Who's got some?"

"Gimme a light, somebody. I've lost my goddamned lighter again."

"Hell, my last pair of socks are wet. Anybody got a dry pair?"

"I've got to wash my teeth or they're gonna fall out. Somebody gimme some toothpaste."

We get to laughing sometimes about what one of us would do without all the others. Even in a family there are *some* things that are private, but in this platoon what one man owns, everybody owns. Well, nobody has asked to borrow a toothbrush yet, but I expect it any day. What I have personally lost from Normandy to the Rhine would outfit half a dozen men. *Now*, I've lost my shaving brush. Guess I can make out with that squirty stuff we get in rations.

Jeff came in lugging a typewriter a little while ago. Miller[6] is tinkering with it & if it can be fixed that boy will fix it. He'd rather take something apart & find out what makes it work, put it back together & *make* it work than to eat fried chicken on Sunday. He's a natural born tinkerer. Once, at Gloucester, we were having classes in mines & grenades. The Lieut. asked if anybody knew how a grenade actually worked — what made it work. Miller stepped up & drew pictures of all the component parts with their right nomenclature. Beat the hell out of all of us. He'd taken one apart to *see* what made it work. Sort of flabbergasted the Lieut. too.

Back in England LaCoste started calling Miller "Ginfoo" & the name has stuck. Most of us call him that. It doesn't mean a thing. LaCoste just makes up words. He couldn't think of

---

[6] Cpl. A. Miller, 2nd platoon.

Miller's name one day & just said "that ginfoo guy that makes things work."

And I found something today the whole outfit is taking "butts" on. It's a book on Greek art, I'm almost sure. The text is in German & we can't make it out. The screwy thing about it is, all the pictures are of statues & carvings & every last one of them is of people having sexual intercourse. I've seen pictures of Greek statues & wall friezes & while they didn't even use a fig leaf, at least the poses were normal. But the Greeks must have had some pornographic sculptors, too.

Told about it in the orderly room tonight & one of the officers gave me a flashlight & "ordered" me to get it. He shook his head over it. Then First Sarge had a look. He has a rubber face & every time he turned a page we went into convulsions. His eyes would bug, his mouth would twist, he'd blink & chew his tongue. He said, "My God, they didn't leave nothing to the imagination, did they?" Then he'd turn another page & sort of back off from it. "This is embarrassing me. Hell, them old boys knew their stuff, didn't they?"

The remarks from various others, looking over his shoulder, wouldn't do to repeat. I don't know when I've laughed as much.

There's a lot of daylight left now after I get off duty. This afternoon a bunch of us were just sitting around in the sun, shooting the breeze. I happened to mention I hadn't been across the railroad bridge yet. Said I'd like to be able to say I had crossed it. Jeff was right in for taking me. He got out his old 2½ ton & we took off. Got in line & crept across. Not so much traffic as there was when we first came. Don't know that I felt any particular distinction in crossing it. The 9th Armored has used all that up. But for some reason I wanted to cross it. We came back over our own bridge — and that's the first time I've been all the way across it.

When we got back to the area I was so hungry I had the weak trembles. Decided to get out & do some scrounging. Found a henhouse with about half a dozen eggs in one nest. Then I saw a hen. Decided I'd latch onto her. Another man to help & it wouldn't have been any trouble, but me, alone, trying to surround that durned flighty fowl was something to see. Every time I'd get anywhere close to her she'd squawk & fly off. I'd about worn myself out & finally I got mad & picked up a rock & waited till she settled down. Then I took good aim & let fly & damned if I didn't hit her right in the head & knock her off first try. Came in feeling pretty superior.

The boys think I'd better load my gun with rocks. Might have better luck hitting the Kraut planes.

We fried the chicken & scrambled the eggs. Hooks had some fruitcake, about that time Jeff walked in with cognac, & a fine time was had by all.

Then we had our sing — Mac & I tuned up & we settled down to it. Spider, the canary, warbled right along with us. Every time we begin singing, he cuts loose. Jeff says Spider thinks he is our glee club leader. He doesn't wait for us to sing, of course. He's the singingest canary I ever saw. But when we tune up, he always joins in.

Even with a war on, that's not a bad way to end a day. Just a little boozey, singing together, & with the best damn bunch of fellows in the world.

Friday, March 16, 1945

And it came very near being the end of us! We were in chow line for dinner today when a damned V-2 landed, so close the wrappings on the rocket fell all over us & around us. There's no warning — not a sound until suddenly you're blasted off your feet, your guts are sucked in, you can't get your breath. It's like all the noise in the world packed into one big jolt. Then, when the explosion is over you can hear the rocket coming in. Sound travels so much slower than those damned things that it's several seconds after the explosion before you can hear the rumble of the rocket's passage.

There's no time to hit the dirt. It's just bang, blast, & over with. We did hit the dirt, of course. That's instinct & reaction, but if one of them is on top of you, it would be over before you could move. We were still flattened when these wrappings began to fall all over us. When we pulled ourselves together & got over the shakes a little, we looked up the hill & by God, half of it had been torn away. Part of what fell on us was dirt sprayed out from the crater.

LaCoste was behind me in the line when the thing zoomed in. His teeth were still chattering when he picked himself up. "B-b-b-y God," he said, "if they don't liberate us from this damned town pretty soon I'm not gonna be nothing but a bunch of fiddlestrings on bones!"

I knew what he meant.

Then he picked up his mess kit. "Look at it! Just look at it. All bent up."

He looked at me & his face was all screwed up & he was shaking, & I knew I was. "Here," I said, "let me have it." He had fallen on it, I guess. Mess kits flew in every direction, I can tell you. I got the worst of the bend out of it & there weren't any holes in it. Gave it back to him & told him it was still serviceable.

He stared at it, then he grinned. "Sure. Sure. Them little dents don't hurt. Some more souvenirs, huh?"

"Sure," I said, "just some more souvenirs." But they're the kind I can do without.

McCarl was yelling at us. "All right, all right. Get moving. We've not got all day."

Form up again & shuffle along. Wash your kit, first in the big tank of hot soapy water, then rinse in the clear. It struck me as very funny all at once, the pains we have to take with our mess kits to keep from getting the G.I.s when a V-2 can blow the whole damn outfit into little pieces any minute. But habit is strong, & I went through the routine.

Coupe & Jeff & I huddled over against a building to eat. I don't know about them but I was still shaking. Could hardly get my coffee up to my mouth & my spoon kept rattling against the pan. Nobody said anything for a minute. We just tried to poke the food down. Then Coupe said, "By God, this outfit's time is running out. They're gonna get us with one of these things one of these days. We've been in too many hot spots. Had too many near misses. The percentage is running out on us."

Jeff turned on him. "Goddammit, shut up!" Then he got up. "I can't eat this damned crap." And walked away to empty his kit & wash it.

Coupe looked down at his kit & said, "I can't eat it, either."

I was having a hard time with mine, so we all dumped the stuff. Then it was business as usual. Back to my gun. I'm sick to death of that truck, though. Feel like I've been living in it for ten years. We have been here just one week today but it seems like forever.

Still plenty of action on the river. The Navy is pretty busy, too. They keep setting off depth charges & putting out things that look like nets & traps. I would guess they are taking precautions against the Krauts trying to blow the bridges from the river. But a Kraut boat wouldn't have a chance of getting by our artillery lined up on the banks. Not even at night. There are tanks with big searchlights mounted on them & the river is as bright as day all night. We never saw these before & didn't know the army had them. Even if the Krauts only send a raft loaded with explosives down the river, it wouldn't work. With those lights & our artillery it would be blown out of the river.[7]

We were given our ribbons for the Presidential citation today, also our new ETO ribbons with the three battle stars. This Remagen deal will probably give us another star. The Capt. says so. The blue ribbon for the Presidential citation is the only one that can be worn on the right side of the blouse. Most of us just put them away. They'd only get dirty if we wore them over here. Maybe when Johnny goes marching home, if he ever does, he can pin them on & be a real hero. But just looking at them made most of us remember the misery that earned them.

One of the boys found the queerest mandolin I ever saw today & brought it to me. I can usually handle any kind of stringed instrument but this is a new one on me. It is shaped like a mandolin, but the neck is only six inches long, there are only five frets, but it has seven strings. Must have been some kind of key to tune it with, but Mac & I used a pair of pliers. Finally got four strings tuned Hawaiian style & plunked away on the durned thing but you couldn't call it very tuneful. Don't think we'll hang onto this, for it can't add anything to our music. What I'm anxious to get hold of is a guitar. Jeff swears he'll find me one, if he has to rob somebody, or buy one. That boy really loves our music. He's a good old New York hillbilly.

Mail call. Twelve letters for me, two from home. Mail hasn't been coming up for several days & normally I'd be crying the blues about it, but there's been so much going on I haven't had much time to think about it. All I've had time to write J. have been V-mails — just news bulletins, for I can't tell her

[7] The tanks with searchlights were top secret and this was the first time they had been used by the Americans. The British had used them in North Africa, however, and the Germans had used them in the breakthrough in December, 1944.

what's been happening. These were good letters, late in February.

Later: Everyone was asleep but me when here came Jeff with a bottle of gin. That boy either knows someone near the source, or has found a cache which he's gradually liberating. As usual, he wanted me to sing. We got the mandolin & very softly, so as not to wake the others, had ourselves a private little songfest. We took the quart of gin down considerably. Thank God for Jeff Elliott & thank God for the booze he finds. The way my knees were aching tonight & after the scare we had today, I needed a good anesthetic.

Saturday, March 17, 1945

The railroad bridge collapsed today!

I saw it happen, watched it happen, heard it happen & still couldn't believe it. Was at my post as usual, about a hundred yards downstream, when there was this screeching, cracking, splintering noise. I looked over at the bridge & right before my eyes it began buckling & caving in. It wasn't hit. There wasn't a plane in sight & no shells falling. It just collapsed. Sort of slow motion at first, the way you'd run a movie at the very slowest speed possible, then it began settling very fast.

There were a hell of a lot of men working on it — it's been closed for repairs since yesterday — & I could see them running in both directions, toward both ends. But they began to slide back down into the river as the middle caved in. Just slide down backward & some were thrown by falling timbers & beams. It was horrible. Horrible! I just stood there goggling. Couldn't think. Couldn't believe it.

Then I could see them struggling in the river & all at once I realized some of them would wash down against our bridge. I thought first I ought to go help, but I wasn't supposed to leave my post. Then I saw a bunch of fellows running onto our bridge & they began pulling them in. By that time I was shaking all over. My God! To *see* something like that. I'll not forget it to the day I die.

Everybody's been talking about it tonight. Jeff especially. He was near enough our bridge that he was one of those who rushed out & helped pull them in. Our Medics got there very fast & gave them first aid before they were sent on to the hospital. Jeff said most of them were in shock as well as hurt pretty bad. Don't know how many were killed. There were a hell of a lot of them, working some air compressors & a crane & welding.

Lieut. Edelstein says the bridge collapsed from weakness. All the traffic over it, all the artillery firing. He says as much vibration as it's taken, even though it hasn't been hit often, could cause the collapse. Thank God it never was our baby. None of our boys were on it.

But I think most of us are glad the damned thing is gone. Maybe the Krauts will quit pouring so much stuff in here, now. Of course, they'll keep trying to knock the pontoons out, but even if they do, others can be thrown across. And we have enough troops & supplies on the east bank we have it made now.

That's all we've been able to talk about tonight. All we can think about. It was such a terrible thing to see. Nobody knows how many were on the bridge, how many were killed, how many were rescued. Some washed into the banks before they reached our bridge & were rescued. So the count is anybody's guess. What it must have felt like to feel that thing going under you. Terror? It must have been pure hell.

Well, we have a little something to numb the shock — about half a bottle each, it sure is welcome.[8]

8 Around 200 men were on the bridge when it collapsed, engineers of the 276th Engineer Combat Battalion and the 1058th Bridge Construction and Repair

My watch stopped today. Miller looked at it but said the balance wheel was broken & he couldn't fix it. Said it would have to have a new balance wheel. Since the army doesn't carry spare wheels for watches, I think I'll send it to Janice to have fixed. Lieut. Hayes said he would send it first class & it ought to reach her safely. We decided the vibration from all the firing I'd done caused it to break. Lord knows there has been plenty.

Linz

Sunday, March 18, 1945

We were finally liberated from Remagen today. Crossed our own bridge to the east bank, came upstream about three or four miles to this place where Battalion has been for some time. We're still on the Rhine, can even see a little bit of Remagen, if anybody wants to look, but it's behind us & I, for one, am damned glad. We got some glory there, but paid for it. 31 of us got hurt, one killed, & the rest of us were shook in one way or another nearly every day. If they could ask what price glory in World War I, we can give them the answer in this war. You can't eat it, you can't wear it, you can't live it. And we can do without any more of it.

We're in houses here — Pinkie & me in a cellar of our own. We got a bonus with it, too. It's full of potatoes.

This was a very short move & we had the rest of the day off, so after we got settled in I decided to do a washing. Found a beat up old washboard & got more ambitious than usual. Heated a big can of water & boiled out some underwear, socks, a pair of fatigues & even, finally, washed out my wool OD shirt. It was stiff with sweat & dirt.

Group. Ninety-one men were thrown into the river. Seven were killed, 18 were missing (presumed killed but bodies never recovered), three saved from the river died of injuries in the hospital, for a total of 28 killed. Sixty-three others were injured but rescued and lived.

About the time I finished, Hooks came in with three chickens, so we washed out the can & put them on to boil with about half a bushel of potatoes. Pigg had seen me doing my washing. He came in a while ago & saw the chickens cooking in the same can. Said, "I don't know whether I'm gonna eat any of that mess tonight or not. I don't think Giles emptied his wash water. Just dumped the damned chickens in his soapsuds."

One of the boys, a little slow on the uptake, said seriously, "No, I saw him empty it. And he washed the can out good, too."

After I finished my washing I didn't do another blamed thing but lie around. It was pretty warm & the sun was shining. Felt good to sit in it & get hot. The trees are almost leafed out, now. There's a lot of green showing in the grass. There's an apple tree out back of this house & the buds are almost ready to bloom. Spring. I suppose not even a war can change the seasons. In the middle of a shooting war the sap is going to rise in the trees, the grass is going to turn green, & flowers will bloom.

Back home Dad is burning his tobacco bed about now & Mama is fussing about getting the garden plowed so she can plant potatoes & early peas. And the old short-core apple tree down by the barn is about ready to bloom. Sometimes I wonder if I'll ever see any of it again & sometimes I even wonder if I haven't just imagined the things I remember. The war just goes on & on & on & you can't see any end to it. I do best if I just take one day at a time & don't think ahead. But I have so much to live for, so much waiting for me when I get back, I can't always do it. I get to dreaming about it & then I get very impatient.

No mail for me tonight. None the last two nights, either. And that's a switch. If the mail comes up, I usually get some. Did get the *Courier* tonight. Been working on the crossword.

Monday, March 19, 1945

Pinkie & I found our cellar pretty cold last night & there were so many potatoes we couldn't keep them from rolling down on us. So finally we got up & dug us out nests on top of them & then slept fine. Only thing, during the night a mouse ran across my face & woke me up. I wouldn't have minded that, but he had the coldest feet I ever felt. Like little prickles of ice all across my forehead. While I was trying to get back to sleep I thought of that Bill Mauldin cartoon in S & S not long ago. Willie & Joe were in bed & a rat had them cornered. Joe was holding a flashlight while Willie aimed with his .45. Joe said, "Hit him between the eyes, Willie. I've heard they charge when wounded."

The potatoes in the cellar are coming in handy. Everybody in the outfit is having potatoes fried or boiled. They are disappearing right fast & pretty soon Pinkie & I can lay our beds on the floor.

Latrine rumors all over the place tonight that some Kraut frogmen were captured the other night trying to swim downstream & blow up the bridges. Seems they were equipped with waterproofed packages of explosives & were swimming down the river when the searchlights on the tanks spotted them & all of them were captured. Don't know whether it's true or not.[9]

Dismantled my gun today & cleaned it & that's all. Late in the afternoon Black Mac & I walked out in the country a little way. No good reason except the day was beautiful & warm, the sun was shining, everything beginning to turn green & it

[9] This story was true. A squad of specially trained swimmers were ordered to a point ten miles above Remagen, to float down the stream and destroy the railroad bridge. They made a false start on March 16, but had to postpone their effort until the next day. When the news of the collapse of the bridge reached them it was decided they should go ahead and blow up the pontoon bridges. All of them were captured because of the giant searchlights.

just felt good to get into the country & be peaceful. We found a pretty little creek & sat on the bank & talked. Mac is a restful fellow to be with. Just goes along easy. But he's looking just as beat as the rest of us. He's a good squad leader but I think he'd just as soon not have had it.[10] You don't only have to get in there & slog yourself, you've got your boys to think about. He's showing it.

Don't know why, but I picked up a stone & skipped it across the creek. He looked at me. "You do that when you were a kid, too?"

I said, "Sure. Didn't you?"

He nodded & skipped one across himself. I told him about Green River & how we used to sneak off & go swimming & try to skip stones clear across. "Prettiest river in the world," I said, "and if I can just get back to it I don't ever want to see another one."

Mac said, "Imagine what it would be like to look at a river & know you didn't have to build a bridge over it. Just look at it, maybe take a fishing pole along & sit on the bank. Just enjoy it."

I said, "I can't imagine it. It stretches the imagination too much."

We saw some fine fish in the creek & if we'd had a pole it would have been fun to catch some. But we didn't.

Time for chow when we got back to the area & then we got out our mandolins & tuned up. About that time, we got drowned in champagne & wine & I do mean drowned. I never saw as much of the stuff in my life! Jeff & Coupe & Hooks had been ranging around considerably & they came back loaded. Everybody but the guys who pulled guard got very well oiled.

[10] Sgt. Geary was wounded at Remagen and Cpl. McDonald was now leader of 1st squad.

Me among them & this writing is deteriorating rapidly. I'm seeing three lines where there shouldn't be but one.

But what a nice state of affairs.

Friday, March 23rd

We've been on something of a spree for a couple of days, but ran out yesterday & the painful process of sobering up began. Also a little sobering, we are assigned to 99th Infantry for this next push. Big argument tonight about whether it's worse to support infantry or armor. Since we've never supported armor, there wasn't much point in it, but many opinions just the same. Until somebody gets disgusted & yells, "Aw, blow it! We gotta be assigned to something long as the war lasts. What difference does it make?"

The kid who got the anonymous letter about his wife paid me a visit tonight. Wanted to tell me everything was fine with him & his wife, now. He looks like a different fellow. Happy as he can be. I sure am glad for him. He had a long sweat over that deal & it's good to see him over the hump with it.

Still no mail for me. The boys are really razzing me about it. "She's found somebody else."

"You'll get a Dear John next."

"Some stateside G.I. has beat you out."

Back in England I did use to sweat some when the mail slowed. I don't like it, now, but it's not because I'm worried about anything like that. She's been too faithful & too good. There's just a foul-up somewhere. Lieut. Hayes told me they were having to bring a lot of the Airmail over by boat now. There's such a hell of a lot of it they can't haul it all by air.

Pigg just came in & said we'd be moving tomorrow. I'd better get some shut-eye.

From Remagen to the Danube

Sunday, March 25, 1945

DON'T know where we are but we didn't come too far yesterday. Up in some very hilly country. In houses here in a very small place & several of us in another cellar. These are farmhouses, I suppose, for there are manure piles stacked to the eaves right by the houses & a stink all over the place. We won't be here long, however.

According to S & S the news is good all along the entire front, now. Even the British up north have got across the Rhine. Patton's boys crossed on the 22nd. And the Air Corps is really plastering the Ruhr. Big formations flying over every day. I don't know. Hope they soften it good. Billington & I were talking about this Ruhr deal some tonight. It's the industrial center of Germany & if we can take it the war has *got* to end pretty soon for they won't have any way of going on. We've said things like that before, though. No way they could keep on, but somehow they do. Billington's folks send him the New York *Daily News* & we usually work on the crossword together. Between us we usually manage to work them.

Jeff brought in another typewriter in his loot today & I'm using it for the time being. Standard American model & nothing wrong with it except it needs a new ribbon. I would guess it got left behind by some of the 99th office boys.

No guitar yet or bass fiddle or clarinet for Loftis. Jeff said he saw an infantryman with a guitar today & tried his best to swap him out of it but he said he wanted to keep it.

I found another German Mauser today. It was broken, but I thought maybe I could fix it. Couldn't. Jeff saw me fooling with it & said, "Giles, forget it. I'll find you a good one." And he probably will.

Heard tonight 7th Armored was about to break through to the autobahn. The 99th is right on their tails, mopping up. Everybody is anxious to hit the autobahn. They say we'll really roll then.

Mail call. *Nine* letters. I waved them around & made some jokers eat crow. These were from March 1 through the 11th. She was guessing we were at Remagen. Said the *Courier* had headlined the railroad bridge on the 11th & there was an article about some engineers building pontoons.

She says she has finished the book but has to revise it & type it. And she *will* send me a copy. Some time ago I asked her, if it wasn't too big a manuscript, to let me see it. I'm too anxious to read it to wait till I get home.

Had to laugh over one piece of news. Nash lost his St. Christopher & was in a big sweat over it. Told Libby to get another one to him as fast as she could for he'd be sweating out every mission he had to fly until he had another one. Only fifteen to go for him. I *sure* hope he makes it.'

near Weilburg
Friday, March 30, 1945
Haven't had time to do anything these last few days, not even write Janice. We hit the autobahn the 27th & we moved, but

not exactly the way we had hoped. We got strung out along it building Baileys. If we didn't set some kind of a record we should have. We leapfrogged by outfits & built 14 of the damned things in 36 hours! We've come some distance, a little south by east. Came through two pretty good-sized places, Montabaur & Limburg. Have seen a hell of a lot of Kraut prisoners all along, being sent back to the PW cages.

Last night when we stopped, some place between Montabaur & Limburg, I was so dead I didn't even pitch a tent. Just rolled up in my blankets with my shelter half laced around them. Some time during the night I woke up & it was sprinkling rain but I just turned over & thought the hell with it, I'll have to start getting good & wet before I move. Then I thought of my mandolin, but remembered I had it wrapped in my raincoat in my B. bag & it wouldn't get wet. Must not have rained much for I woke up only a little damp around the edges this morning.

We left the autobahn at Limburg & headed due east. My "home" tonight is the Kraut version of a puptent — a pyramidal about six feet square, tapered to the center & in four sections of camouflaged material. Good tent. Built for four men, I'd say, but I have this one to myself.

One thing you have to give the Krauts. Some of their equipment is damned good & a lot of it beats the hell out of ours. Gardner, the tanker back at the hospital in Liége, told me his tank commander said it took four of our Shermans to equal one of their Panthers & about eight to equal one of their Tigers. Why didn't we have tanks like that? And their rifles, the Mauser, beats our M 1 s & carbines all to hell, both for accuracy & easy handling. A good four-man tent like this is something we could have used, too, instead of puptents. If they hadn't been fighting for five years before we got here & hadn't had a two-front war on their hands at that, we'd have had a hell of a time licking them. They've been hard enough, the way it is.

Later: Stopped for chow & then Jeff came in & I'm pretty excited. There's a bombed-out ammunition train near us & as usual Jeff was out in his truck following his nose around to find stuff. He just brought me the sweetest little Mauser you ever saw. Not a thing wrong with it except the stock is a little cracked. Brand new, never been fired. It's clip fed (five shots) & bolt operated, with sight graduations up to two hundred yards. I'll sure have me some fine squirrel hunts with it one of these days. I'm going to take it apart & send it home.

Jeff is the hustlingest fellow I ever saw. Never still a minute. I believe the way I'll always remember him is moving around, nervous & restless, that gun of his sloped across his shoulders, yelling at us, "Let's get cracking, boys, let's get cracking." Whether you need food or booze, he can find it if it's to be found. He's always lugging in something that will help make us more comfortable, or something he's heard one of us say we want. Believe me, 2nd platoon is having a better war because of Jeff Elliott. I really appreciate his finding this gun for me. He also brought me a quart of gin, which is being very helpful.

Mac came over to visit me a while. Told him to bunk with me if he wanted to, but he said he'd already bedded down & was too tired to move. I know he is. He's a big guy & hard to wear down, but my God what they expected of us the past several days was too damned much. And Mac is always in there, heaving & shoving his guts out. It took us *all* this time. They were mostly short bridges or we'd never have made it. Mac needed a few drinks & I was glad Jeff had brought me a bottle.

He said he'd just heard he'd been recommended for a cluster for his Bronze Star. I don't think it means a damned thing to him. He said First Sarge had been recommended for the Silver Star for his work on the treadway & so had Dolcha &

Champion. If anybody that worked on that bridge deserved a Silver Star it was Mac.

He told me a good one he'd heard. One of the officers is getting a Purple Heart. Mac said he'd heard his pants got caught on some wire & his tail got scratched. Then we talked a little about the news. We really have some hope, now. The news is just too good. Everybody is across the Rhine, everybody's moving, from the British up north to the 7th Army farthest south. Everything is going good. We can't help feeling the war is really going to end pretty soon. But this Ruhr show we're fixed up in, now. The Krauts aren't quitting on it at all, we've heard & rumors are that they have all their crack outfits, all their best stuff there. Mac said, "Henry, you think we'll make it?"

I said, "Sure. They're on their last legs, Mac. We'll make it."

He said, "I didn't mean that. I meant, you think us boys, the 291st, you think we'll really make it through to the end?"

Well, what the hell! But I said, "We've just about got it made, Mac."

He was blue, though. He said, "I hope we don't lose any more boys in 2nd platoon. Holbrook. Priester. That kind of thing rides you, Henry. If we can just make it & not lose any more."

I know it rides you. I know damned good & well it rides you. But Mac can't huddle them under his wings. Holbrook was a gunner. He had to do his job. Nobody could have done anything about Priester. It could have been me, or Mac, or La-Coste, Jeff, Pigg, any of the boys. When hot iron is flying around, nobody can protect you. Luck is with you or it isn't. It just wasn't with Priester that day. But the trouble is, you know a guy. One day he's with the outfit. Maybe standing in front of you in chow line. Sleeping in the same house with you.

You're so used to him he's like your own brother. All at once he's gone. Nothing left of him at all. He's Graves Registration business. You miss him. Keep looking around for him. Can't believe you'll never see him again.

We're not Infantry & we don't take near as many losses. But just because we don't take as many we are all together for so much longer. They lose so damned many they can't possibly get to know each other as well as we do. We've come so far together that we're like a family. When we lose a man it's like losing somebody in the family.

Well, Mac had enough gin under his belt finally to get to feeling a little better. We were waiting for mail call & about that time somebody yelled it was in. Seven letters for me & two from home. Janice sent a snapshot of Nash & his crew taken at Capri where they were on a rest leave. Ten missions to go. I'm *praying* he makes it. God, when you've got it worked down to that every one of them must seem a year long.

Giessen

Sunday, April 1, 1945

Came here yesterday. Came on through the city & are bivouacked in some beat up old houses on the far side. C company, I think, built a Bailey here across the Lahn River. We're roadmending & maintaining the Bailey.

We have seen thousands of Kraut prisoners the last few days & when we came through Giessen yesterday we could hardly get down one street they were lined up so thick. I must say they are sorry looking specimens. Hitler is down to the kids, now. We have seen some that couldn't be more than fourteen or fifteen years old. Just little boys, not even begun shaving yet. They grin at you as you pass. Look right cheerful. Guess they know the war is almost over & they're just as pleased to be out of it. We have heard the Krauts are surrendering easier these days because they're afraid if they fight till the war is over the Russians will get them.

One surrendered to us here in the area today. He was a warrant officer. Came walking in all decked out with his pack, clean clothes on, freshly shaved, waving his little white flag. The Capt. sent him over to H/S Company to get rid of him.

We have also seen a hell of a lot more happy Frenchmen & Russians. Slave laborers released by the advance outfits. They wander around grinning all over their faces, making the V sign, doing some looting & drinking on their own. It must be a wonderful feeling to be free again. They all have a diamond shaped patch sewed on their coats or sweaters with the initials OST on it.

After we got in yesterday, LaCoste & I went looking for something to eat & met up with three Frenchmen. They were looking for food, too. LaCoste talked with them for a while. They told him they were kept in barracks in a camp fenced in with barbed wire & guards posted all around. These fellows were worked in a factory. Said guards marched them to work every morning, they worked ten hours, then guards marched them back to the barracks. No heat in the barracks. They nearly froze every winter. They were never given enough to eat — were hungry all the time. And if they got sick, they had to work anyway as long as they could stand on their feet. At their camp, though, nobody was taken out & shot if he was too sick to work. They let them stay in bed until they were well enough to work again. I told LaCoste to ask if they were mistreated in any way. They said they got knocked around and kicked, but they hadn't been tortured or beaten or anything like that. They said the badges were to show they were slave laborers so that if any of them tried to escape his clothes would give him away. Said all the Germans, even the civilians, knew what the badge meant.

So that gives the lie to their denial they knew what was going on.

It's hard for me to understand how a whole country, a nation, could be so uncivilized as to do such things as this. Even if the civilians didn't do it themselves, they put up with it. Let it happen. And how could one lunatic man & his gang of thugs get such a hold on people he could get by with just anything he wanted to do. It beats me.

We can't talk to the Russians, of course. Jeff goes around calling them all Stalin & we can tell they get a big kick out of it. They grin every time. They don't understand English but that's a name they know very well. We've heard H/S Company have a couple of Russians they're keeping as pets. They can go along as far east as we go, I guess. Seems they're earning their keep by helping the cooks.

This is a pretty good looting town. I found a nice load of wine which has been more than welcome. Also plenty of potatoes & eggs. Somebody found a guitar today, but it's cracked & the tone is bad. Mac, though, can make it sound pretty good.

After we'd cooked up some food & eaten we settled down for a good sing, my mandolin, the guitar, & several harmonicas. Sang everything from the classics to cowboy songs. One of our best song fests because there was plenty of wine. We sound pretty good when we are mellow enough. At least we think we do. Spider was warbling right along with us. Then one of the boys had to go to the latrine. He was boozey as hell, couldn't walk without wobbling. Mac had laid the guitar down & durned if this kid didn't put his foot right through it. Busted it all to pieces. Well, another day, another guitar.

I left them with it. Turned my mandolin over to Mac & came in my tent to write, but I've been sitting here laughing most of the time. They *were* singing "Red River Valley," but they're improvising some new words for "Rhine River Valley"

& every foul word we use in the army has found its way into it. What this outfit thinks of the Rhine is unprintable.

Have heard we are to stay here a few days. Hope so. Everybody's tired. It's not so much the work, although that's enough, but it's moving so much. When you can stay in one place a few days you get a little bit rested up & bounce back pretty fast. But when you just keep rolling it doesn't take long for all your bones to begin to ache & your stomach gets to feeling funny & you don't know what day it is & don't care. You just want to stop some place & be quiet. My legs need a little rest.

There's a lull in the music outside now. And this is the conversation. "God, I feel as old as my grandpa."

"I feel older than that. I feel as old as Methuselah."

"How old was that?"

"Nine hundred years."

"You believe that? You believe anybody ever lived 900 years?"

"It's in the Bible."

"Well, I don't care if it is, I don't believe it."

Billington spoke up then & finished it. "Hell, Methuselah was a mere lad. I feel as old as God."

Pinkie just stuck his head in & said the mail wouldn't be up tonight. I said O.K. He drew his head back, then stuck it back in. "Did you know today is Easter?" I said I didn't. He said, "It is." And that was that. Just another day to us.

near Marburg
Tuesday, April 3, 1945

Moved again & are angling northeast. Yesterday while we were still at Giessen I took my Mauser apart, rustled up a crate for it, packed it carefully & sent it home to Dad. Also wrote him how to assemble it & told him to go ahead & use it if he liked the way it shot. I think he will.[1]

One of the boys found a pretty good radio today & everybody who can tinker has had a hand in getting it rigged up. Finally got it fixed & listened to the news tonight. It comes from Luxembourg. First in English, then in German. We're glad to have it. The mail hasn't been coming up regularly & without S & S we haven't had any late news at all. Haven't heard what's been happening even on our own front, much less what the score is generally. It's very, very good. 9th Army from the north & 1st Army from the south joined up at a place called Lipstadt yesterday & the Ruhr is encircled. The Krauts haven't given up, but they'll have to. Patton has been streaking off, as usual, & the British are doing all right up north. We got pretty excited about it. It *does* begin to look as if this mess is going to end not too long from now. By summer, we are letting ourselves hope, if not sooner.

Funny thing happened, though. We were all ganged around the radio listening when here came three old women. About the only German we know is *Ja, Hande Hoche, Raus* & we've kidded around with *Verboten* & *Achtung*. But by their gestures they made us understand they wanted to listen to the Luxembourg news. We also understood that the German radio from Berlin is no good, or they no longer believe what is being told them. Pigg said let them come in & listen. I think they believe this is the real dope they are getting for one of them looked over at another & said, "Alles kaput."

It sure as hell is, if not right now, very shortly.

Hinkel came by to see me late this afternoon. He stayed to

---

1 Henry Giles still hunts with the Mauser. His father mended the stock, and when the war was over he took one of Henry's dogtags and sank it in the stock, where it remains to this day.

hear the news. Don't see much of him any more. But I am always glad when I can. He gets some straight dope at H/S & he told me the 99th was moving north to help reduce the Ruhr pocket. Said it would be a big artillery deal. We have them caught, now, & we can just pound them to pieces. Well, that means us, unless we are detached & there's no good reason we should be.

He has seen a slave labor camp. He said the prisoners sure had no comforts — they slept in bunks built up in tiers & from what they left strown about they didn't have much bedding — but very few blankets & those thin & shoddy. But these were better off than the first ones we saw before we got to the Rhine. They had been worked underground on the secret weapons & they were shot when they got too sick to work. He asked about Janice & I asked about Mary. We still would like for the four of us to get together for a good visit after we are settled back home. He had to go, then. I was glad he came by.

Mail call. Ten letters & one from home. One of J's letters was written on December 28th & it hadn't been forwarded from replacement depot. It must have come by way of Australia & on a slow boat at that. The others were recent. On the 17th, she was scared. Radio had reported the bridge collapsed at Remagen & a bunch of engineers working on it had been killed. She'll have to sweat that one out until she gets a letter written since then. O, damn censorship anyway. Why couldn't I have told her what was happening there! Indirectly, I have. I sent her some copies of S & S. She knows that when she gets a S & S whatever the headlines are, we are right in the middle of it. Hell, we were told before we left England that German Intelligence was so good that they not only knew every outfit in England, they had dossiers on every man from every outfit — where he was drafted or enlisted — where he trained — his whole military history. Well, what are we trying to hide?

The letter from home had a real surprise in it. Charlie is at home. Seems his ship had to go into dry dock for repairs & it was sent to San Diego. So he got a 30 day liberty. For a minute or two I was so envious it made me sick. Not that I'm not glad Charlie could get home. But it was such a damned good break for him — & I've got no chances of such a break myself. Then I was ashamed of myself. I know how much it meant to him & Irene to be together again. But I *wish* I had a ship to be repaired.

Near Berleburg
Friday, April 6, 1945

Moved out on the 4th & came north through Berleburg but are now on the other side of it. The towns & villages are so close together it's hard to keep up with them. Sometimes there are no signs to read. Here there are just a few houses. We are ahead of the 99th, however, roadmending for them.

We're in houses & there's a little river down across a pasture from us. When we got in today & got squared around we decided a change of diet was in order. About this time of year fresh fish always tastes good to me. We got some blocks of TNT & a bunch of us went down to the river. Pigg, Billington, Chapin, a few more. Billington said we were using too much big stuff. He said a few grenades would do just as well. But we wanted to get enough fish at one time for the whole outfit. He was right. Damn, what an explosion. For a minute I thought we'd blown the whole river dry!

But when it had settled down I never saw as many dead fish in my life. The current was drifting them down toward some shallow water so we went down there & all we had to do was scoop them out with nets.

We had a fish fry to end all fish fries, then. Everybody had all he wanted. I had pretty good luck with mine, but the

Lieut. was having trouble. His were crumbling to pieces. In fact, he was making mush of them. So I offered him mine & fried me some more. We just kept on frying fish till we didn't want any more. And they did taste wonderful.

Saw some Krauts going down to the river & picking up fish, too. We may have ruined their private fishing hole. Well, I would far rather have had the time & peace to use a fly rod myself. But we get so sick of army chow. McCarl is a good mess sergeant but he can only dish up what's sent him & all too often it's the same old thing day after day.

Saw some dogwood trees in bloom today. They made me so homesick. On a work detail out a side road there was a nice stand of young trees along a low hillside. Several dogwoods among them. Lord, but they made me think of home. Redbud is blooming at home about now. Heard a meadow lark today, also. Reminded me of how foolish I was when I was just a little kid. Mac's squad was the detail & I was guarding them. Told him about it & he couldn't believe it, but it's the truth. Until I was ten or eleven years old I thought I was the only person in the world who could hear the birds singing. I had never, in my whole life, heard anybody mention birds singing. Not anybody in the family nor anybody at school. Nobody ever mentioned the birds. Dad always had a martin box & the martins would swarm around noisy as the devil. He might say something about the martins had come, or the martins were leaving, but he nor anyone else ever said anything about birds singing. So I thought my ears were different from other people's.

I didn't learn better until one day Dad & I were in the woods. Think it was when he was teaching me to handle a gun. A bird was singing up on a hill. Dad stopped a minute, then said, "That's a wood thrush. They sing the prettiest of any birds in the woods."

I was so flabbergasted I couldn't open my mouth — but mighty relieved. I wasn't queer or odd or different. Dad taught me a lot about birds after that.

Mac said, "Why in the hell didn't you ask sooner?"

I told him I was afraid people would think I was a natural.

"What the hell's a natural?"

"Somebody who's not all there."

He just shook his head over it.

I know now that Kentucky hill people are really odd & different. I've been away from home & in enough different parts of the States & the world to know that our ways are curious. But it's all still part of me. When I was a kid I had a morbid fear of being made fun of. And it seemed to me as if every time I asked a question, the folks would laugh at me, & tell it on me & sort of poke fun at me for being so foolish. It was natural for me not to talk much, but I soon got to where I just kept my mouth shut about everything.

That's pretty much the way of everyone around home, anyway. You don't go around shooting off your mouth. It's not considered good manners. A "talky" person is putting on airs, acting proud. I had the guts to begin using good English as fast I learned it, but even that "went quare" to the folks. I was putting on airs, trying to act "proper." Just what the hell was I going to school for? But you don't get out of the ways of your training very easily. I'm still not much of a talker.

I think what started me being afraid of being made fun of was the hollow log. We moved to the Old Place when I was five or six. I know it was before I started to school & that was when I was seven. Where we had been living was in the edge of some woods. There was a hollow log near the house. Brownie, the dog, would jump a rabbit & run it into the hollow log. I don't know how many rabbits we trapped in that old hollow log. Everything was loaded & we were ready to leave when I suddenly remembered the log & went running to Dad. We had to move the log with us. Dad just laughed. I know now that he wasn't making fun, but at the time it seemed to me he was. He told it to everybody, in front of me & everybody laughed. It made me so ashamed I used to go off & hide & cry. A few incidents like that & I quit telling what I felt or thought, or asking questions. Except to Irene. We used to talk a lot together, wonder about things & come up with our kind of answers.

Mail call. Five letters tonight — from March 20 through 25th. She's still worried about the Remagen bridge. Pretty soon that sweat will be over for her. Censorship has relaxed enough that I can tell her about Belgium & up to & including Remagen. It will be a pleasure. At least there will be something to write about for a few days. I filled ten pages, both sides, tonight with no trouble. And haven't yet got to Remagen.

The radio says we now have nine more bridges across the Rhine than the Krauts ever had.

Germeter
Tuesday, April 10, 1945

We have moved right up front with the 99th artillery to build an airstrip for their recon planes. Battalion is at Berleburg. This is all hills & woods, but a fairly level place was found for the strip.

In tents again, but the weather is so nice now I don't mind.

Cornes & some of his squad, including Jeff, who were left behind on detached duty at Giessen have joined us. This is strictly a Company A job & we went to work this morning. One thing that slows us, though, is that the strip is out in front of the artillery. About the time we get to going good we have to fall back, quit work & get behind the guns so they can fire.

This is the first time I ever watched artillery in action up close. It is something to see. These 105 mm. cannons shoot a shell that is four inches in diameter & about two feet long. They have a range of anyway ten miles. The firing is controlled somewhere else, but the first gun goes off, then the next, then the next, right on down the line. Then the first gun again, etc. Only an interval in between. The flame & thunder is amazing & somehow very exciting. The concussion is terrific. But to watch those boys lay it in. And God knows how many more artillery lines are laying it in that pocket. Man, I wouldn't want to be on the receiving end of it. I would guess it's being laid in around the clock & one hour of this kind of barrage would be enough to drive you out of your mind. What the Krauts are taking now is murderous.

A lot of them are giving up. Jeff said H/S Company & I believe B are using all their trucks to haul prisoners back to the cage at Giessen. And any work detail lately is as likely as not to come back with a truck full who have just walked over & surrendered. Whatever Adolf says, the war is over as far as they are concerned.

Spider, the canary, doesn't like artillery fire. When the guns go off he gets so excited he flies around his cage & beats his wings against them. He doesn't quiet down until they quit. It's enough to make anybody beat his wings.

Saw my first Purple Heart medal today. Hernandez got his & showed it to me. Also saw Mac's Bronze Star. The Purple Heart is a very handsome medal. Hernandez said he guessed he'd send it home to his folks. Some of the fellows say I've been a fool not to see Capt. Kamen & be put in for a Purple Heart for my ears. But I don't want one that way. Not when guys have died for them. Some of the boys wear their ribbons but most of us don't. I don't. Mine are in a box in my B. bag. The one I'm proudest of, anyway, is the Pre-Pearl Harbor ribbon.

We heard today we're to get two more Battle Stars — one for the Rhine & one for the Ruhr. If so, my point count will go up by ten. We don't yet know what the essential for demobilization is. If there *is* an essential for us. Most of us still believe we'll be sent straight to the Pacific, via the Suez Canal. There's been a slow build-up toward it in S & S & the brass must be giving them the word.

Found a pretty good guitar today in a farmhouse. It needs some new strings, but the box is in good condition. We had a pretty good sing tonight, but nothing to drink to help us get off the ground slowed us down. We have been very short on anything to drink lately. Not even much of our grain alcohol mix.

Jeff said he'd haul my guitar in his truck. I'm hanging onto the mandolin to take home, but I already have a guitar at home so this one is just for our singing here.

Mail call & six letters for me & whaddya know? One of J's Christmas packages. It was the fruitcake & some homemade candy. The fruitcake was as good as new, but the candy had melted somewhat. Just the same it all got eaten. We're so hungry for something sweet that even the crumbs got raked up.

I must have told Janice too much about our binges over here. She doesn't sound particularly worried, but in one of these letters she does say she hopes they are part of the war & not a habit. They aren't a habit. I don't go on binges in civilian life. But I like good bourbon & I mean, if possible, to have a drink or two every day of my life. There is nothing in this world better than eight or ten year old 100 proof Kentucky bourbon & a little of it, regularly, is good for you. I think she'll understand.[2]

Listened to the five o'clock news from Luxembourg. We feel mighty good about it. This war is going places, now. All the news is good.

2 She did.

Friday, April 13, 1945

It's a beautiful day & much warmer. No Friday the 13th bad luck for us. I'm so glad the winter is almost over. As long as I live I'll never forget how cold this winter has been, how long & how miserable in every way. S & S says it's the coldest winter in Europe for 50 years. Wouldn't you know we'd hit it right on the nose?

We have been seeing deer & rabbit in these woods & today Jeff & Hooks went deer hunting, Jeff carrying a German burp gun he found. And by george, they got a deer. They brought it in & we have dressed it out & hung it up on a tree. Anybody that fancies a venison steak can just walk over & slice it off. It was a young buck & pretty tender. There isn't as much fat on deer meat as on beef, but it tastes mighty fine just the same. There's been a considerable amount of cooking going on since they brought it in.

I'd like to have been along to watch Jeff cut down on that buck with a burp gun. Probably the first deer hunt ever organized with a burp gun. Jeff said, "Hell, I was looking for *meat,* man. I wasn't hunting for sport. I was *hungry."*

Since we finished the airstrip some of the fellows have been hitching rides in the 99th's little Piper Cub. Billington has gone up & a few others. Lieut. Hayes went once but they came home with flak holes in the tail of the plane & he said that ended his tour of duty in the Air Corps. Thought for a while his own tail had had it.

Don't think I'll go. Don't see any use, at this stage of the game, taking any extra chances. And I've outgrown the need for thrills.

By george, there's still a little justice left in the army. Sgt. Love put in for one of the rotation furloughs some time ago. Today he got one. Got his orders. He just dropped by my tent to tell me. They are addressed to the commanding officer of a camp in Texas. Since he is from Texas, that suits him fine. I'm glad for him, but I still think this near the end it's best to stick with the outfit & see it out. If he's caught at home on furlough when this war ends, he'll almost be certain to be nabbed for the CBI. I think there's a better chance we won't be.

He means to go by Joplin. May get married. I wish him the best of luck. He is one more swell fellow.

Mail call. Two letters & one from home. J's last letter was written on her birthday. She didn't get the money I sent in time. I'm sorry about it but I did the best I could. She & Libby & some friend went out to dinner that night. She said, as far as she knew, Libby had her first hard drink. They ordered Old Fashioneds before dinner. Shortly after, Libby was holding onto her hat. J. asked her what was wrong. She said her head was about to fly off. J. appropriated her drink. Said, "Her husband can teach her what & how to drink. As far as I am concerned Libby is as high as a kite all the time without alcohol." This tickled me.

Sometimes, right in the middle of reading a letter from her I have the queerest feeling that I've just made her up — that she isn't real. Then sometimes I get to thinking about her, or looking at her pictures & I want to see her so bad it's a real pain, a real hurting pain & I don't know how I can just keep on slogging it out.

Later: We turned on the radio for the five o'clock news & it really stopped us in our tracks. President Roosevelt is dead. We couldn't believe it at first, thought there was some kind of mistake. But since that was almost all the news there was, we finally had to believe it must be true. He's been president for so long now it's hard to think of someone else in his place.

I never got to vote for him, but the folks did & Janice did. The first two times he ran I wasn't old enough to vote. The last two I didn't have a vote, being away from home. The news told about Mr. Truman being sworn in immediately.

Once we got over the shock of it, we began wondering how much difference it would make in the war. Everything that happens comes down, finally, to how it will effect each of us personally. Nobody knows Mr. Truman or has any idea how well he will do as president. The Republicans in the outfit think he'll mess things up. But I don't. It stands to reason he'll follow along the way Roosevelt would.

Somebody said, "Who the hell is he? I never heard of him?"

Somebody else said, "Oh, he's a hick from Missouri."

I said, "He may be a hick from Missouri but he did a damned good job running that Senate Investigating Committee. He's no fool."

Some of the boys don't ever look at a paper, S & S or any other. Have no idea of what goes on back home.

Sunday, April 15, 1945

Well, the Krauts have quit in the Ruhr. Just heard the news over the radio. They say there are over 300,000 prisoners. Good God, what do you do with 300,000 prisoners. The cages are so full now they're jammed. Somebody is sure going to have a hell of a job hauling them.

There's a rumor going around we won't get any part of it. That the 99th & us with them are going to be transferred to Patton's Third Army. And will be heading south. Why? To reduce the National Redoubt.[3] For some time we have been hearing that when the jig was up in Berlin, Hitler & his gang would retreat to the mountains & dig in down there. S & S has

---

[3] The National Redoubt scare was very real. Both Generals Eisenhower and Bradley admit in their books to have been very uneasy about it. Therefore, when the Ruhr pocket was reduced General Patton was ordered to swing his Third Army south and cut the roads between Berlin and Munich.

mentioned it several times. My God, it would take another year to finish the war if they get by with that. It would be guerilla war, just flushing them out one by one.

I guess the rides in the Cub have come to an end. Billington went along today & when the plane came in it hit a rough spot & nosed over — broke the prop. Nobody hurt. Billington said, "That's the way to crash 'em. So you can walk away."

We finally found a clarinet for Loftis & now we have a good little three piece band. Mac takes my guitar, I stick with the mandolin, & Jack has the clarinet. Man, can he play that thing. He leads off in whatever he wants to play & Mac & I string along. Had quite an audience tonight that turned into a dance. Some of the boys draped towels around them for skirts & went to town. We can do pretty well on a number of songs — "In the Mood," "String of Pearls," "Deep in the Heart of Texas," "Mississippi Mud," etc. With Mac & me backing him up, Jack can almost make the hair stand up on your head. So glad we found him an instrument. We had almost begun to think the Krauts didn't use clarinets.

Jeff & Hooks had taken their trucks & ranged around for some wine. Found enough for us all to feel mellow. When we finally wound up the fun, one of the officers called me over. Said, "I don't know whether you realize it or not, but those instruments of yours & the singing you & Mac are always leading off in, are worth their weight in gold as morale lifters."

I thanked him, but came into my tent laughing. Morale lifting? Who'd have thought I'd live to see the day I'd be accused of it. We're just doing what we like to do. Making a little music, having fun. But I must say we have a good singing outfit. Very few who don't join in & they're the grouches anyway. Nothing would ever suit them. I doubt if there's another platoon in the army that sings as much together, or as well, as we do. And most of the Company come around when we get going.

If it lifts morale, fine. The main idea is to end the day with a little fun.

Mail call. Three letters & one from home. Nash is almost through. They don't know how many more missions he has to fly. He's quit saying. Said he was superstitious about it. But it can't be many more. He has told Libby to prepare for a month's vacation in the south. Said he would have a leave before reassignment. Wonder what it would be like to work that 50 down to the last five, then the last four, & so on. A hell of a sweat, I'm sure. I feel a little like that myself. We have this war so near won, now, that I get edgy some days, scared something will happen yet. I try not to think of it.

Thursday, April 19, 1945

It's official. The whole III Corps, including the 99th & 291st, have been transferred to Third Army. We are winding 'em up tomorrow at daylight & heading south.

Mixed opinions as to how good a deal it will be. Some of the boys distrust the shift & figure we'll be tied up down there the rest of the year. First & Ninth armies have done a fast sweep eastward & when & if the Russians ever take Berlin, or we take it, the war up here could be almost over. We could get into a hot war down in Bavaria. But since they didn't ask us anything about it, I suppose we'll roll down with old Blood & Guts.

There have been some of the damndest stories in S & S lately about some concentration camps the advance has overrun. Patton's boys found the first one & General Eisenhower came over to go through it. It was at Ordrup. Ike said he wanted news of it published through the whole world & he wanted pictures of it to be seen by the whole army, so we would know exactly the kind of enemy we have been fighting. But it's sickening & unbelievable. Torture chambers, gas chambers where

Jews have been put to death by the millions. The boys found thousands of bodies, starved to death, just piled in great piles. They found crematoriums & they found people so nearly dead they were just walking skeletons. Patton made the burgomaster of the town take all the Germans who lived in the town through it. Some of them fainted. They couldn't stand the sight of it. One story said a man & his wife went home & committed suicide. They all said they didn't know anything about it. They knew there was a big camp of some kind there but they didn't know what it was. They said they weren't allowed to go near it. But that's a lot of crap. They *must* have smelled the place. You couldn't burn thousands of human bodies without an awful stink. They must have heard a few things. If you ask me, Hitler & his bully boys have had the whole damned country so scared they couldn't think for themselves. Those Nazis are just a bunch of inhuman monsters. This is something the world can never forget, or ever forgive. This has been going on for years. We used to read about the Jews being put in concentration camps but nobody dreamed they had been exterminated like rats. We didn't know about the slave labor camps, either. It's a thousand times worse than we could have imagined. I don't want to think about it any more. It makes you feel like puking.

Jeff just let the canary out of his cage & gave him a pan of water for his bath. He goes all out when he takes a bath. You wouldn't believe one little bird could make such a fuss over it. Then when he gets through he can't fly for a while because his feathers are wet & heavy. He fidgets & fusses & flutters them to try to dry them out. He's one more spoiled little fellow & gets the best of care.

S & S says Ernie Pyle was killed on some island in the Pacific. I'm sorry. He believed when he left the ETO that his luck had run out & I guess it had. It's strange that within a few days two great men should go — one of the greatest presidents & one of the greatest war correspondents.

No mail tonight except some packages. I had two cartons of Luckies from Janice. Would like to have had some other mail for I imagine with this shift in armies it will be some time before it catches up with us again.

Hammelburg
Wednesday, April 25, 1945

We *have* been rolling, mostly one-night stands down through Alsfeld, Lauterbach, Schluctern & here tonight. Jobs mine clearing, roadmending, bridges & here a Bailey across the Saale. I feel mostly as if we'd done more loading up & moving on than anything else. We zigzag around so much it's hard to tell where we are. Anyway, tonight we are billeted in what used to be an inn, or tavern. Big bar down one side of the place, with beer pumps that still had a little beer in them. I don't like German beer. Too weak & watery. I always heard the Germans made the best beer in the world, but what we've had isn't worth bottling as far as I'm concerned.

Got the radio set up in time to hear the news tonight. It is still very, very good & from what we are seeing in the air, everything ahead of us & into Austria is really taking a plastering. All hell has suddenly busted loose with the Air Corps.

Latrine rumors have it that we are headed for Austria ourselves. Just hope they soften it up a little before we get there. And one *big* river to cross between here & there — the Danube. Maybe we won't get the fire we got on the Rhine, though. But I don't know. Patton's boys got plenty at Regensburg when they crossed the Danube. He has really skedaddled these days. Already down in Austria.

Jeff found a set of new guitar strings a while ago & I've restrung the guitar. It makes a much better sound now. Not too much looting going on nowadays. The first interest has rather worn off. Now the boys are saying, "If you can't eat it or drink it or — — it, leave it!" We still look for food & booze & that's about all.

But I found a rather unusual calendar in this place. It's perpetual. Made of steel, stands about three inches high, and the slot with the date is swiveled so that you turn the panel over & the date changes. No month or day of the week — just the date. It doesn't take up much room & I thought I'd take it home to Robert.[4] He might get a kick out of it. I asked Janice a long time ago if she wanted any souvenirs of any kind. She said a souvenir of this war was the last thing she wanted. Just get myself home & that would be souvenir enough.

Raining tonight. In fact it's been raining for several days. April showers, I guess. The mud makes the roadwork harder, though.

No mail yet. Heard it almost caught up with us tonight, though.

Boys are yelling come on, let's have some music.

Thursday, April 26, 1945

Bridge finished & had the rest of the day off. It has quit raining so Speedy Dymond & I decided to go deerhunting. This is hilly, woodsy country & the fellows have been seeing them in these woods. We didn't have a burp gun. We just took our M1s.

We tried the woods first & I did see one big buck but he was too far away & the woods were so thick I couldn't get a good shot. We tried to close up on him but he got the wind up & ran away. That was the only deer we saw.

Then we decided to try the meadow that ran alongside. It was a fine big meadow of clover. We were walking along & I

---

[4] Robert Giles, Henry's younger brother, was at this time eighteen.

thought I saw another deer ahead of us. Speedy spotted him about the same time. I told him it was his shot, take it. Speedy kept watching him & he finally said, "I don't think that's a deer, Sarge. Durned if I don't think it's a jackrabbit."

I said, "If that's a jackrabbit it's the biggest one I ever saw. Looks like deer antlers to me."

Anyway, Speedy took aim & cut down on him. It was a hell of a long shot, at least 200 yards. But, by george, those eyes of his *were* good & he made one of the prettiest shots I ever saw anybody make, anywhere. It *was* a jackrabbit & he got it right through the head. With an M1, mind you. What shooting!

He was almost as big as a young deer. We thought he'd feed quite a bunch of the boys. But that was all we saw. We flushed the field over & didn't work up another thing. By that time it was getting late & beginning to rain again so we thought we'd better head back for the area. Thought for a while we were lost, though. We had gone pretty far & were a little turned around. We finally worked our way back, mostly due to Speedy's good sense of direction. Had a fine rabbit stew for chow.

Mail call. Only two letters for me, *but* there was the manuscript of Janice's book, which I mean to read tonight if I have to sit up all night to do.

near Nürnberg
Sunday, April 29, 1945

At Würzburg this morning we hit the Frankfurt–Nürnberg highway & thought now, by george, we'd make some time. And we did. Highballed along through Kitzengen & Iphofen, feeling pretty swell about being on a good road & thought maybe we'd get a break on bridges for a change.

We have got used to seeing the sky full of our planes headed for Austria & some few Kraut planes dogfighting around. We had gone through Iphofen when all at once there was this high, snarling whine & by God, some Kraut jets were dive-bombing us.

All trucks stopped. Everybody flattened or hit the ditch. Wham — bang — blast! Heart failure again & sweat. But they are so fast it was over almost as quickly as it began & they were zooming off behind us. A quick check around. Nobody hurt. Barrel on, but feeling pretty shaky now. Everybody keeping an eye on the sky. I was riding in the cab with Hooks. "The war," he said, "is a hell of a long way from being over for us."

I agreed. That deal could have got some of us.

A little farther on we took a rest stop & right on the side of the road was a jet one of our planes had shot down. It is a sleek, deadly looking plane. Some of the boys got some pictures of it, but it was only a ten minute break & on we went.

We are in some dinky crossroads town north of Nürnberg tonight, but as usual there is a stinking little river that needs a bridge. And it will damn well be a Bailey.

One consolation. This is good wine country. For the past few days we have had some of the best wine we ever had. You can drench yourself in it & never have the slightest headache.[5]

After chow, our nerves a little settled by the wine, we were tuning up for some music when the Lieut. came over & told us Capt. Kamen & Sgt. Swift had been killed.[6] They were rolling along with H/S Company at the tail of the column & they got dive-bombed by jets, too. I didn't know them well. Capt. Kamen is the medical officer who looked at my ears & sent me to field hospital. Sgt. Swift I only knew by sight. They were both always with H/S Company & usually we aren't near them. But it sends a shock wave right down to your toes to hear

---

[5] For several days the 291st had been in the Franconia district of Germany where some of the best wines in the world are made. Small wonder the boys loved it.

[6] Capt. Paul Kamen and S/Sgt. Douglas C. Swift were both "Medics."

something like this, especially when you've just had a near miss yourself. And the war is bound to be so near over. Just yesterday we read in S & S that the Russians & Americans had linked up on the Elbe River. That ought to finish the Krauts, but by God until the last one of them is killed I suppose Hitler will keep them fighting. Any one of us can get it any day, from any direction.

I have read Janice's book twice now & I think it's wonderful. It is a wonderful, happy story of a wonderful little girl & her mother. Parts of it made me want to cry & parts of it were so funny they kept me laughing. I know I'm partial but I honestly think it's a lot better than some of the crap that gets published. Have tried to write her about it but I couldn't say all I meant. Did my best, though, & one thing I hope I got across. She must try to have it published.[7]

near Heinheim
on the Danube
Wednesday, May 2, 1954

Well, here we are on the beautiful blue Danube. But it's neither beautiful nor blue. It has rained so much in the last few days that the river is at flood stage, very muddy & with a hell of a current that's going to make throwing a treadway across it a sonofabitching job. And it has, by God, cost us another 2nd platoon man. We rolled up to the river & positioned by squads. Hooks put his truck down pretty near on account of my gun. When we got all staked out, he left to go find some of the other boys & I thought I'd just stay put & maybe catch a little sleep.

Was snoozing away when, by God, suddenly all hell busted

---

[7] This book never got off the ground. Strangely enough, neither Henry nor I remembered this was my first serious writing effort. For years I have said I wrote my first book in 1946 and it was *The Enduring Hills*.

loose. We were getting the living daylights blasted out of us by mortar fire from a cruddy little town just across the river! Good God Almighty! None of us liked the looks of the damned position, none of us liked the looks of the river or that town. Patton had trouble just a short distance away at Regensburg, & we have wondered if there might not be some pockets that hadn't yet been wiped out. We had approached this with considerable squeamishness.

There wasn't time to do a damned thing but hang on. Just grit your teeth & hang on. They threw them in & they were screaming all over the place & every one of them sounded like it was headed straight for me. But they mostly landed up in an orchard & a tree burst was what did for Hall. As good a guy as there was in the platoon. But hell, they're all that. And to get it now, *now* when the Krauts have begun to talk surrender, just makes you sick. Makes you so sick you can't do a damned thing but cry.

Anyway, they threw them in for a while, then quit. I was so shook I just sat there & shuddered. Didn't want to move. Couldn't move. Then here came one of the boys running. He said, "Giles, they got Hall. And Nickell has been hurt." Then he ran away again.

Well, Jesus Christ. I just caved in. Just plain caved in. I began bawling & couldn't quit & couldn't help myself. Just sat there & shook & bawled. Hall was one of the boys in that group picture that was made of some of us with the French kids back at Marle. And the idea that he & Holbrook both were gone now was just too much.

I kept remembering his shaving brush. He had one of the finest shaving brushes I ever used. After I lost mine I used to borrow it sometimes. It wasn't more than a week ago I threatened to steal it. He laughed & said, "The only way you'll get this brush is if I cash in my chips. Then I'll will it to you."

I finally pulled myself together & went up where the trucks were parked. They had Hall & a 99th tanker who was also killed, laid out across the road, already wrapped in blankets. I was glad I couldn't see Hall's face. They said he never knew what hit him. He was asleep in Jeff's truck. Whatever consolation that is. Jeff was there & saw it all. He has tried to tell us about it, between spells of crying so hard he couldn't talk. He nearly got it himself.

We got settled down a little, but thank God we have plenty of wine tonight. We have three five-gallon cans full. I'm half drunk now & mean to get drunker. It doesn't make any sense. None of this makes any sense. Why doesn't that lunatic Hitler give up & *quit!*

[Jeff Elliott says: I first got to know Hall well at Giessen where our squad was on detached duty maintaining that bridge across the Lahn. Second squad's job was to maintain the Bailey there. We moved in and set up in a house near the bridge. I put the truck on the side of the house & Cornes put some men on the bridge. Cornes then told me and another fellow to go find some potatoes and anything else we could find to eat and drink.

We had C-rations there and soon sickened of them. We found a couple of bushels of potatoes, a large bag of rice, three chickens, one rooster and a hell of a lot of booze. Cornes was boss of the bridge and he cooked in his off times.

We had a big party one night and, much in his cups, Hall somehow got behind the door between the rooms. He thought he was locked in some place. Yelled, "Nazi! Let me out!" And he damned near knocked the door off the wall getting himself out from behind it. We kidded hell out of him about that and all of us got to know him well there.

Convoys would come over the bridge and we would stop

the first truck, check the driver's papers, let the rest go through to the last truck, stop him and check his papers, too. While the last truck was getting checked two men would go on the back of the truck and throw off six or eight cases of whatever they had on it. We were well supplied with eats and gasoline *and* booze. Some officers' liquor rations never found their way home.

When we got to the Danube we moved by the squad down near the river. Cornes in charge of our squad, Bossert down near the river which was about 300 feet from the road where we were parked. The road sloped off toward the river and there were some apple trees near the road and on down to the river. Some tanks moved into the apple trees.

In the town across the river there was a church with a tall steeple. I thought I could see somebody moving in the window in the steeple. I was lying in a ditch on the right side of the road talking with a tanker. I had a pair of field artillery glasses hanging in the cab of my truck along with Henry's git fiddle. Cornes was sleeping across the seat.

I stood up and went to the right side of the truck cab. Hall was asleep in the back on the floor between the demolition chest and a tool box on the other side. Nickell was sitting up beside him cleaning his rifle. I reached up in the cab to get the glasses and I heard the Nebelwerfers come screaming. I flopped down beside the truck. One of the shells hit in the apple tree beside the truck. It killed instantly the tanker in the ditch where I had been lying. A big chunk of hot lead went through the tire I was by, through the frame of the truck, into the oil pan and all the oil ran out on the ground. Another chunk went through the windshield, nearly scared Cornes to death and nearly got him. Another chunk went through the steel side of the dump box, through the demolition chest, killed Hall and went on into the tool box on the other side of him.

Nickell had flopped down on top of Hall when he heard the shells screaming in. He was hit in the face.

The blood ran out of the bottom of the truck into a red pool on the ground. I had been hit by pieces of flying dirt and stones on the back. When I saw Hall's blood, I thought it was mine and I thought I was a goner. I put my hand on my back to see if the blood was still squirting out. Couldn't find any so I got up and ran like hell across the road and into a German fox-hole, a nice deep one, that I had seen earlier.

They quit shelling after a while and I heard somebody yell for help to get Hall out of the truck. Diaz went and so did I. Diaz took his feet and I went to take his head. I couldn't! The blood was still pouring out of him. I had to turn away and puke and then I started crying. I couldn't lay a hand on him.

I was very ashamed after it was over. I liked Hall very much. I thought I would write to his wife but I went and got drunk instead.]

Friday, May 4, 1945

We got the 99th across the Danube on a floating treadway, but it wasn't easy. It took the whole damned Battalion to do it. C Company finally finished the bridge while the rest of us fell to & built 300 yards of plank road for an approach. The mud was almost knee deep. I never saw worse mud. No vehicle could get through it. But 17 hours after we reached this god-damned river the 99th was crossing. I sure as God hope they pour it on the Krauts from here on.

We are bivouacked tonight in some cruddy little town whose name I don't know & don't give a damn to know. Too tired, too beat, & still too shook to care. But whatever it is, when we came into it, here came marching out a little delegation, the mayor & some citizens, waving their little white flag. 99th had bypassed the place & it hadn't yet been taken. But please,

Yanks, be nice & don't mess up our little homes or bother us. They surrendered to us. The Capt. laughed & said he guessed we'd get credit for taking *one* town, at least. Nobody cared. We just wanted to get bedded down. And forget the damned blue Danube.[8]

Before we left Heinheim I went around and asked for Hall's shaving brush. Don't really know why, except he said I could have it. I felt sort of sentimental about it. I'd borrowed it so often & I couldn't forget how he'd said if he cashed in his chips he'd will it to me. Had a sort of feeling he would want me to have it. What a good old boy he was. Big fellow, strong as an ox — and he always pulled his part of the load. What a damned shame he didn't make it.[9]

For the news is good. Very good. Himmler has tried to surrender to the British & Americans, but not the Russians. Boy, they don't any of 'em want anything to do with those Reds. They know what they'll get. The radio says he made surrender overtures to Churchill through somebody in Sweden. Well, now, that's not a damned bit of good. If we accept surrender from any of the Krauts without the Reds in on it, we'll have them to fight next. And I sure don't want to have to fight those Reds.[10]

Mail came in early tonight. I hit the jackpot with 12 letters & they're all recent. They have been a long time catching up with me, but were well worth waiting for. One of these letters tonight *ought* to make me feel wonderful. But I'm too beat to feel anything. Anyway, we decided a long time ago to be married as soon as I could get to Louisville. Then after a few

[8] Company A did get credit for taking this town. But no one now remembers its name.

[9] Henry Giles shaved with this brush for ten years, until it was worn down to a nub. We hope his wife didn't mind Henry's having it.

[10] Himmler made his overture to Prime Minister Churchill through Count Bernadotte.

days alone we would go down home & see the folks. In this letter she asks if I would like a quiet wedding, in the apartment,
with just Dorothy & Lloyd[11] & Dr. Sherrill marrying us. I would
like it. I wouldn't know how to behave at a big affair, but I
have left the wedding strictly up to her. She wants me to wear
my uniform & this once, at least, my ribbons. Well, I doubt I'd
have time to outfit myself in civilian clothes, so that sounds all
right to me, too. But I wonder, I really do wonder, if I'll make
it. If there *will* be a wedding.

Five of us from Hq. squad always are in the same room together. We know all there is to know about each other. For
some reason I started making down my bed before writing my
letter to Janice tonight. Everybody stopped & stared at me.
Finally Pigg said, "Aren't you going to write your letter tonight?" It really rocked me back on my heels. We know each
other so well that to change the routine the least bit seems
strange. They have been used to seeing me dump my bedroll,
get out my writing equipment & write my letter, then tend to
other matters. I'm always afraid I'll get caught by dark & won't
get to write. That's why I always write the minute we get settled
in. I can make my bed down in the dark, but I can't write.

I don't suppose our wives will ever know us as well as we
know each other. We sort of look after each other the way the
members of a family do. You don't really have any family but
the boys, nor any home except the one you make each night
with them. I said, "Do you really think I should?"

Pigg said, "You goddamned better. As good as she's been
to you!" Well, of course I meant to. But we got in a little early
& there was plenty of time.

The news is so exciting these days that almost the first thing
we do is get the radio hooked up & gang around & listen. And
it is wonderful. The Krauts in Italy have surrendered uncon-

11 Mr. and Mrs. Lloyd Naveaux.

ditionally. This is bound to be the beginning of the end. It does look, it really does, as if the end is in sight. Within another month even Adolf ought to see the handwriting on the wall.

We have read in S & S about another concentration camp very near us. Dachau. It seems to be the worst of all. The 7th Army overran it the other day when they took Munich.[12] They found lampshades in the superintendent's home made from human skin! The Krauts stripped the skin from prisoners who had been tattooed, so the tattoo marks would make a design & made lamp shades out of them! This is the very worst yet. This is the foulest thing we have read. What kind of monsters are these Nazis? S & S says they are all considered war criminals & there will be a big trial of them after the war is over. Why try them? They don't deserve a trial. They ought to be taken out & hung to the nearest tree by meat hooks through the chin.

We have read about them freezing people, just to see at what temperature the human body dies. We have read of their using human beings as guinea pigs, cutting them open, putting highly infected stuff into the wounds, to see how much infection filth would cause. We have read of them beating people almost to death, then when the wounds were almost healed, cutting them open again & putting red pepper & vinegar into them just to hear them scream. These people aren't human beings. They are monsters. Try them? My God, they don't deserve the justice of a trial. The methods of the Inquisition ought to be used on them. And on Hitler first. This is worse than the Middle Ages. At no time in the history of the world, not even during the Roman Empire, have a people set out with more determination to conquer the world & to destroy their enemies so systematically and so cruelly as these Nazis. No, I

12 On April 30, 1945.

don't see any use of trials. I just think any member of the
Nazi party ought to be boiled in oil.

Wornsdorf

on the Isar

Sunday, May 6, 1945

The war is ending. Tonight we got the S & S announcing
Hitler's death. We had already heard it on the radio. It is
said he "died at his post in Berlin." Well, it's very good news
that he's dead. At least he didn't try to make a getaway down
here. But it was too good a way for him to die. He ought to
have been drawn & quartered. He ought to have been made to
suffer all the agony he has caused — endless hours and days of
it.[13] If he really did die at his post, it was much too easy for him.

We have had a lot of thrills today listening to the radio. We
heard the surrender in the north. All the Kraut troops in north
Germany have quit & surrendered to Monty. We heard it all,
even when the Germans signed. Things are really cracking, as
Jeff says. It can't be but another few days until the rest of them
give up. They have quit in Italy, they have quit in northern
Germany. Hitler is gone. Germany is *kaput*.

We have had a wild day. For one thing a bunch of Czech
PWs in a cage near us broke out & got into Pinkie's photo
trailer. They mixed up some stuff & drank it. Guess they
thought they were getting grain alcohol but what they got was
developing fluid with cyanide in it. They have died all over
the place & we've been hauling them to the firehouse & laying
them out. Then the Capt. went to see the mayor of this dump &
told him he'd have to bury them.[14]

---

[13] At the time it was accepted that Hitler had "died at his post."

[14] General Patton's Third Army had advanced into Czechoslovakia as far as
Pilsen. These prisoners must have been taken at that time. This was as far as
the Russians would allow the Americans to advance into Czechoslovakia. A great

We have been more than slightly drunk all day ourselves. Jeff & I decided to go find some more wine. We somehow managed to tear the doors off a barn trying to back his 2½ ton truck out. I think we are all "victory" happy.

Hq squad & 1st squad are quartered in the home of some very religious people. We can hear them praying all the time. Everytime they come out of the house or pass any of us, they cross themselves. They must feel like the end of the world has come — but who gives a damn. — Let them. We just took the place over. Pigg told them to move upstairs. Said we needed the place. Let *them* feel fear, for a change! They have sure, by God, made enough people feel fear before we got here.

We had a good sing tonight — one of the best, well oiled with wine. And Jeff liberated a generator so we even had electricity.

[Jeff Elliott says: Wornsdorf was a cruddy, dirty little German town. We had all dirt roads through there. The CP, the kitchen & H/S platoon were set up in one house. 1st and part of 2nd were in another. 3rd was across the road. The motor pool was up beyond the crossroads. This was the place where you and I, Henry, nailed the calf hunter's wooden shoes to the steps of the CP. Somebody had looted his calf. While he was inside complaining to the C.O. we nailed his shoes to the steps. When he came out he slipped into them, then tried to walk & fell all over himself. Wonder *who* liberated that calf of his?

We did a lot of singing & I had liberated a generator so we had lights for a change. Wornsdorf is also the place where the Czech prisoners died like flies after getting into Pinkie's photo supply trailer. We hauled them to the firehouse for the mayor

---

many Czechoslovakians were of Allied sympathy, but General Eisenhower was following his set rule to honor all Russian directives.

to bury. Then, I don't know why, we tried to take my truck out of a barn. So drunk we tore the doors off. It was a wild time because we figured the war was practically over.]

Monday, May 7, 1945

THE WAR IS OVER! All we can think is thank God, thank God. Next, I'm sure everybody thought exactly what I did. I made it! I made it all the way! Nobody is going to shoot at me any more. I can't be killed. *I have made it!* It is selfish, but it's human. You can't help being glad. We have lost some. And we all wish they could have made it, too. But, instinct is very selfish. What counts tonight to me is that I, me, myself, made it. And unless we draw the CBI, the war is over for us.

The radio has been crackling with news & tomorrow is offcially VE-day. We went sort of wild. Everybody whooping & shouting & yelling. It's over! It's all over here in Europe! We still have the CBI to sweat out, but at least this one is over!

It's still sort of unbelievable. Mac came around & sat by me. "Do you believe it, Henry?"

"Sure. Don't you?"

"I dunno. It's been so long. Maybe there's been a mistake."

I said, "Mac, look. We heard them signing the surrender. There's no mistake. It's *over!*"

"You don't think it's a false alarm?"

Well, there is that queer feeling that it might be. Some kind of mistake yet. But it seems there isn't. And yet there is a queer kind of let-down. We have waited for this day so long. We don't yet much believe it. And there isn't a drink in the house. Not even any grain alcohol. We have had the most sober celebration in the ETO. And once the first wild excitement was over, there's been some sadness for the ones who didn't make it.

I wrote Janice & home immediately so they would know as soon as possible I made it, all the way.

And over the radio, BBC via Luxembourg, I heard for the first time a song Janice has especially liked all through the war & written about — "My Shining Hour." She first wrote about it when we were in England. I never could hear it. But tonight they played the record from London & I finally heard it. There was never a better time to hear it, for it is indeed our shining hour.

But when I think back how far we have come, all that has happened, I feel more sad than glad. We tuned up our instruments & sang for a while. And a song that tells it the best was one we hit on first — from World War I — "There's a Long, Long Trail." Not many of us knew all the words. But it has been a hell of a long trail. And we are finally at the end of it.

As usual, my reaction has been a feeling of terrible weariness & then weakness & sleepiness. But I *am* happy. So *damned* happy. It's over. There will be no more shooting & killing in Europe. What Hitler started, we have finished.

Brückenau — Munich

Tuesday, May 8, 1945

No WORK details today since it is VE-day. All we have done is listen to the radio. We heard Churchill's victory message. It made you blink back a few tears. He got very emotional over it. He reminded the British people that five years ago all he had to promise them was blood, sweat and tears. Today there is victory. The Krauts are through, *finis, kaput.* For the second time in 25 years they have tried to conquer the world. I hope this has taught them no nation can conquer the world. I'm still afraid I'll wake up & find I've been dreaming. Last night I dreamed I was with Janice & I told her I hoped I wouldn't wake up & find I was dreaming. But I was. Imagine dreaming a dream!

London is having a big celebration. We have heard most of it. No doubt Janice has heard the President today as we have heard Churchill. What a celebration they are having in London. BBC is letting most of the noise come through. Here we sit sober — stone cold sober. There ain't no justice!

But just think, next spring I'll probably be burning my own tobacco bed. I'll probably be setting out my own plants. Next spring Janice & I will probably be married. May be living at the Old Place. I can't believe we'll have to go to the Pacific.

I just *know* I'm going to be demobilized. I have all the necessary points. My job isn't essential even for Army of Occupation. S & S says the required number of points is 85. I have 90 & if we get the other two Battle Stars I'll have 100. There are only five of us in the whole Company who have as much as 85. The rest of the boys are sweating.

Of course, since a lot of the excitement of the victory is wearing off, we are thinking & talking of nothing but what happens next? Where do we go? And when? Billington & Mac & Jeff are all moaning. Saying they'll be in the army the rest of their lives. I do feel sorry for them, at the same time I am glad, glad, that I am a high point man. That good old longevity of service of mine. Billington looked at my count & said, "Where the hell do you get 60 points?"

I said, "Sixty months in service, friend. Sixty damned long months."

I'm short on dependents, for parents don't count — short on decorations. But I've really got 'em piled up on that longevity, time overseas, and five Battle Stars if we get the last two. I have 90 even if we don't.

We're just sitting here. We're still with the 99th so I guess we'll go in whatever direction they go. There aren't even any rumors yet. Guess the brass has got to do some tall figuring about what to do with all the outfits.

Mail call. Six letters. She is doing a lot of dreaming about our farm. Drew a plan of the kitchen she'd like & for the umpteenth time mentioned the fireplace. The rest she leaves up to me.

Bad Brückenau
Saturday, May 12, 1945

As LaCoste says, we are back up in the "bad" country. When we went through here on our way to the Danube we kept noticing that nearly every little place we went through was Bad something or other. "Bad, bad, bad," LaCoste finally said, "Don't they have any *good* towns?"

I think it means "spa." Something like our Hot Springs and Warm Springs in the States.

On the 9th we & the 99th were ordered to do a right about face & come back up here. A two day convoy back across the Danube, through Nürnberg, Kitzengen, Würzburg, etc. We got to use many of our own bridges, but the Krauts had bombed a few so we had a little building to do.

This is a pretty nice bivouac area. We're back in the hilly, woodsy country & near a small river for bathing & doing our laundry. In tents, but it's so warm now nobody minds. I have mine pitched with the sides rolled up — more of a sun shelter than anything else. I'm glad to be back up here. I didn't care for the Danube and Isar country — too flat & level. Just an old hillbilly, I guess. I like a line of hills to break the monotony.

We are taking it very easy. Don't have reveille until 7:30, then B Company's bugler rolls us out swinging. Nothing much to do but keep the place clean, a little guard duty, & one day a week I have gun inspection & cleaning. Once in a while there's a little work detail. Construction for the 99th usually.

We get a ration of "schnapps" by the kegs, through 99th, now, and we are to start getting A-rations for food soon. That will be a bit of all right.[1]

Most of the platoon have been loafing in my tent today, the guitar & mandolin much in use, a considerable amount of schnapps being drunk, much talk about the point system. Capt. Gamble talked to the whole Company this morning & confirmed what we've been reading in S & S. The minimum

---

[1] A-rations had more variety than K or C rations. There was a meat and several vegetables, all to be cooked. K and C rations were cold.

number of points for demobilization *is* 85. Big groans at that announcement. Most of the boys only have between 60 & 75. He went on to say that having enough points to be demobilized didn't necessarily mean a man would be sent home & discharged. His MOS might keep him in.[2] There *does* have to be an army of occupation, too. He also gave us our new APO number, without explaining it. This is the first change we've had since we got settled down in England. If it wasn't changed when we shifted to Third Army, why now? Much speculation as to what it means. A shift to some staging area? Army of Occupation?

Hinkel came by during the afternoon & we went down by the river under some trees to talk since my tent was full. He said it was pretty straight dope that what was going to happen was that the low point men would be transferred out of the Bn. into some other outfit. High point men from other outfits would be transferred in & that the new 291st would likely be shipped home, then, for demobilization. Well, if that's true, it's good news for me, but at the same time I sure would hate to see the outfit split up. Hinkel doesn't quite have 85 points himself. Feels pretty blue about it. He thinks the low point men will draw an outfit headed for the CBI. "You're a cinch," he said, "you've got it made. With your MOS even if somebody gets saintly & decides engineers ought to rebuild all these roads & bridges for the Krauts it won't affect you."

I don't think it would either. With the war over, who needs a Weapons Sergeant?

Mail call. No letters for me but another of J's Christmas packages. A book of crossword puzzles, four cans of boned chicken & some homemade candy. All very welcome.

2 Military Occupation Specialty.

Saturday, May 19, 1945

Moved into a better area yesterday. Still near the river but we're in some trees for shade here. Also a nice field for some recreation.

This morning I signed my demobilization papers, so I feel pretty fine. S & S today had a list of "essential" men — men who can't get out no matter how many points they have. I sort of held my breath as I read through it, then whooped. My job isn't listed. Didn't see how it could be, but you never know.

We had to see a pep-up movie today, "Two Down & One to Go." The two down are Mussolini & Hitler — the one to go is Tojo. But if they think a movie is going to pep this outfit up & make them wildeyed to go after Tojo, they're nuts. Let some of the stateside boys get him. We really razzed the thing.

Good bit of "fraternizing" going on now. This has become a right no-care bunch of boys lately. As long as there was a war on there wasn't too much of it, but the bars are down somewhat. It's so hot the Kraut girls go around in shorts & barelegged. Right provocative to see a well-stacked girl in shorts ride by on a bicycle. Some of the girls don't tumble but mostly they're anxious to be friendly & nice.

I spent all this morning fixing up my tent. Hustled around & found some planks & made a frame about 16 inches high, then stretched my tent over that. It gives me more space & headroom. Then I laid a tarp for a floor & had myself a rather cozy little home.

It rained pretty hard last night & most of the boys just had up sun tents, but I pitched a pretty good tent when we got in. I've been caught too often with water flooding me out when I was tired or careless. So while everybody was scrambling around trying to get some shelter up, I just lay there & enjoyed the sound of the rain on the roof.

The boys are calling my abode the "Waldorf."

Mail call & I had nine letters. Nash made his final mission & they were expecting him in Louisville around May 10th. If he made it by then his visit there is over & he & Libby are now in Florida. He was to go to Miami Beach for a month's rest. And finally J. has heard from me since the 7th & knows I made it all the way. Such a happy letter she wrote when she heard. It's been a long sweat for her, with many bad scares.

Censorship has been lifted to some extent. We can now tell where we have been up to the end of the war. Are allowed to seal our own letters, too. Of course there are still some things we can't tell — where we are & what we're doing now, etc. But I just wrote probably the longest letter of my life — 14 pages on both sides. Funny, but I've forgotten so many of the little places already. The big deals I'll never forget but there were so many little villages & crossroads & even my notebook wasn't much help, for I often didn't know where I was at the time.

I'm still pretty tired but am beginning to bounce back a little. This hot weather is wonderful. I was lying in the sun this afternoon, dreaming. Speedy was sitting alongside plunking the guitar. He said, finally, when he couldn't rouse a song out of me, "What are you in such a study about?"

I told him. The corn has been planted at home by now & maybe the tobacco has been set. Mama has already had the first mess of early peas & she has all her garden planted by now — pole beans, tomatoes, cabbage, peppers, sweet corn, etc. I said, "This time next year that's what I'll be doing."

He bopped me over the belly with the guitar. "You mean you're going *back* to the farm? I used to hear you say nothing would ever make you go back there."

I had to laugh. He sure has heard me say it & many others have, too. But that was before I knew I was going to be married. That was when I meant never to marry & meant to make the army a career. "Love," he said, disgustedly, "it sure does make a damn fool out of a man!"

Maybe. But maybe it brings him to his senses.[3]

Saturday, May 26, 1945

We're playing a good bit of softball these days. This afternoon we played a doubleheader with 3rd platoon. I'm beginning to feel like a human being again so I got into the second game. They beat the socks off us in the first game, 9-0, but we squeezed by with 9-7 to take the second one. Just by accident I got two walks, a single & a double. Only flied out once. When the game was over 3rd platoon ganged around trying to sign me up with them for the rest of the season. Much tomfoolery. I finally told them they didn't pay enough, I'd better stick with the 2nd.

After chow, Jeff came around & we mixed some schnapps with a little music. He & Coupe both met nice English girls while we were at Gloucester & Jeff is thinking a little about trying to get a furlough back there to see if perhaps it'll work permanently. There's been some talk if you can pull a furlough to England, you can sail for home from there. I don't know. Must be a lot of red tape to it.[4]

When Jeff had gone the fellow who got the anonymous letter came along to shoot the breeze. Stayed about an hour. Mostly

---

[3] Speedy Dymond says: "At Brückenau we had a long lull until someone apparently thought it looked bad to have us in camp doing nothing. So they made a work detail not far from camp. We shoveled dirt from the side of the road to the center of the road and patched some holes. Only trouble was, the road didn't go anywhere. I was resting on my shovel when a man drove up in a jeep, got out, came up to me and asked what we were doing. I said, "Beats the heck out of me, sir." He shrugged his shoulders and as he headed back to the jeep my eyes bugged. The guy was wearing *three stars!*"

[4] John Coupe married his English girl, but Jeff Elliott came home to marry a girl he had known most of his life.

talked about the point system. He's low point. Anyway he got up after a while & said he'd better get on back to his own area. Then he floored me by saying, "I suppose you've heard I'm a single man now."

Well, I hadn't. The last I heard everything was fine. He was the happiest man in the army. I said, "No. I hadn't heard it."

He said, "Yep. She divorced me last month."

That was all he said. Just walked away.

Then Cornes & Pigg & Mac & some others drifted over. They figured he'd told me something. Since he didn't say it was a secret I told them. All agreed he got a very raw deal. Mac said, "Hell, it was true all the time. She just lied to him right down the line. But why? Why make it up with him & lie to him if she was going to divorce him?"

I said, "Maybe she hadn't made her mind up yet. Didn't want to turn loose of him till she had the other one good & hooked. A bird in the hand, you know."

"Well, that's a rotten way to treat a guy."

Pigg said, "Aw, hell, when he gets over it he'll be better off. If she's that kind she's not worth losing sleep over."

I know. That's true, I know. But right now he's hurting. It does something to you to have someone you trust let you down. I know. I had it happen to me one time. It takes a long time to get over it. I didn't really trust another woman until I met Janice.

About then it was time to go to the movie. First we've had in a long time. It was John Wayne in *Tall in the Saddle*. Durned good western. But before the movie began there were some of the Grand Ole Opry troupe in person — Roy Acuff, the Duke of Paducah & some others. The Duke was a riot. It will be a long time before we forget, "I'm goin' to the wagon, boys, these shoes are killing me!"

They had the show & the movie in the field & it was nice sitting there, so warm, the stars shining. I think, maybe, for the first time I really felt like peace had come, felt peaceful in myself.

Friday, June 1, 1945

Moved again, not far, to do a little work for the 99th. This is the best bivouac area we've had — a long row of trees for shade, the river for bathing & washing. I got real ambitious when we got in the other day & built myself a *house*. Found plenty of boards & worked on it all one day. Had plenty of advice, of course. And Pigg said, "Hell, Giles, what are you going to so much trouble for? About the time you finish it we'll move on."

No matter. If I don't live in it but a couple of days it was worth it. I like to be comfortable & then I sort of like carpentering. Now that it's finished it's being much admired & I might add, *used*. It's the hangout for everybody. I'm thinking of naming it "Giles' Tavern — bring your own schnapps."

The Col. was in the area today & he said it was his opinion that we'll *all* go to the States. That's not much consolation, though, for the low point boys. It could be they would go to the States all right, but just passing through. I didn't get to talk to the Col. but one of the other 85 plus boys did. He told me the Col. said the high point men would probably be on their way sometime in July. Sounds good to me. But I don't put too much hope in it. I don't think anybody knows anything for sure yet.

We were afraid the Col. was here to put us on garrison routine again — drills & inspections & such. But nothing was said about it. It's been so long since this outfit stood an inspection I doubt if any of us could pass one.

We've all been talking about so many kids in this area. Don't believe we've ever seen as many before, not even in France.

These range from babies up to eight & ten years old. Billington said, "They're Hitler's state babies."

Somebody said, "What the hell's a state baby?"

Billington told him. Said, "German girls were told to have babies whether they were married or not, so as to build up the state. Hitler told 'em it was their patriotic duty. I think the state helped pay to raise them."

The kid shook his head. "What the hell all went on in this country under Hitler, anyway?"

Plenty, as we have found out.

Played softball today, another doubleheader, & tonight I'm pretty stiff & sore. I know better than to get in two games, but I like to play. My knees are giving me fits tonight, though.

Mail call. Three letters. Nash made it home on the 12th of May. And this tickled me. Libby had been planning for weeks what she would wear when he got there. Then when he called her from Camp Dix he asked her not to meet him at the airport in Louisville. Said he would call her when he got there but he wanted to see her the first time at home. Well, he didn't call. Just walked in. Caught Libby in an old bathing suit, oiled all over with suntan oil, her hair up in curlers. Janice said one lovely, expensive uniform got ruined right then & there. But what a beautiful way to ruin a uniform. I wouldn't mind ruining two or three that way.

She went to stay with a friend a couple of days & let them have the apartment. Then they went to see his folks, Nash bought a car, & they left for Florida. Lucky kids.

Friday, June 6, 1945

Much talk today about what was happening a year ago today & all of us glad we're not sweating out our move to the continent. Glad we have it all behind us. But we also did a lot of remembering. Remember old Bedcheck Charley? Remember that damned Tucker bridge? Remember the gas attack? Remember Giles chasing the washwoman all around the bench? Remember Paris? Remember — remember — remember. Marle — Luxembourg — Salmchâteau — the Battle of the Bulge — Malmédy — the snow & the cold & the damned everlasting Baileys. The one at Lanzerath. The one over the Roer. Remagen. Remember Remagen. We still have one souvenir of Remagen — Spider. Then the lootin', tootin' war when we could hardly keep up with the 99th. A hell of a long way we've come. We were trying to figure the mileage & all of us think it's around 3,000 miles, if not more.

"What was the time you were the worst scared?" somebody asked.

Billington said, "I think — I believe it was when those Kraut tanks were shooting at us. Hell, I don't know. I was scared so many times. But there was something about those tanks . . . you could *see* the damned things. I mean they were coming right at us!"

Pigg said he thought for him it was the night of the gas attack. LaCoste said the same. Mac? "I think when the Krauts hit us at Malmédy. We didn't get any sleep for days & then they hit us that morning. I thought our time had come."

Cornes? He thought maybe when the chunk of hot lead went through the windshield on the Danube. Jeff thought that was his worst time, too.

Me? I just said, "Hell, I been scared to death the *whole* time." But I guess the time that shook me worse was the Danube, too. We weren't looking for that. The war was over. And we were so damned tired we didn't have anything left to fight fear with.

In the afternoon suddenly LaCoste came chasing himself in.

"Sgt. Giles, there's a two-star general in the area & he's madder'n hell because nobody is salutin' him. And we all got to put our shirts & caps on. It's an order."

Well, what the hell! We quit saluting when we got to France.

I got my shirt on & scrummaged out my cap. We still have winter clothes & it's too hot for a wool shirt & cap, but a little piss-ant general can make it right uncomfortable for you.

Then we had a softball game with a team from the 99th. We got the living daylights beat out of us. What a pitcher they had! He could make that ball do everything but talk. We didn't stand a chance. Just got up to bat & struck out as fast as we got up. Got beat 8-0.

The Col. was here again today, too. He took it real easy about us getting caught so sloppy. Just laughed & said, "Well, you know how Third Army is. Pretty spit & polish."

Then he spoke to us & told us what I, at least, have been wanting to know. Said the Bn. would be home by September. Said he didn't know just when we would leave or how, but we could count on it. We'd be back in the states by early September.

But who'll be in the Battalion? All of us? High point boys? Or low point boys? I kept remembering what Hinkel said, so I figure I'll be kept with Battalion.

Mail has been pretty good for me all week & there are five just now. Latest one, May 28th. J. says unless I can give her enough warning she *may* have to work a little while after we're married. Says she must train someone to take her place. Have just written her that she can count on me getting home sometime in Sept. Hope that's enough to help her plan.

In another letter she tells where Nash was in Italy & some of the places he bombed. And by george Munich was one of the cities he bombed most often! We weren't far from there when the war ended.

Munich
Thursday, June 14, 1945

Yes, dammit, back down that long haul to Munich! We've had a rest but now it's back to work again. Job here, working PWs cleaning up the mess Nash & his boys made of the city. And I do mean they made a mess of it. There is hardly a whole building left. Block after block nothing but rubble, walls standing but the whole inside of buildings gutted out. The streets are full of craters & even the sidewalks are pockmarked all over.

None of us like this job. None of us wants to help the Krauts begin to clean up. But I suppose something had to be found to keep us busy while we were waiting to find out what's going to happen to us. So, we were detached from the 99th & sent here. A military government has been set up here & this looks like an army of occupation deal to us.

My job is pure hell on my feet & knees — walking guard. The PW cage is outside the city. They are brought in on trains. We meet them & deploy them by details. Then I walk, block after block after block, from one detail to another. I can't think what use it is. The boys working the prisoners can handle them all right. Guess I'm supposed to rush up with my trusty M1 to shoot somebody if necessary.

We moved down here the 11th. They hauled us into the courtyard of what had been a Kraut prison. Told us this was it. Unload. We didn't like the looks of the place & all began bitching about it. Who the hell quartered us here? Who's idea was this? We got off the trucks but were slow about starting to unload.

First Sarge had gone inside with some of the officers & the jeep drivers were beginning to unload the officers' stuff when Sarge came highballing out, hell-bent-for-election & yelled, "Don't even put your stuff on the ground! This place is working alive with fleas!"

It was a good thing we *hadn't* unloaded, for when we got to looking around even the ground was hopping with fleas. We got back onto the trucks like greased lightning. First Sarge was going around clawing at himself & cussing & when the officers came out they were walking fast & looking pretty disgusted. Don't know who billeted us there, but we sure got the hell out in a hurry. Stayed in the city park that night & all of us deloused ourselves good.

Today a hotel with the lower floors in pretty good shape was found & we moved in. There's plenty of room, the electricity works most of the time & there are showers in the basement. We spread out & took over the joint, two men to a room. Arlie Wall & I decided to bunk together. We're on the third floor.

I suppose the furnishings are standard for a second class German hotel. There is a double bed of some kind of dark wood, a dresser, an old rug on the floor, one light bulb hanging down from the middle of the ceiling & curtains of some kind of dark red, thick material.

We deloused the bed & decided since neither of us is a heavyweight we could sleep double in it all right. Then we went down & tried the showers. We stayed pretty clean up in the Brückenau area but it was still fine to have a hot shower. That river water was cold! I had just done a big laundry the day before we moved, so I had clean underwear & clothes to put on.

Mail hasn't begun coming up yet. After chow I went down to the Red Cross canteen to read the S & S. Not very encouraging. 3rd & 7th Armies have been picked for Army of Occupation, to be made up, probably, they say, of high point men. Low point men will be transferred out to the Pacific.

I think it's worth mentioning that the Red Cross canteen is located in Hitler's old beer hall. The 45th Inf. which took Munich nailed up a big sign over it, saying Hitler started the war here, but the 45th ended it here. Then, curiously enough, I picked up a *Life* magazine & there was a picture spread, showing the beer hall & the 45th's sign.

Sunday, June 24, 1945

Ten days since I wrote here. Too tired most nights after walking all day. All the Weapons Sgts. are doing walking guard. Arlie & I come in beat every night. My feet have been blistered, the blisters have broken & new blisters formed over them.

Some Hungarians are mixed in with the Krauts & the boys say they are giving them the most trouble. The Germans will mostly work, but there's no work in these Hunkies. They don't get by with much, though. The boys have a way of making them stand with a brick in each hand outstretched until they're begging to go back to work. A shovel looks pretty good after standing an hour or two holding out a brick at arm's length. We're not allowed to touch them, of course, & don't suppose anybody wants to.

But I saw an ugly thing driving to the station this morning. A truck load of prisoners was just ahead of us. Suddenly a prisoner jumped off the back end & tried to get away. He was caught by two Kraut police. They beat the poor bastard almost to death with the clubs they carry, then turned him over to the MPs to take to the prison hospital. He was nothing but a bloody pulp when they got through with him. Our boys would have roughed him up a little, I guess, hustling him back onto the truck. But these Kraut police nearly killed him.

The trains don't run on Sundays, so nobody works. And we are just getting over one real wild binge. There is very little to drink around here except the German beer they serve in the cafes & bars. We get a liquor ration once in a while but it's mostly wine or champagne. And you have to have a military permit to get anything extra — which takes so much red tape it isn't worth it.

Anyway Pigg & Jeff found a grain alcohol distillery the other day & they brought the stuff in by the G.I. can full. For two days the whole outfit was too drunk to work & the hotel was running over with women. All bars were down. Even the kitchen went out of business. Cooks too drunk to work. The binge ended when Lieut. Hayes, the only sober man in the outfit, got disgusted & made the boys pour the "spirits" down the drain. Jeff smuggled about 20 gals. away, though, so we've all had enough to go on a little longer. But back to work. I promoted some fruitjuice from McCarl & have been walking my beat with a canteen of the stuff instead of water.

We wouldn't have done this during the war. Nobody was drunk when a job was coming up. But the whole outfit is so disgusted with this deal, we feel like there's so little to look forward to if we're stuck here, anything goes. And that includes the frauleins who are all so very, very willing.

But I've had to laugh & take a razzing. Three evenings in a row I've run into the same girl in the park. She *loved* my kickapoo juice — fairly guzzled it down. But the minute a certain little T/5 Medic hove into view, she left me flat! A T/5! My self esteem has suffered considerably.

One of the boys is shacked up with a girl right here in the hotel. He calls her his little Nazi. With Lieut. Hayes on the prowl, they have to be careful. When they hear him coming she rolls out the back side of the bed & hides under it. Hayes hasn't found her yet.

There's a captain (not one of ours) in the room just over Arlie & me. He's shacked up, too, for we can hear a woman talking up there. This morning, though, we were just waking up (slept late) when we heard the biggest row up there. She was screeching at him & things were banging & knocking around. Then all at once a rain of suitcases, clothes, what have you, started pouring down outside our window. We said, what the hell. I went out in the hall & we could still hear the woman yelling. Pretty soon here came a Pfc down the stairs, laughing fit to kill. He was really doubled up. Seems the woman had got mad at the Capt. & thrown all his stuff out the window & he was up there in nothing but an undershirt. The kid was going down to try to collect the Capt's clothes for him.

We lost Spider during the binge. Jeff let him out of his cage to take a bath. The window was open & he flew out. Nobody in any shape to chase him. We just hope he finds a good home.

[Concerning the grain alcohol binge, Jeff Elliott says: Pigg & I were out looting and we got to talking with some fellow who said here was a drinking alcohol plant. We went in and there were three stainless steel tanks that held about 8,000 gals. each. We went back to the Co. and got seven G.I. cans, came home with 35 gals of the straight. Had to cut it 2/3 water and 1/3 booze to get it down & keep it.

Went back with eight water cans. The whole Company got drunk with the exception of Lieut. Hayes. The kitchen even quit serving meals. It came to an end when Lt. Hayes caught one of the fellows chasing a girl down the stairs. Both were very lightly clad. Hayes said, enough, get rid of the booze, get back to work. We managed to keep a little around to fight colds and snakebites with, although he stood over us and watched while we poured about 25 gals down the drain.

Everybody was so low over the move to Munich and it was so hard to promote any booze that that binge was about the only bright spot for days.]

Friday, June 29, 1945

A couple of days ago I was detailed to go about fifty miles
south of Munich to a place called Seeshaupt to guide a convoy
of Kraut trucks & prisoners back to the cage. Jeff drove me & we
made it there & back without any casualties — except Jeff's
watch. He left it in the cab of the truck & some PW stole it.
He was cussing about it all the way back.

Both of us were glad to get out of Munich for a little while
& it was a pretty drive down there. The place was on a beautiful big lake. Don't know the name of it, but there were
boats on it & the water was a very deep blue.[5] Also it was within
sight of the Bavarian Alps. Some fine, snow-capped mountains
in sight. Munich is rather flat & in flat country, but it's not far to
the mountains. I could have stayed down there several days
& been right happy about it.

Some of the boys went on a tour of Hitler's hideaway at
Berchtesgaden while we were on this convoy. They came back
full of it. Said he really was holed up there. Elevators going up
the inside of the layout & a wonderful view of some beautiful
scenery from the terraces of the buildings on top. Well, he
never made it back down here to hole up again. That National Redoubt sure did fizzle out.

I've had another good break. Was pulled off walking guard
today & sent out on the train to bring the prisoners in. But we
only have one guard to a coach & I know we're losing a few.
Told the Lieut. so. He just said, "Well, do the best you can."
When the train gets into the city & the PWs are turned over to
the work details, I'm through with prisoners until time to
take them back out to the cage.

Have also found me a private source for some damned good
wine. Was walking down to the Red Cross canteen after get-

[5] Seeshaupt was on the Starnberger See.

ting through yesterday & as usual had forgotten my lighter. Asked a Kraut for a light. He spoke English. Asked me what part of the United States I was from. When I told him he said he used to live in Kentucky — worked in Louisville and Cincinnati. I wondered at first if he might not wish he had stayed in the States, but he went on to tell me he worked at a winery. Seems he is manager & has a good job. He asked if I would like to have some good wine. We went around to his office & he gave me four quarts. Told me I could have more when I wanted it. And it is *very* good wine. I wish I could get enough to go around, but can only share with Arlie & one or two others.

There was enough for a bunch that gathered in our room tonight to sing, Mac, Jeff, Cornes, Arlie, Speedy, etc. Not as many gather around to sing as there used to. Too many other things to do — but there's still a bunch of us that like to make music.

The mail comes pretty regularly. Janice is in Arkansas, but by now is starting back to Louisville. Dad got my rifle. Mama said he had shot five squirrels, two crows & a chicken hawk with it & said it was the best rifle he ever shot. I'm looking forward to using it myself.

Wednesday, July 4, 1945

We have a holiday today. Slept late this morning then took it easy the rest of the day except for doing a washing.

There are an awful lot of kids in this city & I guess the civilians aren't having a very easy time. We're suckers for the kids, as usual. As much as you might hate the Nazis for what they've done, you can't hold it against a bunch of innocent children. All of us give them the candy & gum we get in rations & whatever else we can pick up.

I was passing an open window on my way to the Red Cross

today & two little fellows about five or six years old were standing in it. They didn't say anything — just held out their
hands. I had some fruit bars in my pocket that I could give
them. They laughed & went running to show it to someone in
the room. An old woman came to the window then & smiled
& said, "Dankeschoen." These people are lucky they aren't in
the Russian zone & they know it. Our military government is
firm, but the people are being treated as fair as possible. The
procedure seems to be to help them get back on their feet as
quickly as possible. I hear we are supplying them with some
food from our army surpluses.

We had an official notice today saying our two Battle Stars
had come through. It was almost a cinch & I had counted
them in, but it's good news to have it official. We were also notified that the 291st is definitely Category IV — that means
slated for demobilization. But that doesn't mean much. All
of us could be shifted out & a whole new Bn. reorganized to be
shipped home.

We got our liquor ration last night. I drew a quart of champagne but Arlie got a quart of Scotch. We divided it half &
half. One reason I slept late this morning was because I took
my half down considerably before hitting the sack.

But the damndest thing happened. Arlie had gone out & I
was sitting in the room, drinking, writing my letter, when suddenly Gann[6] came barreling in, rolling drunk. He must have
jolted his whole ration down all at once for he barely could
stand up.

I know Gann, of course. He's one of the boys. But I've never
known him well. He came weaving in & said, "Giles, I'm going to beat the hell out of you."

I put my writing stuff down & got up & said, "I don't know
what for, but if you think you can do it, Gann, just start."

[6] Pvt. Herman Gann, 1st platoon.

He's a big bruiser, would make two of me, but I had judo in the old 19th. I can take care of myself with anybody. He stood there for a little while, blinking, weaving back & forth, then he said, "Aw, hell," and rolled back out.

I asked him this morning what the hell got into him? What was wrong? He didn't remember anything about it at all. Was totally blacked out. He had a hangover to end all hangovers & looked pretty sheepish when I told him about it. Said he hoped I wouldn't hold it against him. Told him to forget it.

Ran into Paul Hinkel at the Red Cross & we talked a while. He said things would start cracking pretty soon. Said the dope was official & the Col. would announce it in the next few days — and it's the way he first said, if he's right. Low point men transferred — high point men staying. But you don't know what to believe until it's official.

Saturday, July 7, 1945

This is official. It was announced & posted today. Low point men will be transferred to the 112th Engineers. High point men will remain here in Munich with the Battalion. 93 men are to leave Monday, more will be leaving all next week. I feel very blue over the split-up. All of my best friends in Company A will be going — Jeff, Pigg, Billington, Cornes, Black Mac, little LaCoste, Speedy, all of them I like the most, have been with the most. Even the Col. & Capt. Gamble & most of the other officers are transferring out. The boys are even bluer than I am. They feel sure the 112th is slated for the Pacific.

It is also official that the 291st will be built up to Battalion strength with high point men from the 112th & other engineer outfits. That we will definitely go home & be demobilized — we will not be kept here for army of occupation. If we could just all go together, that would be wonderful news.

Black Mac & LaCoste & I tried to drown our sorrows in some

Kraut brew at a little cafe tonight. Under our military occupation government all Krauts have to get out of public places at 7:00 P.M. & only Americans can be served after that hour. It was a sad evening. A little three piece band tried to play some American jazz & made a very poor effort. Our own band, all split to hell, did much better. I felt very much like weeping in my beer & so did Mac & LaCoste.

We got to remembering again, which wasn't good for us. There's so much to remember & mostly what a damned fine outfit it has been.

McCarl has his boys working on a big banquet for noon tomorrow. A sort of farewell & send-off for the fellows. I don't even like to think about it.

Janice is back in Louisville. Nash has been sent to Santa Fe, New Mexico. Some big government hospital there & he is to be the Air Corps liaison officer. That is the best of news. I didn't think he would draw another overseas assignment but am glad he will have a desk job for a while.

Very little news in S & S now, except the war in the Pacific. It seems to be going well. Much pounding of Japanese cities by air force. It would be wonderful if that war could end pretty soon too, but nobody expects it to.

Thursday, July 12, 1945

They're gone. All of them. Just a few of us left who feel like the last leaves on the trees.

The banquet & celebration in farewell was a big flop. Everybody was too sad over the split-up to have any fun & there wasn't enough liquor to ease the pain. I went for the food because it was the only way I could eat, but I sure left in a hurry. I couldn't face speeches & the break-up. We've been together two & a half years — cussed, bitched, griped, been scared to death together, got drunk, chased women, razzed the hell out of each other, borrowed & loaned, helped each other & been helped. I love every damned one of them, but saying goodby to some was about the hardest thing I ever had to do in my life.

I packed my mandolin today & shipped it home. Won't be needing it any more. The picking & singing bunch has gone.

I'll be going home in a few weeks, either with the Battalion or as a high point man. I have a wonderful future waiting for me & what I have to do is set my sights on that.

I don't think I'll write any more here. No point in it. There's no 2nd platoon left, no Company A, and not much of a 291st.

But what we had together was something awfully damned good, something I don't think we'll ever have again as long as we live. Nobody in his senses wants war, but maybe it takes war to make men feel as close to each other as we have felt. We'll never feel toward anyone else the way we have felt toward each other, for the circumstances will never be the same again. We are all a little homesick for it already.

[The war in the Pacific ended before the 112th Engineers, which included so many of Henry Giles' friends, left Europe. These boys reached home in December of 1945 and were demobilized.

Henry Giles left Munich, as a high point man, ahead of the Battalion. He received his orders on August 25, and left on August 28. He sailed from Marseilles, France, on September 15, on an old Liberty ship that had engine trouble the entire way across the Atlantic.

He arrived in New York on October 7, 1945. He was discharged from the army at Camp Atterbury, Indiana, on October 10. He arrived in Louisville, Kentucky, in the early morning of

October 11, and we were married at nine o'clock in the evening of the same day.

The Old Place had been sold before Henry reached home. In 1949, however, we bought our first farm in Adair County and have been living and writing only a stone's throw from Green River where Gileses first settled in 1803, ever since.]

Appendix

Historical Division, SSUSA

Battle Organization as of May, 1945

Awards and Decorations

Appendix

WE WERE not able to reach all of the men mentioned in the *Journal*, but those we were able to contact are presently located and occupied as follows:

Lt. Col. David E. Pergrin is now Regional Engineer for the Pennsylvania Railroad. He is married and has five children and lives in Clarence, New York.

Capt. James H. Gamble is now Dr. James H. Gamble. He has his own clinic in Lovingston, Virginia, and we were told by friends of his that he is doing a very fine work in that area. He is married and has a family.

Sgt. R. C. Billington lives in Harrisburg, Pennsylvania, where he is a claims adjuster for an insurance company. He married in 1955. His wife, Rosemary, has a managerial position with American Telephone and Telegraph Company. They have no children.

Sgt. Abe Caplan lives in Albany, New York, where he is employed in the New York State Department of Public Works, Bureau of Office, Service, Reproduction Unit. He is not now married and we did not learn if he had ever had children.

T/4 John Coupe married his Gloucester girl, Molly. They live in Corning, New York and have four children. John works for the New York Central Railroad as a fireman, but is due to make engineer shortly.

T/4 Merlin E. Dixon is married and lives on a small farm near Caldwell, Idaho. Merlin went into the National Guard after the war and had another war to fight in Korea. He has two children and two step-children.

Pvt. George J. Courvillion lives in Abbeville, Louisiana. He is married and has one son and one daughter. He is employed by the Louisiana State Highway Department as Machine Operator #1 at Abbeville.

Pfc. Louis (Speedy) T. Dymond lives in Washington, D.C. and works at the Smithsonian Institute. Louis married in 1957. He and his wife have no children. Although he lives in Washington, he considers Charlottesville, Virginia, home and has property there in the country which gives him great joy with its orchards and gardens.

T/4 Jeff Elliott did not marry his Gloucester girl. He returned to his home near Clinton, New York, where he married a girl he had known most of his life. They still live near Clinton, have five children, and Jeff teaches in Utica, New York.

Pfc. Vincent A. Fresina is now deceased. He died on February 4, 1964. His wife, Ladieruth, continues to live in their family home near Baton Rouge, Louisiana. They had two daughters.

S/Sgt. Paul J. Hinkel lives in Canton, Ohio. He is married and has seven children. We did not learn what his work was.

Cpl. John A. King went to school on the G.I. Bill and obtained his engineering degree. He now lives in Oklahoma City, Oklahoma, where he is an engineer with LTV University. He married in 1955 and has two daughters.

T/4 Louis (Hooks) Kovacs lives in Greensburg, Pennsylvania, where he is employed by the New York State Natural Gas

Corporation as a truck driver in a gas storage field. He married in 1955 and has one son.

Pfc. Paul LaCoste lives in Morgan City, Louisiana. Before the war his family operated shrimp boats, but Paul is now with a steel boat company. He is married, has nine children and three grandsons.

Sgt. J. B. Miller, "the hero of Trois Ponts," calls Opelousa, Louisiana, home. He is not now married, but is divorced. He has one son. Currently he is a caterer on an offshore boat.

Cpl. John D. Pink lives in Rochester, New York. After the war, "Pinkie," as he was called by 2nd platoon, returned to his old job at Eastman Kodak Company in Rochester, New York. He is a sheet metal worker and takes over for his boss when he is away. He has been married for eighteen years. His wife's name is Greta and they have three sons and three daughters ranging in age from five to seventeen. In the last few years they have built a new home of which they are very proud.

Cpl. A. C. Schommer lives in North Chelmsford, Massachusetts, where he is a process engineer with General Electric Company. He is married and has three children.

It caused us much distress to be unable to locate some of the men who are most often mentioned in the *Journal* and who were very close to Henry Giles. We could never find Cpl. Isaac O. (Black Mac) McDonald; Sgt. Bill Keenan; 1/Sgt. Wm. H. Smith; Sgt. Edwin Pigg; Lt. Alvin Edelstein; Sgt. Jack Loftis; Sgt. Arlie Wall. Short of private detectives we tried every source from Military Personnel Service last known addresses to correspondence with state automobile license bureaus. These men we could not find, but we are grateful, after twenty years, for being able to find as many as we did and for their cheerful cooperation.

Historical Division, SSUSA:
Unit History Work Sheet

DESIGNATION: 363d Engineer Combat Battalion

CONSTITUTION: Constituted 19 December 1942 in the Army of the United States as 2d Battalion, 82d Engineer Combat Regiment

HISTORY: Activated 25 January 1943 at Camp Swift, Texas
Redesignated 291st Engineer Combat Battalion, 29 March 1943

Inactivated 20 October 1945 at Camp Patrick Henry, Virginia

Redesignated 363d Engineer Combat Battalion and allotted to the Organized Reserve, 6 May 1947

Activated 21 May 1947 at Louisville, Kentucky

BATTLE HONORS:

World War II

Normandy	Rhineland
Northern France	Ardennes–Alsace

Central Europe

UNIT DECORATIONS:

Distinguished Unit Streamer embroidered MALMEDY
Streamer in the colors of the French Croix de Guerre with
Silver Star embroidered MALMEDY

Battalion Organization as of May, 1945

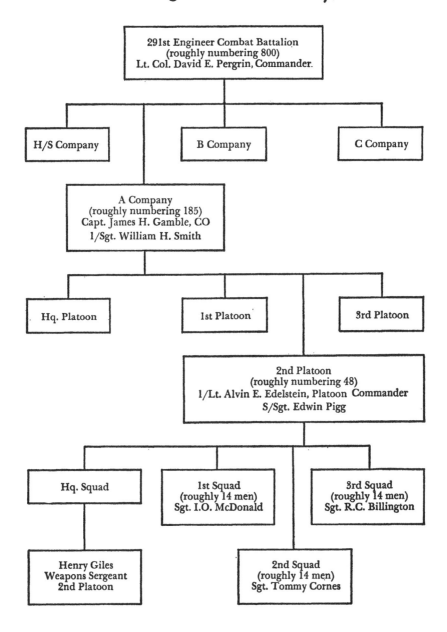

Awards and Decorations

Silver Stars

Lt. Col. David E. Pergrin
2d Lt. Ralph W. McCarty
* 1st Sgt. William H. Smith
* S/Sgt. Malvin E. Champion
* Sgt. Frank C. Dolcha
T/5 John H. Noland

Bronze Stars

Lt. Col. David E. Pergrin
Major Edward R. Lampp, Jr.
Major Lawrence K. Moyer
Captain John T. Conlin
* Captain James H. Gamble
Captain William L. McKinsey
Captain Frank W. Rhea
Captain Lloyd B. Sheets
1st. Lt. Wade L. Colbeck
1st. Lt. John C. Kirkpatrick
* 1st. Lt. Archibald L. Taylor
* 1st. Lt. Albert W. Walters
2nd. Lt. John K. Brenna
2nd. Lt. Ralph W. McCarty
T/Sgt. John L. Scanlan

* Sgt. Jean B. Miller
* Sgt. Joseph H. Geary
* Sgt. Floyd W. Wright, Jr.
* T/4 Walter J. Landry
* Cpl. Isaac O. McDonald
  (Cluster)
Cpl. Edward C. Woertz
T/5 Vincent J. Consiglio
* T/5 Cleo H. Blanchard
T/5 Herbert F. Helgerson
* T/5 Pasquale A. Zegarelli
Pfc. Camilio A. Bosco
Pfc. John F. Iles
* Pfc. John D. Rondenelle
* Pfc. Robert B. Schaer

* Company A men.

Pvt. Norman F. Fisher   * Pvt. Sergio Pasquale
Pvt. Thomas J. Olden   * Pvt. Roger E. Sandle

In Memoriam

Captain Paul (NMI) Kamen   Pvt. William C. Mitchell
S/Sgt. Douglas C. Swift   Pfc. Lorenzo A. Liparulo
* Pfc. Wiley A. Holbrook   Pvt. Edward L. Barker
* Pfc. Merion A. Priester   * Pvt. Arnold K. Hall

Purple Hearts

Pvt. Robert J. Milositz   Pfc. John C. Stackhouse
* S/Sgt. Paul J. Hinkel   T/5 John H. Noland
Pfc. Patrick J. Libertelli   Sgt. Augustine M. Martinez
Pvt. Francis J. Buffone   Pfc. John J. Berardi
* Pfc. Walter M. Street   Pfc. Calvin J. Dupre
2nd Lt. Robert S. Marshall   Pfc. Scott E. Petterson
Pvt. Bernard Goldstein   * Sgt. Lee M. White
Pfc. Joseph Descak   Pvt. Raymond A. Jackson
T/5 Ronald L. Hall   Pvt. Paul M. Bucklew
* Pvt. Joseph A. Spires   * Pfc. George R. Clark
Pvt. Edward V. Gutowski   Pfc. Daniel P. DeLoreto
Capt. John T. Conlin   * Sgt. Hazen E. Perkins, Jr.
Pfc. John J. McVey   Pvt. William L. Jackson
T/4 Burnie J. Hebert   Pvt. John T. Antlitz
Major Edward R. Lampp, Jr.   * Pfc. David E. Baldwin
T/5 Joseph P. Zureich   Pvt. Angelo J. Coscia
Pfc. William H. Hildebrand   * Cpl. John J. Flaherty, Jr.
* Pfc. Austin J. Bendon   Pfc. James W. Phillips
* Pfc. Frank E. Teston   S/Sgt. Douglas C. Swift
T/5 William A. Wieberg   Pvt. Willard I. Farley
Pvt. Stanley L. Reed   T/5 Curtis Ledet

1st. Lt. Leroy H. Jochnck
T/5 Lloyd G. Eaton
2nd. Lt. Coye R. Self
Pvt. Walter P. Gomez
T/4 Isidore Rosenberg
T/4 Francis X. Conroy
Pvt. Joseph P. Conners
Pvt. John J. Moze
Pfc. Peter E. Nassis
Pfc. James N. Lane
Cpl. Richard L. Frey
Pvt. Frank P. Baumann
Sgt. Windsor W. Vorce
Pfc. James R. Duncan
Pvt. Allen C. Nickens
T/4 John W. Chapman
Pfc. Victor (NMI) Gramm
Sgt. Charles J. Dishaw
Pvt. Ernest (NMI) Palmer
Pfc. John (NMI) Abraham
Pvt. Walter R. Mosteller
Pfc. Ormond Exferd
Pfc. Gilbert R. Chavez
T/5 Ralph K. Hocking
* Pvt. Earl L. McCorkle
* Pfc. A. H. Storrs

* Pvt. George J. Courvillion
* Pvt. Talmage V. Nickell
Pvt. Leo O. Roach, Jr.
Capt. Max Schmidt, Jr.
Cpl. Montie M. Beaken, Jr.
* Sgt. Joseph R. Downey
* Pfc. Merion A. Priester
* Pvt. George A. Bignar
* Cpl. Frederick E. Lederman
  (Cluster)
* Sgt. Joseph H. Geary
* Pfc. Louis O. Hernandez
* Pfc. Robert R. Schaer
* Pfc. Roger E. Sandle
* Capt. James H. Gamble
* Pfc. Edward S. Pysz
Pvt. Carmine E. Servello
T/4 George W. Werner
Pvt. Viree B. Stephens
T/4 Ronald L. North
Lt. Col. David E. Pergrin
T/3 Mack E. Barbour
Cpl. Peter J. Piar
T/5 Michael J. Popp
Sgt. Charles J. Dishaw, Jr.
* Sgt. Jack Loftis

Index

Index